When MARTHA YATES' husband died in 1970, she found it necessary
to work, for the first time, to support their four children. She entered
broadcast journalism, worked for the Internal Revenue Service
in their Atlanta office, and is now editor of the alumnae quarterly
of Agnes Scott College, of which she is a graduate. Author of numerous
articles in professional magazines, Martha Yates is an expert
at seeking out helpful information and organizing it
so that her readers can put it to practical use.

Coping

COPING

A Survival Manual for Women Alone

MARTHA YATES

A SPECTRUM BOOK

PRENTICE-HALL, INC., Englewood Cliffs, New Jersey 07632

Library of Congress Cataloging in Publication Data

YATES, MARTHA.
  Coping : a survival manual for women alone.

  (A Spectrum Book)
  Includes index.
  1. Single women.   2. Divorcees.   3. Widows.
4. Finance, Personal.   5. Conduct of life.
I. Title.
HQ800.Y3   362.8   75-37837
ISBN 0-13-172221-2
ISBN 0-13-172254-9 pbk.

Prentice-Hall International, Inc., *London*
Prentice-Hall of Australia Pty. Limited, *Sydney*
Prentice-Hall of Canada, Ltd., *Toronto*
Prentice-Hall of India Private Limited, *New Delhi*
Prentice-Hall of Japan, Inc., *Tokyo*
Prentice-Hall of South-East Asia Private Limited, *Singapore*
Whitehall Books Limited, *Wellington, New Zealand*

To my four reasons for coping . . .
  Scott, Mark, Elaine, and John

  and always and forever . . . to George

Contents

Prologue

Why this book?

Because I found nothing like it when I desperately needed it after my husband died. Because I knew little or nothing about raising my family, about working, about handling money, or about facing the world—all alone. In short, I knew nothing about coping and could find no practical advice to help me.

But as I plunged into the complex world of credit and cars, of furniture and finances, of sex and Social Security, I discovered that the problems I faced varied only in degree from those confronting any other woman alone, whether she was unmarried or had lost her husband by death or divorce. So this book is for all of you who are single for whatever reason.

A recent survey conducted by the University of Chicago showed that the happiest group in America is that vast number of women who are alone. I agree, but with the stipulation that that state of contentment is never achieved easily. It involves preparation, hard work, anxiety and some falls, faith in yourself, a few triumphs and a few mistakes, and a whole lifetime of dedicated coping.

Acknowledgments

My list of people who merit acknowledgment for their assistance to me in preparing this book is lengthy because it must, of necessity, include those who helped me through the dark days following George's death (without their help I couldn't have emerged to cope with the future), as well as many others who have given me every type of supportive aid.

During those first agonizing days, I couldn't have made it without the loving help and concern of Ann and Lewis Ledsinger, Alice Vaughn, Ann Thompson, Mia Walter, Kathy Martin, Saralyn and Gene Oberdorfer, Hazel and L. J. Iseman, Jack Walter, T. J. and Jo Perkins, Charlotte and Walter Rodgers, Hugh Winn, and the Reverend Charles Mann.

In addition to those above, there were others whom I knew I could call on for help without a minute's hesitation on my part—or theirs—and they are Ann and Stan Smith, H. T. Weaver, Ken Sargent, Al James, Frank Beckum, Frank and Evelyn Atkinson, Beth and Dick Osgood, and Don and Lib Boyle and Ruth Melber.

For encouragement and practical advice about money matters, I will always be grateful to Rose and Alva Miller, John Yates, and David Ulrich. And in a category of her own must be Elaine Yates, who not only gave me financial and moral support, but the name for this book as well.

For technical advice and assistance, I am indebted to Hunter Clotfelter, Jerry Sewell, and Evelyn V. Freeman—all of Atlanta Federal Savings and Loan Association; to Lou Fortuna, Kathleen Miers, Evelyn Shepherd, Joe Daniel, and Sue Brown—of Citizens and Southern National Bank; to Frank Bentley of Merrill Lynch, Pierce, Fenner and Smith, Inc.; to Jack Townsend of Metropolitan Life Insurance Company; to Detective D. L. McCoy, and Ms. Pola Eisenstein of the Atlanta Police Department; to Mark Yates, martial arts practitioner; to Jim Deemer and Irene Sabatka of the Social Security Administration; and to Ann Lockett, Betty Davis, and Eleanor Pickett of the Internal Revenue Service.

I owe a debt of gratitude for their aid in the completion of this book to the unfailingly helpful members of the Reference Department of the Atlanta Public Library; to Sherry Fowler, Scott Yates, Ruby Owens, Jackie and Homer Bishop, the *Random House College Dictionary,* the Bureau of the Census, the Department of Labor, the Federal Bureau of Investigation, and the Internal Revenue Service for their various—and varied—contributions to my research.

I would be remiss if I failed to mention those who have loved me, encouraged me, believed in me and made life—and coping—much more pleasant than I had any reason to expect: My cronies of the early-morning radio news shift, Walt Wuthrich, Dick Garrett, Art Collier, and Harry Davey; Chuck McGivern and Michael Hunter; Mary Cobb Bugg and the ladies in my first lecture class at Emory University; my constant companions as I worked, the family pets, Fancy, Doggie, Eat, and Pye (they never offered a word of criticism); my friends and co-workers at the IRS who have been as excited about this book as I, Charleen Beneker, Connie Robertson, Terry Watkins, Don Farrell, Carla Maguire, Nell Needom, Brenda Greene, and all the rest; my supervisor and section chief, Jean Pate and Charles Haggard, who have both been understanding and accommodating about my erratic work schedule; and always, every day, for their encouragement, love, belief, support, and assistance—my four wonderful chlidren.

Coping

1

COPING WITH A NEW PHENOMENON

Single, Widowed,
or Divorced—You're It!

You may not know it yet, but because you are a woman, you will probably someday be part of a new phenomenon on the contemporary American scene: the woman alone.

Never in history has there been such an unprecedented number of women who, whether by choice or circumstance, are establishing themselves as heads of their own households.

From the agonizing birth throes of the Sixties has emerged a new world, a newly structured society with new morals and new mores, new rules, new values, and you—a new woman.

You may be young, middle-aged, or old; black, yellow, white, or red; single, widowed, or divorced; but *you* are the new phenomenon, the woman alone.

Of the twenty-three million women who are unmarried, more than fifteen million of us must maintain homes, raise families, work, pay our bills, provide guidance for our children, and struggle to achieve stability in our financial, moral, emotional, spiritual, social, and sexual lives—and all of this alone. Whether we live in an apartment with other single women or in a house with our children to raise, we are alone. Solitary. Accountable to no one, and dependent on no one but ourselves. We have the sole responsibility for every decision, every action, every whim that will affect not only our own lives but those of our children as well.

The dictionary, sparing no feelings, defines "alone" as being "apart from others, without anyone else, only, isolated, unaccompanied," and, bluntly, "companionless."

THE PROBLEMS WE FACE

That lack of companionship sums up most of the problems confronting the woman alone. Whether she has never married or is alone because of death or divorce, she must grapple with a society predicated on the family unit, on pairs, couples, *two*.

We make society uncomfortable. "What do you *do* with a single woman? How do you invite her to dinner? 'One' makes an odd number. It's a pain to worry about providing an escort. Let's just not invite her." Thus we find ourselves excluded from most normal social functions and must make our way alone—again. True, the social aspect is only one part of our lives, but, unless we are recluses, it *is* important, and it does hurt to be excluded.

Almost worse than the exclusions are the worn-out jokes about the woman who lives alone. There are still the sly winks and knowing asides insinuating that every woman living alone welcomes and maintains sybaritic orgies, and that she has or would like a succession of lovers to share her bed and abode.

Speculations about her love life are, of course, irrelevant, immaterial, and quite beside the point. The point is that whether she establishes herself in a one-room walk-up, in a houseful of other singles, or in her own home with her children, she has assumed the status of head of her own domicile. She has undertaken the responsibilities that were formerly the exclusive province of the male, and for which she is, too often, woefully unprepared.

Not only must the woman alone establish herself as an individual in our couple-oriented society, but she must make a life for herself that encompasses every facet of existence. She must work, learn to handle money, establish credit, and maintain her home. She must acknowledge and live with her sexuality, and try to achieve an identity with which she and society can be easy, content, comfortable.

HOW DID IT HAPPEN?

How did this modern phenomenon occur? Why are there these millions of women living alone? Of course, this hasn't happened overnight. It has been developing over the past several decades, but in such a gradual way that it has caught us unprepared.

For one thing, through modern medical technology, today's woman is living longer than could have been imagined a century ago. Because she is no longer the victim of childbed fever and other complications associated with giving birth, woman's natural resilience has guaranteed that she will probably outlive her mate. The built-in health safeguards peculiar to women have finally been given a chance to do the job for which they were designed. Our natural protection from heart attacks during our child-bearing years is our biggest safety factor; and until recent years and increased feminine smoking, we were protected from the dangers of lung cancer.

We are only now falling prey to the stress connected with work, which has decimated the ranks of our husbands; but we have been forewarned, and so may better pace ourselves. And with gynecological progress in menopausal hormone therapy and early detection of uterine and breast cancer, the primary female cripplers and killers of a generation ago are presently being better controlled. The result is that we are now in the majority in this country, outnumbering men by about 5 million.

A quick breakdown of the country's population, as of 1973, shows that of all the women in America who are age fourteen or older, one-third of us are alone. According to the United States Bureau of the Census, 10 million of us are single, 10 million of us are widowed, and 3 million of us are separated or divorced. Of course, not all single women live alone, but tens of thousands establish themselves in homes of their own every year.

SINGLE WOMEN

No longer is a stigma attached to the girl who leaves home before marriage. Only a generation ago, a girl stayed safely in her father's house until she was delivered into her husband's care. A "nice" girl had to be looked after and protected, since she was considered incapable of taking care of herself. At least, that was what was assumed, and the few brave souls who dared to strike out on their own were looked at with a doubt only slightly tinged with envy. Girls stayed at home, where they "belonged." It was unthinkable that any young woman would even consider wanting a place of her own before marriage. She would have been called "fast"; eyebrows would have raised and tongues wagged at the very thought of her shocking independence.

Today, as other mores have changed, so has this pattern—and usually with no bad feelings between parents and daughters. The young single woman living alone is no longer the exception, but the accepted norm. No longer must she prove herself by "catching a man," nor are her parents haunted by the specter of an old-maid daughter. The young woman of today is not marking time until marriage. Whether she decides to marry or not, living alone has become an accepted and acceptable way of life.

DIVORCEES

Divorce is another reflection of the changing manners and customs of the world today. Although divorce was scarcely discussed openly, and was considered shameful a generation ago, it is now largely looked upon as a workable solution to an unworkable situation.

This is not to say that divorce is any easier, emotionally, than it ever was, but it is no longer the rarity of the past. Our annual divorce rate is now about one-third of our annual marriage rate. This simply means that, each year, there are thousands of formerly married women who must learn to make a go of it on their own. But unlike single women, they are usually bringing to their homes children, added years, probably little or no work experience, and, all too often, a burden of guilt or bitterness over a failed marriage. So in addition to her other problems, the divorcee must overcome and adapt to changes in herself as well as in her drastically altered circumstances.

WIDOWS

Unlike her single or divorced counterparts, the widow is alone through circumstances over which she had no control and which have left her totally unprepared for the future. Her single sister chose to establish a home alone. The divorcee, whether or not the decision to divorce was hers, had some period of time in which to weigh the results of the action and, usually, to make some kind of adjustment to her new life. The widow, however, has been thrust into a situation staggeringly different from anything she could have imagined. She enters her new life shattered, in shock at the blow fate has dealt her. She is now half of a whole, an emotional cripple, an identity-less part of what may have been a warm, loving, functioning marriage to the man with whom she had wanted to spend the rest of her life. Now she faces that life alone.

The widow is a pathetic addition to the growing phenomenon of the woman alone, and the one with which society is not yet equipped to cope. Only as far back as the times of our great-grandmothers, many women died in childbirth. Their husbands, understandably, remarried to provide a mother for their children and to produce more progeny to work on the farm. Large families were desirable in then-rural America, no matter how many wives had to die in the process of creating them. Many a husband only several generations ago was buried alongside two or more young wives.

Only rarely was a woman left a widow, and then it was usually the result of war or accident. Men outnumbered women, so that a widow, usually considered an experienced homemaker (and sometimes also well-to-do), did not remain alone for long. Not that she was actually alone during her widowhood. She usually went to live with a relative until she remarried, and the widowed sister, aunt, or cousin was a familiar member of many homes. She helped with the mending or baking or caring for the children—her own and those of her relatives—did the spinning and weaving, and generally made herself useful. Sometimes she sewed to make some money, or if times were hard, she took in laundry. A few generations later, an occasional widow worked outside the home, usually as a school-teacher, but most still remained within the sanctuary of the family.

The picture wasn't all dark, however. Our forefathers, in their adherence to biblical injunctions concerning the care of widows and orphans, were watchful over them. Very few dared to incur God's wrath by harming a widow; some of the classic villains of literature were those who threatened and mistreated the widow and her fatherless children.

There were strict rules governing the behavior of the widow, especially during the Victorian era. She draped herself in "weeds"—black dress and veil—so that all the world would know of her loss. This labeled her as one alone and requiring the protection and solicitude of others—particularly men. It also let those same men know that within a certain period of time she would be available for marriage and willing to listen to any attractive proposals. Naturally, she was not expected to live the rest of her life alone. She was a rare commodity, and much in demand.

It's different today. There are too many of us, and we are rapidly ab-sorbed into society. Widows are no longer easily identified, and that is probably a change for the better. But it must have given the widow of the past some solace to know that her loss entitled her to special treatment.

My Widowhood

I would be less than honest if I didn't admit to a longing, every now and then, for a little special treatment. As a woman of the late twentieth century, I'm not supposed to need it, and am expected to be capable of facing my new life alone. I certainly had never been alone until my husband died in 1970. I was married at eighteen and had spent my entire adult life wrapped in my husband's love and cushioned against the harsh realities of the world.

I was God's golden girl. All my wishes had been fulfilled, and I had every reason to expect life to continue as I had planned.

George and I had been sweethearts since the day we met, when I was fifteen and he was nineteen. As young as we were, we both believed that we were meant to spend the rest of our lives together. Miraculously, our love had ripened to a richness that even I hadn't anticipated in my wildest dreams.

And I *was* given to daydreams, as were most of my contemporaries. A child of the movie-going Thirties, I truly believed what Hollywood told me —that every story must have a happy ending. I expected my life to reflect that deliciously deluding philosophy.

Before George's death, if I had taken time from my busy, fulfilling life to assess its condition, I would have realized the extent to which all my dreams had come true. George and I had wanted to marry; we did, and never wanted anyone else. We had wanted to have a large, loving family (this was before the days of zero population growth), and we were the parents of four bright, attractive, outgoing children.

We had wanted to raise our children in as rural a setting as his architectural practice would permit. So we had bought twenty beautiful wooded acres outside Atlanta in what became the most desirable neighborhood in town. Our house, which George designed, was comfortable and large enough for us, the children, and their constant stream of friends.

George's architectural practice was growing every year and had earned professional recognition. Gratifyingly, it had supplied us with a handsome income. This, too, was another fulfillment of my dreams. Not just the success of George's practice, but that I was a part of it. In this, as in everything else, we shared our lives. I was George's consultant, responsible for all the public relations work, and for writing articles for his architectural journals. I handled the office's business details, which he despised, freeing him to do the creative work he so loved.

Nor was this sharing one-sided. Just as I was involved in George's professional life, so was he equally absorbed in the upbringing of our children. For many years he had maintained his office at home so that we could share in the wonderful experience of raising our family. The children grew up with two parents in the home, and felt as close to one as to the other.

There was no one disciplinarian, as so often happens if the father is infrequently at home. We shared the discipline, the fun, the illnesses, the joys and sorrows and triumphs which made up the fabric of our children's early years, and, in the process, wove a close, loving, supportive family. Every response and reaction our children have had in the years since their father's death can be attributed to their childhood, and to the love and care they received from both George and me. They have returned that love a hundredfold.

In short, my every dream had come true. George and I were busy, happy, successful, productive people. We had our love for each other and our family, community respect, good friends, and a firm faith in God's abiding love and care. We were sure that we would live to be very old people and would die in each other's arms.

In the space of one heartbeat, on a beautiful sunny July morning, all of that ended, and nothing will ever be the same for me again.

George woke up that last morning of his life, had an early breakfast, prepared to attend a business meeting, was stricken with a heart attack, and died instantly.

The autopsy which his doctor and my friends insisted that I authorize showed that a massive blood clot had blocked a valve to his heart, and that he was dead before he fell to the floor. All the medical teams in the world could not have saved him.

Thank God I consented to the autopsy; I was at least spared the agonizing self-recrimination common to most widows. If I had not had the post-mortem performed, I would have spent the rest of my life torturing myself with "what ifs": "what if" I could have gotten him to the hospital, "what if" I had suggested he have an examination by a heart specialist, "what if" I had urged him to slow down. These are all middle-of-the-night horrors, to which every widow is prey, and they can cripple her so that she ceases to function normally. There was nothing I could have done to have prevented George's death. I accepted that fact, and so could turn my attention to the immediate problems with which I was confronted.

And the problems were many and complex.

I, like millions of other women, had to assume responsibility for myself, my children, our finances, and our future. I was not prepared for the task and didn't know how to start. I wanted nothing so much as to withdraw, to hide, to whimper, to suffer in seclusion. But I couldn't, any more than any other widow.

Our impulse—and it's a valid one—is to delay, but we must begin coping with our new world immediately after our husbands' deaths. We think it can't happen to us, and it is a cruel shock to realize that it can, it has, and we must move forward.

I knew that I needed guidance, a road map for the new world of widowhood. I didn't need the slim volumes of inspirational verse or uplifting passages that well-meaning friends press into the unresisting hands of every widow. I needed practical help and I knew it. There may be some women who are so completely self-reliant and independent that they don't require outside help and advice, but most of us hunger for it. I desperately needed to know that I was not unique in the way I felt and in the problems I now confronted—alone. I wanted to be told, "Yes, this grief is more than you can bear, but you *will* bear it, it *will* lessen, you *will* be able to make it."

But no one will sit the widow down—or the divorcee, or the single women beginning life alone—and tell her, "This is the way it is; this is the way you'll feel; this is what needs doing; these are the problems you'll face; these are the rules which will now govern your life." That's what I needed, and I also needed someone to tell me how brave and capable I was, even though I was quivering with fear at the awesome responsibilities confronting me, and even though I knew that my capabilities were limited to worrying at a problem, like a dog at a bone, until I was forced into a solution, whether good or bad.

Following immediately upon the shock of George's death (which I could neither comprehend nor believe) was the impact of the discovery of our disastrous financial situation.

George's estate consisted of the house, the twenty acres on which it stood, his insurance, the business assets, our cars, and his personal effects. Theoretically, this made me a very wealthy woman, because of the value of the land; however, in actuality there was very little cash except for the fees outstanding on the jobs under construction and on the insurance money.

I was dealt quick blows in all cases.

First, and most importantly, it would be impossible to sell the land, or even to take out a loan on it with which I could educate my children and which I could repay with the Social Security money we would be receiving. In our not too well-to-do youth, George had bought the land in partnership with a male relative. Over the years the co-owner had refused to consider selling the land, either to us or on the open market, so that now, having inherited George's half of the title, I found myself in the uncomfortable position of being co-owner of an increasingly valuable piece of property which I could not sell and against which I could not borrow—because of the selfish obstinacy of an elderly man.

Nor was the picture any brighter as far as the fees and the insurance were concerned. There would be heavy expenses involved in finishing the construction jobs, and most of the insurance was tied up in a "family income policy" which would pay me a monthly income for the next ten years.

That seemed like a comfortable arrangement, but we had taken out the policy when the children were babies, and the monthly income had been predicated on living expenses of the Fifties. Now, in 1970, a month's insurance check would just about cover a week's grocery bill, and prices were still climbing. Of course, we would be receiving Social Security and Veterans Administration survivors' benefits, but it was frighteningly obvious that we would no longer live in the affluent style to which we had become accustomed. (I learned later that our income would be exactly one-tenth of that on which we had been living before George's death.) We would still have all the accoutrements of wealth without the income necessary to support them.

As far as the business was concerned, I decided to complete all jobs under construction with the help of George's able chief draftsman, who would work under the aegis of another friend, a registered architect. I decided not to sell the practice; it was a creation of George's talent and spirit and imagination, and without him, it was dead. I closed the office within the year.

I knew that it was just a matter of time until I would have to look for a job, and I knew it wouldn't be easy to find one. True, I had served as George's promotional consultant, but I had never had to work for a living, and didn't know where to start.

I needed a practical guide to the dozens of unexpected things I would have to handle alone. The children, money, work, credit, bills, home and car repairs, taxes, faith, sex, and the constant search for some kind of stability and security. I found none, and I learned very early that no matter how much advice I might receive, the final decisions were always mine, and the knowledge was frightening. It always came back to the one inescapable fact that I was alone. Ill-prepared and alone. I also learned that, granted the differences in age, circumstances, and family and financial status, all of us who are widows, divorcees, or single have one common denominator—the very fact of our aloneness. The decisions are ours, the responsibilities are ours, the course of our lives are ours—alone. We are asked to cope with problems and pitfalls undreamed of by our predecessors. We are expected to survive and—hopefully—to conquer them. The definition of "cope" is "to struggle or contend on fairly even terms or with some degree of success"; coping requires some knowledge, some help, and a lot of guts. I learned that I *could* cope, and do it well.

COPING

And I learned the most valuable lesson of all—that being "alone" does not have to be a negative condition. It hasn't been an easy lesson, but I have learned that in today's world, with so many women outliving men, there will continue to be more and more women alone. We must be able to rely on ourselves; we must do what we can to prepare ourselves for the possibility of spending many years—perhaps the rest of our lives—alone. We need to strengthen our inner resources, and we need to know how to cope with the practical aspects of daily life.

But we can't reach these goals without preparation. It is vitally important that before women are widowed or divorced or leave the parental nest they take the steps that will qualify them for that almost inevitable day when they *will* be alone.

Women who are married now or who ever expect to be—again or for the first time—must take certain steps to prepare for widowhood. Some women face widowhood two and three times and are no more prepared for it the third time than the first.

Widows and divorcees must acknowledge and accept the fact that they must cope alone with the complex situations they used to share with their husbands—situations for which neither training nor society has prepared them.

Single women leaving home for the first time must learn to budget their time and money, and to establish themselves as women of property, substance, and consequence.

All women alone must adapt to drastic changes in lifestyle, finances, and status. We must guard against becoming victims of everything from rape to discrimination—to the woman alone, one is almost as damaging as the other. We must confront problems and overcome them.

Our horizons are limitless; there are no heights we cannot reach. The future is opening to us in career opportunities that were unheard of two decades ago. We can create rich, full, productive lives, and we *can* do it by ourselves.

We may be alone, yes, but we are not helpless. We can now—for the first time in the history of womankind—realize the potential within ourselves. We *can* achieve; we *can* succeed; we *can* survive; we *can* triumph—and we can do it alone.

2

COPING BEFORE WIDOWHOOD

It's Easier Now
Than Later

The woman who faces the greatest emotional shock—the most traumatic experience that causes her to enter life alone—is the widow.

Studies show that the loss of a woman's mate creates more stress than does any other single event in her life. There is no way to prepare for the emotional agony she will suffer. But I have learned from bitter experience that there are sound practical steps every woman and her husband can take to make those days alone a little easier.

There were so many steps that George and I could have taken to have made my widowhood more bearable. But we didn't, and I had to find my way through its complexities alone.

My problems were not unique. Almost every woman in America— whatever her current marital (or nonmarital) status—is a potential widow, and if there were one message I could get to each of you, it would be, "Take care of his will and insurance *now*, before he dies." Nothing else is so important to the welfare of the widow, with or without children.

THE WILL

If your husband dies intestate—a word lawyers love that simply means "without a will"—it is possible that all he has left will revert to the state in which you live. If there are relatives who could make a claim against his estate, you are facing potential trouble. And without a proper will, there is the possibility, in some states, that the mother would have to be appointed her children's guardian by the court, and that she would have to post a bond and make regular reports concerning their care and upbringing.

Frightening? No question about it, yet thousands of women have to go through this heartache, which is added to the grief they are already experiencing. It need not have happened—if only their husbands had made good, specific wills.

Too many men, with the best intentions in the world, simply put off making a will as one more unpleasant chore, and some feel that when they sign their "last will and testament" they are hastening their own deaths, or acknowledging their own mortality. These feelings are understandable, but the unpleasantness facing a widow left without an adequate will far outweighs any masculine squeamishness.

The cost of having a will drawn is minimal, and the time required to meet with a lawyer is negligible, so there is no excuse for your husband to delay. Laws vary from state to state, as do rules governing property ownership and guardianship of minor children, so each individual will must be drawn by an attorney familiar with those laws. (It's a good idea, if you move to another state, to have a lawyer check the will to ensure that nothing has been invalidated by local laws.)

But one thing is applicable nationwide, and that is the "marital deduction" allowed by the Internal Revenue Service, permitting a person to leave the surviving spouse up to 50 percent of the adjusted gross estate free of tax.

In simple language, and using figures provided by the IRS, this means that if your husband's adjusted gross estate, less deductible expenses, amounted to $70,000, the estate tax, with no marital deduction, would be $500, while with the full marital deduction it would be zero. Jump up a few brackets, to an adjusted gross estate of $150,000, and the tax without the marital deduction is $17,900; with the deduction it is $1,050. It is obvious that this can make a great difference. So be sure the marital deduction is written into your husband's will.

THE ESTATE

And don't say to yourself, "Estate! That's just for rich people." Don't fool yourself. You'll be surprised how rapidly a man's worth increases when he dies!

Does he have insurance? You won't have to pay *income* tax on it, but it *will* be included in his estate. Do you own a house? That goes into the estate. Is there furniture in the house? That goes into the estate, too. Carpets? A refrigerator? Does he wear clothes? Does he own a camera? Guns? Cars? Stocks and bonds? Savings? A bank account? If he owns his business, what are the assets? They'll be counted in the estate. How about office furniture and equipment? Does someone owe him money? That adds to the sum.

But don't be discouraged. From all of this you'll be able to deduct the cost of his funeral. (But don't go overboard on that account; insist on the next to the lowest price. It will look nice, and you're going to need that money.) You'll be able to deduct the cost of flowers you order for the funeral, the cost of his hospital bills, the ambulance, and the marker for his grave. If he was a veteran, the Veterans Administration will supply a handsome, flat bronze plaque. (I used this, added his Airborne insignia for eight dollars, and bought, through the cemetery, a marble base and bronze urn. It makes a simple, beautiful memorial. All of that is deductible, except the part supplied by the VA.) The cost of the cemetery plot is deductible, but don't get the most expensive because of that. Select one in an area that is not isolated, however, so that you will feel comfortable visiting the grave alone. But *don't wait until it is needed.* Select and buy one now; you can sell it if you move before it's used.

You will also be able to deduct the cost of the attorney who will handle your legal affairs, as well as the amount it will cost to have the will probated. A word here about legal fees. Have a written agreement with the attorney or Certified Public Accountant who will prepare the estate return to be filed with the state and national revenue services. Do *not* allow the fee to be based on a percentage of the value of the estate. Too often, as in my own case, the value on paper and the actual available cash are two entirely different things. Shop around for an attorney or a CPA and retain the one who is most reasonable. In this, as in every other area of your life, remember that it is *your* money, and you are entitled to expect the best service for the most reasonable charge.

Other items deductible from the value of the estate are outstanding loans not canceled by credit life insurance and all debts owed when your husband died.

You will be able to deduct the United States income tax due the next year, which will be based on your husband's earnings in the year of his death. (The IRS mercifully grants a special rate for widows with dependent children on their own returns for the two years following the husband's death. This is a tremendous help.) You can also deduct any losses incurred in the administration of the estate, as well as various other incidental expenses.

THE ESTATE TAX RETURN

If you're lucky, the deductions will decrease or eliminate any estate tax you might have to pay. But don't count on it, and don't hope for the best. Hope has nothing to do with it, but good planning *now* can save time and money and agony later when you'll be coping with all of this alone.

You're not given much time, either. The final return must be sent to the Internal Revenue Service and your state revenue department within nine months after your husband's death. Any debts still unpaid or any monies still due you can be estimated and included on a fiduciary return later.

Legally, you will have a year in which to pay debts incurred before your husband's death, but if he owns his own business or professional practice, pay the business debts during the calendar year in which he dies. That way you will be able to deduct them on that year's tax return, and you'll need them that year because your own future returns will probably never involve as much money as your husband made. Sad, but true.

THE DUTIES OF AN EXECUTRIX

When your husband has his will drawn, be sure that you are named the executrix. There are duties involved, but unless you are so wealthy that the estate is cumbersome, there will be nothing you can't handle. However, if you feel that you cannot execute the duties, have your husband name a bank or a competent, trusted individual. You'll have to pay a fee for the services, but that is deductible, too.

By remembering that state laws and the customary legal practices in certain locales will vary some of these items, you can safely follow the list below, prepared by Louis M. Brown, professor of Law at the University of Southern California, in performance of your duties as executrix. You will need to:

Have an attorney petition for probate, obtain a court order appointing you as executrix, and publish a notice to all creditors

Assemble, inventory, and protect assets of the estate

Give notice to debtors and creditors of the estate that all bills will be paid to or from the estate

File claims for insurance and other benefits applicable

Decide whether to continue, liquidate, or sell the business

Obtain appraisal of assets

File preliminary estate returns where required

Collect income and other funds owed decedent

Pay just claims and bills

Prepare income tax return

Have lawyer or accountant prepare and file estate return

File the fiduciary tax return

This list is rudimentary, but should cover any ordinary estate with ease. If the estate is involved and takes several years to close, you may have to file a fiduciary return each year. Don't be alarmed. It is a simple form reporting any estate business transacted during that year. And if, years later, you find that there was something to be done that wasn't completed, just file an amended final return with all the necessary information with the IRS, and any necessary adjustments will be made.

TRUSTS

I have deliberately omitted anything about trusts from the above list. I am ambivalent about trusts. If there is a great amount of money involved in the estate, I would recommend a trust. Otherwise, no. The trustees will invest the money and will dole out a certain amount to you, but their charges are steep. So if money will be limited, you will be able to do a better job of handling it yourself. Living trusts are different, and will be discussed more completely in Chapters 5 and 6.

One more word about the will. Be sure you are named as your children's guardian, and have your husband name a contingent guardian, someone on whom you both agree, in case you are disabled or die while the children are minors. Let your own will (more about that in Chapter 5) repeat this.

INSURANCE

So much for the will—now let's talk about insurance.

I've told you how woefully inadequate George's coverage was. Our agent was entirely blameless in this. He had been gently but firmly urging George to take out additional insurance, especially because we had several small loans outstanding on the policies. These amounts would be deducted from the final payments to me. He also stressed to us that the family income policy was not large enough to meet living costs as they stood in 1970, and wanted us to increase the amount.

We knew him, and knew he was truly concerned and not simply trying to sell insurance, so we discussed the pros and cons, and decided to delay. The nation's economy was undergoing a tremendous downswing at the time, and the building industry had been especially hard-hit. We reasoned that George was in perfect health—hadn't he passed his recent physical with flying colors? And our business and personal expenses were at a peak.

There was Scott's college tuition—high by any standards and rising every quarter; there were the payments on the two new cars; and there was, at this particular time in George's practice, more money going out than was coming back in to us.

So we decided to postpone taking out the $100,000 policy that our agent felt would give the children and me the necessary coverage to maintain our standard of living and to insure the children's education.

We decided to delay; we gambled, and we lost.

Profit from my experience—do not delay. Get out your husband's policies (you *do* know where they are, don't you?) and examine them in the light of the constantly increasing living costs. Don't think, as I did, that when your husband dies you will be an old lady, with few needs of your own because your children will be grown and no longer need your support.

Look at those policies and the provisions in them as if you were going to have to use them tomorrow. And as if that were all the money you will have for a long, long time to come, as it well may be.

Granted, you will probably work; but what if something happens to you and you can't? You'll receive Social Security benefits, but not enough to cover medical bills or child care. There is *never* enough money for the woman raising a family alone, or for the woman beyond retirement age.

So look closely at that insurance, and urge your husband to increase it to the maximum your budget will stand. (Metropolitan Life Insurance Company recommends the amount should be no more than seven times the wage-earner's annual income.) If that means that you will have to take a part-time job to pay for the premiums, or that you will have to do without something you had planned to buy, it will be worth it. Just make sure that you will be adequately provided for when your husband dies. Too few families are alert to the dangers of insufficient coverage. As a result, it is exceptional for a widow to have been left as much as $10,000 in insurance if her husband's income was in a below median bracket. Men in the middle income range usually carry more insurance, $50,000 to $70,000, but even that's too little.

So much for the amount of the policies. There are two other important items that you must see to now. What kind of policy does he have, and to whom is it made out? From my own experience, I would vote against a family income policy unless it has a feasible cost-of-living clause written into it, whereby the premiums would increase (or possibly decrease, in the case of a depression) to meet your projected annual living expenses. Make sure the amount you will receive monthly will be adequate if it were your sole source of income. But be warned—the premiums will be high.

Personally, I prefer the lump-sum type of payment. That way, you will have the money on hand when you need it most. And you will be able to invest it so that you may realize the maximum amount of interest. I petitioned our insurance company to convert our family income policy into a lump-sum payment, but was refused because, in their words, "minor children are involved." Of course, the fact that I need the money to educate those minors boggled the company's corporate minds, so I'll still be receiving my little monthly checks long after the children have all left home.

So don't go into a family income policy without careful thought; it can tie up the bulk of the insurance money during the very years you'll need it most.

Equally as important as the type of policy is the way in which it will be paid. *Do not let it name you as the beneficiary!*

Surprised? I imagine you are, because the majority of policies issued in the United States are written naming the wife as the husband's beneficiary, although nothing could be worse.

What is wrong with it? It enters into the estate if written that way, and you want to avoid that. Remember that I told you that you will not have to pay income tax on the proceeds from insurance policies, but that the amount will be included in the estate? True, but there is a childishly simple way to avoid this. Have the policy written naming you as the *owner*. It doesn't change a thing as far as the premiums are concerned, and if a loan is ever taken out on the policy you will have to sign the forms, but other than that the policy is exactly like any other. Except that it is free and clear of the estate.

Many men shy away from having a policy on their lives owned by someone else, as if it were a death warrant. That is a foolish and selfish attitude that doesn't make sense. No man who loves his wife and is truly concerned about her welfare will hesitate a minute in having such a policy. Nor can he balk because of the possible loss of investment in the policy in the event the wife dies first. He would simply bring the policy to his agent and have it reassigned. In other words, there is no valid objection that a husband can make to such a policy, and every wife should insist on it.

I realize that I seem to be harping on the estate, but remember that any legitimate way you can avoid paying taxes is something you cannot afford (literally) to overlook. And don't think that because your income is small now it will necessarily remain so. You can never tell what might happen to make your husband's net worth increase. The state might want to buy your property for an airport site; a developer might need it for a subdivision; your husband might strike it rich in his business. You just never can tell, but you *can* be prepared.

WHY PREPARE NOW?

Don't think that any of these preparations make you seem like a ghoul, counting the days until your husband dies. That kind of thinking is not only unrealistic and ridiculous, it's downright dangerous. The fact

that the number of widows in America is increasing so rapidly, and that
we are becoming widows at earlier ages should add an urgent sense of
immediacy to your preparations.

I know it isn't pleasant to contemplate, but read the obituary column
in your daily paper for a few days, and notice the ages of the men. They
are dying younger and younger (leaving younger and younger widows)
every year. Their high, early mortality rate is attributable to many factors,
stress among them, and I think we cannot overlook that peculiar stress
associated with modern war. Surely a constant heightening and lowering
of the level of adrenalin flowing throughout the system damages our men's
bodies. I believe that we are seeing the results now, in the abnormally
early deaths of veterans of World War II, Korea, and Vietnam.

Widowhood can and does happen unexpectedly every day, so prepare
now with those things you can do in advance. There is nothing you can
do to prepare for the wrenching emotions you will feel when it happens
to you. But you can take many practical steps to make those days alone
a little easier.

Although the will and insurance take top priority on the list of preparations you must make before you become a widow, there are other matters
you should attend to as soon as possible.

VITAL DOCUMENTS

Know where all the family documents are, and get them together in one
place so you can locate them when necessary. Where is his will? Keep
it in a metal box at home, but keep all the others in a safe deposit box
at the bank or savings and loan. (You can rent a small but adequate box
for as little as $5 to $10 a year.) If your husband was in the armed service,
you'll need his discharge paper. Do you know where it is? You must have
it to file a claim with the Veterans Administration. Do you know his
Social Security number? Do you know where your marriage license and
the children's birth certificates are? These, together with a certificate of
his death, will be necessary to file a claim with the Social Security Administration.

You'll need to file those claims as soon as possible after your husband's
death. Don't think it will be something you will do automatically. Remember, you will be in shock and probably not functioning normally.
I know one widow who is a college director of admissions—obviously a
woman of intelligence—who didn't file a Social Security claim on behalf
of her minor child until eighteen months after her husband's death.

TITLES

Where is the title to the house? The car? You'll have to have all of these changed after his death unless they are already made out to you as co-owner, or, better still, as sole owner. But *not* as joint owner—that presents tax problems. To quote the trust department of the Citizens and Southern Banks in Georgia,

> By placing property in joint and survivor names, a person may unknowingly make a taxable gift. This would occur, for example, should you purchase a U.S. Government Savings Bond in your name and your wife's and she later redeemed it for cash. On the other hand, the entire value of the bond could be taxed in the estate of the first co-owner to die. Later, the same property would be taxed again at the death of the surviving owner.

This last condition applies to my own case in respect to the property. It has already been taxed as part of George's estate, and, unless I can dispose of it before my death, will be taxed again as part of mine.

Do not hesitate to go to the Internal Revenue Service for advice. It is part of the Service's duty to collect the taxes to which the government is entitled, true, but the part of its duty which is too often ignored is service to the taxpayer. And that service includes helping you find the most advantageous and legitimate means to avoid paying unnecessary taxes.

If you have a savings account is it made out in both names? If so, you'll be able to withdraw from it with no trouble, and it will not enter into your husband's estate.

Of course, the ideal would be to have everything in your name now —house, car, checking and savings accounts. But there are very few men so secure in their masculinity that they would agree to so drastic a move. They know that the control of money is the control of power—women are just learning that fact—and they are unwilling to relinquish that control.

But on the other hand, perhaps you've heard the apocryphal Rose Rappaport story. Rose arrived at the cemetery gates with an armload of flowers for her husband's grave. She was stopped by an officious young guard who told her she could not enter.

"What do you mean, not enter? My husband is buried in there."

"I can't help that," responded the guard. "This is a new rule, and you can't enter unless the name of the deceased is on our list."

"Oh, well," said Rose, "there's no problem. The name is Rappaport."

The guard checked his list and shook his head.

"I'm sorry, there's no record of your husband."

"What?" cried Rose. "Of course there is; he's been here eleven years."
"No," said the guard, "there's only one Rappaport, and that's Rose."
"Well, of course," said Rose. "We put *everything* in my name!"

Farfetched, but I'll bet Rose didn't have the problems the rest of us face in changing titles and establishing ownership after our husbands' deaths.

So you'll probably have to settle for co-ownership. Check with your lawyer or the institutions involved to be sure there are no local laws that could create problems later when you will change title and establish ownership after your husband's death.

If you and your husband have a mortgage or any other outstanding loans, make sure you also have credit life insurance on each. This is an inexpensive policy attached to each loan that will pay the entire balance due upon the death of the insured. I cannot recommend it too highly.

Your Own Credit Rating

Now is the time for you to establish your own credit rating.

Borrow a small sum from the bank. Try to negotiate a loan on your personal signature, if you are known to the officials. If not, you may have to offer something of your own as collateral. It might be a piece of jewelry or a savings bond. The important thing is to have the loan in *your* name, and without your husband as co-signer. Have the loan in your legal name, Mary L. Smith, not Mrs. John G. Smith, and repay it promptly. Keep doing this until you have firmly established a credit rating quite apart from your husband's.

Try to open a charge account in your name, if you are working, and list only your income. On the line requiring "name of spouse" leave a blank. Again, do not have your husband co-sign. If you are refused the account, challenge it. Go to the president and demand that he allow you the same privilege he would accord an employed man. It won't be easy, but if you can establish your own credit now, you will have fewer problems when you become a widow.

The picture is grimmer for those wives who are not employed outside the home. Their plight is identical to that of widows, single women, and those who are separated or divorced. I'll discuss it further in Chapter 11.

Miscellaneous Preparations

Now is the time to train yourself to earn a living if you're not already employed. Don't expect to be able to throw yourself into a glutted employment market and get a job easily. Especially if you have no skills. So go now to night school and brush up on your typing. Or your college major. Or a field in which you are particularly interested or adept. Work a couple of mornings in the library, or a department store. Take a course that will train you to become a medical assistant. *Anything* to gain experience and to give you self-confidence. You'll need both!

Other, more mundane things that you can do now in preparation for your days alone are as simple as knowing where the cut-off valve for the water is located. Do you know where it is? There might be a leak or a broken pipe and you'd *have* to know—fast. Do you know the capacity of your oil tank if your house is heated by oil or butane? Do you know when and from whom to order refills?

Do you know how to replace a fuse? A washer? Do you know where your husband takes the car for repairs? Do you know the size of the tires? They'll wear out, you know. If you live in an apartment, do you know where the lease is? Is there any sort of escape clause in it which would allow you to move to a smaller apartment when you're alone? Or to move out entirely? Do you know how much of the initial deposit you are entitled to if you move?

Do you know good repairmen who are reliable and honest? A reputable television repairman? If you have new kitchen equipment, do you know where the warranties are? And how good they are? Can you replace a float in the toilet tank? (I didn't even know they existed, but I've become a minor plumbing expert.)

I've had to learn all these things alone, and so have millions of other women, but you now have an advantage; you are forewarned and can prepare in advance. Have your husband show you how to take care of all these matters now. He's the best one to teach you, and I guarantee that you *will* need the knowledge. It is your dowry to take into widowhood.

And now that you've taken care of all of the practical details *before* you become a widow, you will be able to cope with them much more easily later, when they're necessary.

So relax, and treasure your man while you've got him. Don't take him for granted. Make some beautiful memories. Love him, and let him know you do.

He may make you a widow tomorrow.

3

COPING WITH WIDOWHOOD

"Widow"—The Loneliest Word in the World

In the old romantic novels, a bereft lover frequently died of a broken heart.

Don't count on it. It doesn't happen that way, and those of us who are widows have been left to cope with a life unlike anything we could ever have imagined.

All of us, at one time or another during our married lives, have tried to picture what it would be like if our husbands died. Believe me, the reality is something for which the most vivid imagination cannot prepare you.

You can—and I hope, will—make practical preparations for the state of widowhood, but there is little you can do in advance that will brace you for the wrenching emotions of grief and sorrow you will suffer.

It's a pity there cannot be some wise, all-knowing personage to induct us into widowhood; someone who can warn us of the strange, lost feelings we will endure; who can map the pitfalls ahead of us; and who can caution us to beware of the searing agonies ahead.

But there is no such person or ceremony. We are thrust into limbo by the death of our mates, and become overnight, different women. Lonely, frightened, alone—women apart.

THE WIDOW

A widow is a mutant, grafted onto the species; a source of anxiety and discomfort to a society that favors pairs and couples. We are neither maid nor married, yet we carry about with us all of the appurtenances of marriage—the name, the ring, the possessions, the children. Each one of us feels alone and helpless, and we wonder, "Am I the only woman who feels this way? Am I the only one tortured by these fears and doubts about my life alone?" The answer, of course, is "No." You are *not* unique. Other women have suffered as you are suffering, and they have become normally functioning human beings once more; so will you.

It isn't easy. You will not arrive at that state soon, or without additional scars. You will suffer intense grief, sorrow, rebellion, and anger. But you will live through it. You will survive, and you will, incredibly, adapt to your new life alone. Gradually you will begin to see ahead a glimmer of your ultimate goal—acceptance.

I hope your marriage was happy. I hope that you had many years together; however many they were, they were too short. But you will have to face the fact that from now on you will be living with memories. Treasure them, but don't burden yourself with them. We all wish that we had been a little sweeter or more patient or more loving. But we are only human. Don't torture yourself with regrets and remorse. If you had a good marriage, he understood and forgave, and the way you might have responded on a given occasion days or months or years ago did not subtract one minute from his life. He loved you—remember that.

The hardest thing for you now is to face the trite fact that, although he is dead, life does go on; you are alive and must make a life for yourself, alone.

Consider yourself blessed indeed if you have children still living at home. They will give you a reason for living when it seems that there can no longer be one. The simple mechanics involved in managing a family household will *make* you get up each day and accomplish something, no matter how little.

And that is no minor feat, because you will find yourself beset by a plague of mental paralysis.

After that week of near-hypnosis following your husband's death and burial, you suddenly find yourself gripped by the most exhausting let-down. You have held yourself together while you planned the funeral. You greeted and talked with all the callers; you maintained a facade of calm acceptance and stability. Now the funeral is over. The flowers have withered and the callers have gone, and the doubts and fears descend upon you like dark birds of prey.

For a while you—and society—have held them at bay. There had been, hanging protectively between you, the tapestry of death, woven of the small, everyday things society has devised to ease those who are grief-stricken back into the routine of daily life. There have been the decisions to be made about the casket, the funeral, the songs and verses, the flowers, the pallbearers. These details following a death keep the mind and hands busy, and that is their purpose.

The Rituals of Death

I used to think that all the trappings surrounding death were foolish and hard on the family, but I feel differently about them now. They help. They get the family's minds on something besides the terrible, inescapable fact of death. And anything that helps is valid. For this reason, I do not believe that the family needs to see the body of the deceased more than once, and then only briefly. I do not think children should see it at all. I do *not* believe that love and devotion are shown by viewing a dead body, and the nightmares and unnecessary pain it can cause should be avoided.

I was adamant about not going to see George's body. I was determined that my final memory of him would not be of his body lying in a casket. (I insisted on his body being in the casket until burial; I think "slumber rooms" are an obscene travesty—a hypocritical denial of the fact of death, as are terms such as "passed away" or "gone to rest.") But a friend who knew I had not yet absorbed the reality of George's death insisted that I allow her to take me to the mortuary the day before the funeral. Wise friend. I will be forever grateful that she insisted I go. But not for any of the sentimental reasons commonly voiced. Not because George looked "natural"—he didn't—but because he looked *dead,* and seeing his body was the first step on my long, tortuous journey toward the day when I could finally acknowledge the unalterable fact of his death.

Denial of Death

There would be months—no, years—ahead of self-delusion, when I would tell myself that he wasn't really dead, and that he would come back to me. I have run the length of a shopping mall because I thought I saw him at the other end; I have followed a car for miles until I could see the driver again, because he had turned his head as George had; I have answered the telephone expecting to hear his beloved voice on the other end of the wire.

But every time I indulged one of my fantasies the nagging memory of seeing him in death would come back to me, and I would have to admit that he is dead, that he will never return, that I will never see him again in this life.

So I am thankful that I saw his body. This self-delusion is common among widows. It is a natural last-ditch fight against accepting the fact of death. And we *must* accept that fact. The loss of touch with reality is a very real danger for every widow—when her grasp on reality is tenuous at best. Reality is often too painful to face—but the alternative is madness.

SHOCK

Fortunately, during those first weeks, you will be in deep shock. This state is a gift of nature that cannot be too gratefully received. It enables us to discuss the death in a normal way, for example, while in years to come it will be almost impossible. It makes us able to make all the decisions necessary to the ceremony of death, while later the simplest one will cause us agonies of delay and self-doubt. If it were not for this blessed cushion of shock the pain would be unbearable and we would be unable to function.

The anguish of the widow is inconceivable to anyone who has not loved deeply and lost that love. Only in the last few years have studies been conducted showing the ravages of her grief. Research by psychobiologists has found that all significant life changes—whether good or bad—are stressful, but that nothing exceeds the stress created by the loss of a mate. Psychiatrist Thomas Holmes and physiologist Minoru Masuda of the University of Washington School of Medicine list life changes in descending order of stress, and show a direct link between illness and the magnitude of life crises. Their study has shown that during the year or two following major changes in your life, you are more susceptible to illness, probably because your general resistance is low, and you are more vulnerable to sickness or accident. The most catastrophic event on the scientists' stress chart is the death of a spouse, at 100 "Life Change Units," followed by divorce, 73, marital separation, 65, and death of a close family member, 63.

So it is comforting to know that we are finally coming to the attention of the medical community, which will consequently be better equipped to deal with the after-effects of our loss.

The effects of the stresses created by the death of a mate are apparent immediately. There are the delusions, the refusals to accept. It is impossible to emphasize too strongly the fact that we are not normal. By any psychological test, a widow during the first year after her husband's death would be ranked far from the accepted norm of mental stability. Our minds seem to atrophy; we feel that the world is passing us by. And we don't really care. Some women, formerly active and well-informed participants in the community, withdraw completely into themselves. The classic example is Queen Victoria, who went into seclusion for many years following the death of her Albert, and whose only contact with the outside world—her family or her realm—was through a servant. It is a wonder either Victoria or the British Empire survived.

Victoria's was an extreme case, but nevertheless there are women who withdraw from reality and court self-destruction by neglecting themselves.

They are indulging that death wish that entices every widow. We think longingly of the peace, the serenity, the forgetfulness of death. Fortunately, few of us do anything about it; mercifully, we gradually overcome this dangerous fancy. Just keep in mind that this is not an unusual reaction; others feel the same. When George died I wanted to die, too. I thought wistfully of the old Hindu custom of suttee, whereby the widow was placed on her husband's funeral pyre. It solved so many problems. But, realistically, I had my children to care for, and I knew that I couldn't leave them, so I kept on struggling, one day at a time, until I vanquished that seductive call to oblivion.

BITTERNESS AND REBELLION

Once the widow is over the initial shock and disbelief, she enters into another stage of her grief, probably the most damaging of all—the bitterness and rebellion she feels against the fact of her widowhood. This is when all the excruciating agony she has been feeling is distilled and focused into one cry, "Why?"

You will be torn to bits asking that unanswerable question. You will hear, like a drumbeat in your brain, "Whywhywhywhywhywhy?" It will take you closer to the brink of insanity than will anything else. But there is no answer, so you will draw on whatever sustains you—your faith, your will power, your courage—until you finally reach a day of acceptance. Not of comprehension; of acceptance. It takes a long time to come, and it will be a hard-won victory, but one day your gratitude for what the two of you had together will outweigh the bitterness at what you have lost. But for the rest of your life, you will struggle with the resentment and anguish that are always ready to destroy the peace you have found.

The fight will be particularly difficult when you see some of the apparently unworthy men still alive. Don't think you won't ask yourself why they weren't taken instead of your husband. There is no answer to this unpleasant question—it is one you will have to put out of your mind, for your sanity's sake. You must become selfish and concentrate on what is best for *you*—mentally, physically, and emotionally. Your husband's death is unfair and impossible to understand, but it is an incontrovertible fact, and the sooner you can accept it, the sooner you will reach the stability for which you must search.

You may as well make up your mind right now to learn to live with not only the unfairness but also some of the inanities you will hear from the most well-meaning people. They will say, "I wish it could have been me," and you will have to struggle to keep from agreeing with them. You will hear, "At least he didn't suffer," or "At least his suffering is over." As if that is any comfort or eases your loss. Or someone will say, "At least you had so many years together." Don't people know that there are never enough years to spend with the man you love? Worst of all is the phrase, "We must remember that everything is for the best." To this you want to scream and cry out, "Shut up, you fool! Can't you understand? The man I love is dead. *How* can his death be for the best? How can it be for the best that my children are fatherless and I'm alone? How can it be for the best when I need him and want him and love him so desperately? How can anything good ever come of this? Just leave me alone if you don't have the answers, because that's all I want. Answers. *Then* maybe I can understand and accept."

But there are still no answers, and you must learn that failure to accept reality leads to self-destruction of the worst sort—from within—and you are not going to permit that to happen. So you *will* learn to accept, even though, far back in your mind, there will always be the question, "Why?"

You will have to learn to live with and control the resentment toward some of the living, especially husbands and wives together, that will be particularly difficult when you have to go out alone. There is no easy way to overcome these feelings. But you are going to be a part of the world, and so, eventually, you will have to grit your teeth and endure. You will want to go up to every woman you see with her husband to tell her to love him while she has him. You will even find, in time, that you will have a tiny feeling of smugness, knowing that the agony of loss is ahead of her, while you have already faced that particular hell.

More complex is the resentment some widows feel toward their dead husbands. There are often terrible surges of fury that the husband has died and left them alone. This too must be resolved if a woman is to resume a normal and healthy life. In some cases therapy may be helpful in coming to accept the death, in coming to understand and then leaving past conflicts behind.

FAITH

Much worse is the loss of faith, whether temporary or permanent, following the death of your husband. This is something so personal that I can only deal with it from my own experience, hoping that it will strike a responsive chord and be of some help to you.

I have mentioned that before George's death I *knew* I was God's beloved. My faith was strong, and the few times it had been tried resulted in a feeling of prayers answered and strengthened belief in God. I was grateful, and tried to live the life I felt He wished. As Christians, George and I did not fear death because we firmly believed in a life after death. We felt close to God and warm, in His love and protection.

But when George died, I felt an utter disbelief that God could do any-

thing like this to me. I believed in a personal relationship with God, and
I also believed that everything happened as a result of God's loving plan.
How then, could He have taken George from me and my children? Hadn't
we always obeyed Him? Hadn't we lived as He wished? Hadn't we witnessed to our faith? Hadn't we been *good?* How could He strike us like
this? Was it conceivable that there was no God?

For the first time in my life I came face to face with this awful possibility.

Nothing was right, because George was gone and I would never see
him again. Could I *really* believe in a God who would do this to me? If
there was a God, didn't this mean He had abandoned me?

I won't go into the soul-searching, the anguish, the sleepless nights, I
suffered as I sought an answer. I can only tell you that I wept as much for
my lost faith as for my lost love. I felt more alone and helpless than I would
have believed possible, because my loss was double. I no longer had George,
and I knew that God no longer loved me.

Some people of faith can accept anything that comes, with a meekness
that has always seemed to me to be more (less?) than human. *I'll* never
inherit the earth because meekness is foreign to my nature. I'm a kicker
and screamer against fate. I can't accept unquestioningly. Perhaps that is
why my favorite historical figure is the Countess of Salisbury. When Henry
VIII was chopping off the head of anyone with a remote claim to the
throne, the Countess, who was unfortunate enough to have been Henry's
cousin, was arrested, taken to the Tower of London, and sentenced to
death. On the appointed day, she was led to the scaffold for execution.
But, unlike her predecessors who went gallantly and nobly to lay their
aristocratic necks upon the block, the Countess ran yelling and shrieking
around the platform with the executioners in hot pursuit. They finally
caught her and killed her of course, but wasn't she magnificent? She didn't
like the whole thing, and wasn't going to ease Henry's conscience with
meek acquiescence. She fought all the way to the end. That's my kind of
heroine.

I have never been able to accept fate or God's decrees meekly. I want
to know why, or in lieu of an answer, I want my protest heard, loud and
clear. Poor God, during those long, long months of my rebellion. I don't
know how He had time to get anything else done for listening to me
scream and cry in protest. But in that, as in everything else, He worked in
His own way, and finally, one day, He won.

I wish I could tell you of a celestial revelation, with choirs of joyous
angels singing anthems while I looked heavenward. But it didn't happen
that way. It happened in a much simpler, and I am sure, much deeper way.

One morning I was beginning my daily harangue with God. "Why did
you take George? Why did you leave me alone? Why have you caused such

suffering? Whywhywhywhywhy?" Suddenly it was as if I were in the eye of a storm. All around me there was turbulence and distress, while at the center, where I was, there was an indescribable stillness and peace. And suddenly my heart was filled with gratitude for the fact that I had had George and that he had loved me as few women are ever loved. At that moment the bitterness left, and at last I was at peace. I could only utter a prayer of thanks for the miracle of my life with George, for our children, and for the blessings that God continued to bestow on us. Now I know that whatever the future holds, He *does* love me and will give me the strength to face any pain or adversity.

I hope that you will be able to find your own peace, whether it comes from your religion or from within yourself. Whatever it is, or wherever it comes from, you will need it as you make your way through your grief.

THE TRIALS OF GRIEF

There are so many things for which you must brace yourself. You must be prepared to suffer through special occasions such as Christmas, birthdays, and your anniversary. These days bring a special kind of anguish. It will be especially difficult for you to do anything without him for the first time, but, for whatever comfort you may find from the knowledge, it will be easier the next time. And the next.

If there is some special time of the day that you associate most strongly with your husband, try to be busy when that time comes. Eventually it will come and go and you won't think of it any more. Until then, protect yourself in every way you can. Don't torture yourself. Life will do that for you, in the most unexpected ways and at the most unexpected times. You will be somewhere in complete control, not even thinking about him, when suddenly some word, some tune, some scent will trigger a memory. The wound will open anew. There is nothing you can do to avoid these times. They happen to us all, but they will pass.

One of the most helpful realizations is that the feelings you are experiencing are not unique. Misery loving company? Probably, and why not? One of the most painful things is that feeling of aloneness, so remember that others have felt the same way. We have survived, and so will you. If you try.

REGRETS AND GUILT

Do *not* burden yourself with regrets and remorse and guilt.

We all have regrets. "Why didn't I tell him I loved him more often? Why wasn't I more interested in his work? Why didn't I take an interest in his hobbies?" We all feel like that. Realize that you and he were just two normal human beings, and you were bound to have had arguments and differences. Your remorse is not going to change the past or bring him back, and you are only doing yourself harm by dwelling on it.

As far as guilt is concerned, survivors often feel guilt just because they are still alive. *Stop punishing yourself.* This was not your choice nor the way you wanted it to be. But it is the way it is. Remember that you are extremely vulnerable now to illness. And you will *make* yourself ill with anxiety, depression, and fatigue if you permit destructive emotions to claim living room in your mind. Stop thinking of the negative and remember all the positive and happy times you had together. You loved him and he loved you. Nothing else matters.

There were days when I walked around wringing my hands, crying, torturing myself by looking at old photographs and rereading old letters. I had been aghast, years before, when I had seen my mother-in-law fling herself across the grave of her husband. Now I found myself staying at the cemetery for long hours, talking to George as if he were there. Mercifully, that stage didn't last long, but only because the human mind and body cannot sustain such protracted grief. There comes a time when the tears stop and we gulp in some fresh air, take a look around us, and try to assess the damage.

THE PHYSICAL TOLL

The first and most dramatic change we notice after losing our husbands will probably be physical. Many widows age overnight. They turn gray, their eyesight fails, their teeth give trouble. Frequently they suffer symptoms of the illness that killed their husbands. (I was sure that I was having a heart attack on the day of George's funeral.) This leads to worry about health, and to vague, unidentified aches and pains. Go to your doctor for a checkup. When you are assured that there is no physical problem, you can put that worry behind you. Not that the psychological ailments can't cause as much trouble, or more. They become the ones against which you will need to guard. You will suffer from worry, self-delusion, indecision, insomnia. If your doctor prescribes a mild sedative to help you sleep, take it. You're not going to become addicted. You'll stop when you're stable again. You are probably going to substitute one physical gratification for another. You are without sex, so you'll probably overeat or oversmoke or overdrink. At this time self-indulgence is decidedly more important than self-discipline.

You will become self-absorbed during these first months; just be careful not to let it become a habit. Your goal is to become part of the world again, and when the time comes you want to be ready.

THE MENTAL TOLL

But it won't be easy. Your mind will betray you. You'll have difficulty making decisions. Your mental processes will be entirely different; you won't be in command any more. During the first year after George's death, I couldn't read a book. I could read magazine articles or short stories, but I just couldn't concentrate enough to pick up the thread of a long story from one reading to the next. And I couldn't remember names. But these are minor peculiarities; they will pass and you will function normally again.

AVOIDING NEW PAIN

While you are guarding yourself against additional pain, *don't* read anything that is sad or especially romantic. Avoid any movies except those with an upbeat ending. Keep yourself involved in pursuits that are light and happy and positive.

It is because of the tendency to avoid anything that can remind us of our loss that we sometimes stop seeing old friends and going to familiar places. It is easier to withdraw than to subject ourselves to unnecessary pain. If you find yourself doing this, explain to your friends. They may be hurt until they understand, but they will be more deeply hurt if you stop seeing them without any explanation. Not communicating your feelings may cause a permanent break. Treasure your friends; you'll need them.

You'll need a lot of things that you used to take for granted. You'll hunger for appreciation. You'll need to be understood. You'll desperately want something as simple as a hug. You will cry out for the man you love and who loved you. Because you still love him. Love doesn't end at the grave, and this is the most difficult thing to try to convey to people who have not experienced this loss. When friends say, "You'll marry again" you'll want to cry out, "Don't you understand? I *am* married."

WHO ARE YOU?

But of course you are not married, and that presents one of the problems your friends will have to face in knowing how to treat you. Who are you? Mrs., Miss, Ms.? What do they call you? I sometimes think the old-fashioned "Widow Yates" would be a nice touch. It left nothing to the imagination. It said, "Here is a woman who has lost her husband. She is alone. She needs consideration. Maybe, in a year or two, she'll marry again. In the meantime, treat her as someone special, because she has suffered." We don't get any of that now, and it's too bad. Now we are absorbed into society with scarcely a ripple.

Society doesn't know what to do with us.

YOUR FRIENDS

As far as your friends are concerned, you will find that they will fall into two categories: disappearing and matchmaking. It hurts when friends disappear, but you can sympathize with their predicament. Whereas there was always room for a couple at the next party, there seems to be no place for just one person.

There are few words more beautiful than "we." Remember how casually you used to say, "We're having a party," or "Yes, we'd love to come"? The invitations are saved for the "we's." It's understandable. There are just so many buffet suppers your thoughtful friends can give, and just so many outings for an unspecified number of guests. Then it all goes back to couples again, and that leaves you out. Eventually you will feel comfortable about asking a man to accompany you, but there are more times that you will *not* go out than you will, so plan some parties of your own. This is part of making your new life—an important part you shouldn't neglect.

There is another thing you will find about your disappearing friends, and it will come as a shock. You are suddenly a threat to them. You are suddenly that mysterious, intriguing woman alone. Men are, traditionally, supposed to fall all over themselves when they hear the magic word "widow." You will find, in fact, that there *are* some men who are eager to comfort the widow—in every way possible (some of them before your husband's side of the bed is cold). Don't let your loneliness lead you into what can become an unhappy situation. Remember that you are vulnerable to any attention right now, and wait. See how your would-be suitor looks in a few months when you will be better able to evaluate your actions—and reactions.

Let this be your guide in regard to those friends who are doing some well-intended matchmaking. If you want them to introduce you to men, fine, but if you're not ready for it, tell them. Dates can wait, too, until your judgment is more reliable.

In this respect, as in everything else, no one should expect too much from the widow during the first year. She should be allowed the traditional year of mourning to stabilize her battered emotions.

For how can she be rational now? She is an emotional cripple. She must learn to live without part of her being. She has lost her identity. The one human being in the world who really *knew* her is gone. No one else has seen her in every mood and under every circumstance. With no one else has she ever been as relaxed—as much herself, without pretense or artifice.

Now she no longer has someone to whom she can pour out her heart, to share her deepest thoughts and feelings. And her loss is twofold. Never again can she do anything to make her friend, her confidante, her lover happy.

This knowledge will set you back on your heels. This is when you will finally realize that from this time on, your mental and emotional recovery will be up to *you*. You won't have him to help you; it's going to be up to you to rebuild your inner resources, in any way you can.

USING ANYTHING THAT HELPS

Go to a qualified counselor, whether religious or secular. There are many organizations that counsel widows. Join a group of other widows and talk together. Forget your inhibitions and tell them of the emotions you are experiencing. You'll find that they feel the same way, and you can help one another recognize fears and overcome them.

If you don't already have a hobby, find one—fast. Keep your hands busy. Learn needlepoint, macramé, découpage. Paint by numbers, take piano lessons—*anything* to occupy your mind and time. You *can* do something useful while you are helping yourself. I made chair seats, pillows, bell-pulls for nonexistent bells. If anything stayed motionless for long, it was in danger of being embroidered. I was ferocious in my concentration on keeping grief at bay.

REACHING YOUR GOAL

Ultimately, as the numbness about your heart wears off, you will begin to see a glimmer of light ahead, and you will begin to live in the real world again.

One of the cruelest lies ever spoken is "Time heals all wounds." Those wounds of grief and sorrow and loss are *never* healed; they are simply covered over by layers of living and coping and experiencing new situations —good and bad. The emotional aftermath of your loss is like the path torn by a tornado. But you *can* build on that devastation. And you will. You will laugh again. There will come a time when you will no longer live by rote. You will open your arms wide once again to embrace life and all its richness.

Treasure your memories of the past, but don't dwell on them. Turn your face forward, to the future, to the new life you are going to make alone. You're going to become a part of the great big wonderful world of the living again—and you'll love it!

4

COPING WITH DIVORCE

Picking up the Pieces

The undeniable fact that our era is unlike any other is in no way more dramatically emphasized than in the contemporary attitude toward marriage.

No longer is marriage the ultimate goal of all—for male *or* female. People now have no trouble establishing themselves as entities in homes of their own, without the stigma formerly attached to the single state. They can rent or buy apartments and houses previously denied them; they don't need someone to maintain their homes for them—they can hire house-keepers, use laundromats, eat out. Many men and women now find marriage a debatable commodity, one that is not necessary to their current lifestyle. They can live with a chosen mate without marriage, and frequently consider marriage only if they decide to have children. And not always then.

Nor is marriage, when it is entered into, thought of as a lifetime agreement. Options are being written into the marriage vows. Couples are standing before the officiating authority (if any) with their mental fingers crossed, and with the subconscious reservation that they are marrying "for better or divorce." Or are rewriting the marriage ceremony to achieve contemporary relevance with words such as those used in a popular TV series, when the couple promised to remain married "as long as we both shall love."

THE RISING DIVORCE RATE

Among vast numbers of our population marriage is no longer considered a sacred institution. Nor is this feeling confined to areas thought of as sophisticated or avant garde; even those states with the most historically religious strictures (the Deep South, Massachusetts, Utah) have relaxed their grounds for granting a divorce decree.

There has been a steady decline in the number of marriages per year, with a commensurate increase in the number of divorces. It is expected that 1975 will see one million marriages and 300,000 divorces, an alarming one to three ratio. The peak in recent years was reached in 1968, when the "baby boom" children were adults and we were involved in the Vietnam War, with the usual hasty wartime weddings. There were two million marriages that year, a number surpassed in our history only once, in the postwar year of 1946. As marriages have decreased, the rate of divorce has steadily increased, so that if a chart were drawn with lines showing the number of marriages and divorces, they would look like an enormous X, marking, perhaps, the spot where family life as it has been known in America has met its end.

Divorce transects all social, racial, economic, religious, and age barriers. There are more divorces among the socially elite—because they can afford them—but there are more desertions among the less affluent. The divorce rate is twice as high among blacks as among whites. Churches that once were staunchly opposed to divorce have relaxed their restrictions. And a leading sociologist, Dr. James A. Peterson, Director of Liaison Services for the Ethel Percy Andrus Gerontology Center of the University of Southern California, contends that marriages deteriorate with years. He feels that time is corrosive to marriage, and that because we are living longer than ever before, marriages are becoming vulnerable to the strain of coping with additional, unexpected years.

Government figures disagree with Dr. Peterson, however, and show that more divorces occur during the first few years, with 25 out of every 1,000 marriages breaking up during the third year. But whenever they occur, early or late, divorces are increasing at an alarming rate, and prove that the longevity of a marriage isn't as important as its quality.

Added to the alarming statistics of divorce is the overwhelming number of children affected by the dissolution of their parents' marital ties. According to the U.S. Bureau of the Census in 1970 (the last year for which figures are available), there were four million children whose lives had been drastically altered and whose love and loyalties were subjected to stress for which they were unprepared. These children face and create problems that are another new condition of our changing mores.

And they *are* changing. Only a few decades ago the only grounds for divorce in most states was adultery, and the sordid little business of providing proof through an arranged tryst, to be photographed as evidence of infidelity, flourished. Now, in states such as California, Colorado, Florida, and Iowa divorce has been replaced with "dissolution of marriage," usually requiring only that both partners agree that the marriage has suffered an "irretrievable breakdown." Although some states still require that the participants in a divorce action have lived in the state granting the decree for two years or more, it has been lowered to as little as sixty days in Wyoming, ninety days in Colorado, and only six weeks in Nevada and Idaho. So-called "quickie" divorces are no longer available in Mexico, but can be obtained in such Caribbean countries as Haiti and the Dominican Republic. The cost is higher than in the States, however, even though the residency requirements and grounds for divorce are mere formalities. They can also present problems in the future if the divorce is contested, so it is generally safer to avoid the hasty approach and take the divorce step by step to its conclusion.

To state that it is becoming easier and easier to obtain a divorce begs the question—*why* are there more divorces today than ever before? Is the family as an institution doomed?

The Causes of Divorce

My opinion, shared by others more knowledgeable about the subject, is that it is simply too easy for a couple to marry. While the divorce laws are being relaxed, it would be well for the marriage laws to be tightened. In our country too many people are looking for the end of the rainbow in marriage, as a panacea to cure all ills. They marry to get away from an intolerable situation at home; they marry because of a passing sexual attraction—but with nothing else in common. They marry hoping for a life of romance and rosy happiness; they marry (still) for children. They marry for all the wrong reasons and then wonder what happened when the marriage falls apart.

The marriage that has a chance of succeeding is one that both partners enter into with wide-open eyes. They know there will be days when one or the other may want to be alone; that there will be differences over money, religion, sex; that divorce isn't the only answer to the inevitable problems. They will know that they must work hard to make the union a success, and that there have to be generous amounts of trust, understanding, give and take.

We enter into marriage too lightly and too poorly prepared. It only requires two bodies, a license, in most states a blood test, in some states a three-day waiting period (not for any altruistic reasons on the government's part—it takes that long to get the results of the blood test), and someone to perform the ceremony. And that, supposedly, is enough for two people to pledge their lives to each other for eternity. I wish we would do as some other countries are doing and really prepare the participants for the practical side of marriage. In Hungary, for instance, people applying for a marriage license take courses in budgeting, family planning, sex education, and interpersonal relationships—all aimed at establishing a stable marriage that will not end in divorce. This is something that every couple could well institute on their own.

Lack of pragmatic preparation may well be one factor in the sharp upswing in divorce, but there are other reasons, too. Religious leaders decry the breakdown in morals and spiritual values as the central cause of disrespect for the family unit. They cite the rise in premarital promiscuity as undermining the necessity of the institution of marriage. Certainly the availability of unattached sex partners can be a strong argument against monogamy. Infidelity is still the number one cause cited in divorce cases throughout the nation. In 1972 there were approximately one million families deserted nationwide, and estimates suggest that a third party was responsible for more than half of those desertions.

THE AFTERMATH OF DIVORCE

A woman who is deserted or whose husband initiates the divorce faces severe emotional traumas. Not only is her entire life changed sexually, economically, and socially, but she is likely to be overcome with guilt at the failure of her marriage, bitterness over the causes, feelings of rejection of herself as a woman, and, frequently, hatred of her former mate.

There are very few "friendly" divorces; the reasons for divorce—infidelity, drunkenness, physical abuse, or whatever caused the marriage to dissolve—obviously cause acrimony, distress, and dislike. The couples who can calmly sit down with each other and their lawyers and discuss the arrangements to be made in regard to the children and the finances are rare indeed.

But no matter how much a woman suffers from a supposed loss of self-esteem or a sense of failure, she must be practical. She must plan, from the moment she knows that the divorce is inevitable, for her own welfare and that of her children. Except in the case of desertion, she will have some period of warning before her husband leaves and she enters into a divorce action. *That* is the time to put emotion aside and to take a long look at the future.

The two main concerns must be who will have custody of the children, and how much alimony and/or child support will be paid. Generally, custody is determined individually and on the merits of each case. Unless the mother is proven to be mentally, physically, or morally unfit to raise her children, she is usually awarded their custody. Only in rare and unusual cases will a judge divide the children between the parents; the rationale is that this would further destroy the family structure. In some cases, when the children are old enough and the parents in agreement, the children are allowed, after a certain age, to choose the parent with whom they will live. The mother is usually given sole control of the children, but in some cases she will agree to consult with the father on major decisions, such as a choice of schools or colleges. Stipulations such as this *must* be written into the decree, however. This brings us to the most important single element in a divorce.

If you now—or think you will ever in the future—contemplate divorce, decide on the terms you want and be sure that they are spelled out in the decree. *Nothing* should be left to chance or to an "understanding" between you and your husband. This is not cold-blooded, but is extremely practical.

THE INCOME TAX RETURN

Begin with something as basic as your income tax return. Even though you have customarily signed jointly with your husband, if there may be a refund on the current year's return, don't sign it with him. If there is a refund due, the check will be made out in both the names as signed on the return, and cannot be cashed or deposited without both endorsements. Have a *written* agreement with your husband that if such a check comes you will both endorse it and will divide the money in whatever way you mutually decide. The main thing is to agree to endorse the check; otherwise the check will be returned to the Internal Revenue Service as undeliverable, and neither of you will benefit from it.

Another precaution to take in regard to the IRS: if you have previously filed jointly, you each may now, under Section 6212 (B) (2) of the Internal Revenue Code, notify the IRS of your new addresses so that any future notices of audit may be delivered to you both. (You are responsible for the return if you signed it, whether you had income or not, and whether or not you know the contents of the return.) Remember too that a wife is *never,* according to the IRS, a husband's dependent—she is his exemption. After the divorce, even if he supports you totally, he will not be entitled to claim you as his exemption because you no longer qualify under the relationship. (I'll get into preparing an income tax return in Chapter 15, but don't let him tell you that he can still claim you —he can't.)

ALIMONY

Now we come to that thorny question of alimony. The feminist position is that alimony maintains a woman's status as a man's dependent. However, I feel that there are circumstances in which it would be wrong for a woman to refuse the payments. Most courts will not order a man to pay more than half of his income to support his former wife and their children. In a case involving more than one child, and if the child support payments are going to be inadequate, then I would insist on alimony as well. If there are no children and the woman feels that she has been gravely wronged, as in the case of infidelity, I can see no valid objection to the wife insisting on alimony. If she works at the time of the divorce, or plans to in the future, she may as well accept the fact that she will not be making the amount of money her husband made, and so her standard of living will be reduced. In these cases I believe alimony to be justified and acceptable.

Sit down and itemize your living expenses and the amount of money you think you will be able to earn, remembering that unemployment and retirement are always possibilities. Decide in the coolness of reality—not the heat of fury and passion—exactly how much you will need to live comfortably and let that be the factor determining whether or not you ask for alimony. Remember that alimony is counted as income, so you will be taxed on it, if the payments are defined by the Internal Revenue Service as being "periodic." Their definition of periodic payments is:

1. Payments of a fixed amount for an indefinite period; i.e., $50 per month for life; or
2. Payments of an indefinite amount for either a fixed or an indefinite period; i.e., 25% of his income for five years, or, as an example of an "indefinite" period, for life.

Remember that the federal government allows the husband who itemizes to deduct these payments and the wife must include them under "Income other than wages, dividends and interest" on her Form 1040.

Installment payments generally are not considered to be periodic and so are not taxable to you. There are, of course, exceptions, and under certain circumstances they might be counted as alimony and be taxable, depending on the period specified during which they must be paid. For instance, if the period specified is less than ten years, the payments are not periodic and are not taxable. However, if the payments are subject to termination because of contingencies (if the court has the power to modify, alter, or amend the terms; if you remarry; or if there is a death or economic change of either husband or wife), they would be considered taxable periodic payments even though the decree specifies that they are to be paid in less than ten years.

If the period specified in the terms of the installment payments is over ten years, the amount will be taxable, but only to the extent that the sum of the payments received during your tax year does not exceed 10 percent of the total specified. This 10 percent limitation applies to installment payments made in advance, but not to delinquent installment payments received during your tax year.

Confused? It sounds more complicated than it is, and before you enter into any divorce agreement you should know all the ramifications as far as your taxes are concerned. In this, as in everything else, you are entitled to seek the way that will give you the greatest tax benefits. If you need further help, remember that the Internal Revenue Service has a taxpayer service branch that is designed to help you. Go to the nearest office or call the toll-free number in your state and ask for help. They cannot give you *advice* as to the best course for you to follow, but they will give you all the information you will need to make the wisest decision.

One way to avoid having anything taxable coming to you is to demand a lump-sum cash or property settlement.

SETTLEMENTS

When you have sat down and determined your needs, you may be willing to accept a nontaxable lump-sum cash settlement. Be careful, however; you may not receive as much as you would if the payments were spread over a number of years. Be wary and examine the situation with caution. Don't act hastily or without professional advice when you are dealing with what may amount to large sums of money. Take your time and study all the contingencies involving taxes, cost-of-living expenses, and your future anticipated income from your work.

As far as a property settlement is concerned, there are two things to remember. First, when the husband transfers property (that has appreciated in value) as full settlement of his wife's marital rights under a divorce decree, a taxable event has occurred, and the husband will be liable for the tax on the gain. The gain would be computed as the difference between the appreciated value of the property at the time of transfer and his basis in the property. (*Basis* can be defined as the cost of any item plus any capital or permanent improvements to that item.) The second point to keep in mind is that if both husband and wife were owners, jointly or as in a community property state, and if they make an equal division of the property, there is no taxable event, but simply a partition or property settlement.

If you live in one of the eight states that recognize community property rights whereby both partners equally own all of their possessions (Arizona, California, Idaho, Louisiana, Nevada, New Mexico, Texas, and Washington), keep in mind that laws within those states vary. For example, in Texas the wife's income is also considered as community property. In most of these states, during a period of separation before the final divorce decree, each spouse is generally liable to taxation on half of the other's earnings. Washington, however, is different. The state courts there have held that when for all intents and purposes a marriage has been terminated and the spouses have shown their intent not to maintain the community status, the community property laws do not apply. You will have to consult with an attorney in your state so that you will comply with its laws and make the most advantageous decisions.

If your marriage is a common-law union that does not require license, ceremony, or witnesses, it is recognized by the Internal Revenue Service if you were considered to be legally married in the state in which the common-law relationship *began*. There are thirteen of them, plus the District of Columbia, and problems are encountered in states such as California that have community property laws but do not recognize common-law marriages. This condition is being challenged in the California courts at this writing, and will probably reach the United States Supreme Court for a ruling as to whether or not the common-law wife is entitled to a share of the property.

If your husband suggests that he pay for an insurance policy on his life, in lieu of alimony, find out exactly what kind it will be before you accept it. If the policy is not assigned to you, and if you are no more than a contingent beneficiary, the premiums are not deductible by your husband as alimony, and they are not taxable to you. But beware—such a policy can be changed without your consent and you could receive nothing. If, however, he pays premiums on a policy absolutely assigned to you, on which you are the irrevocable beneficiary and owner, the premiums are taxable to you and deductible by him. If money is no problem now and you are more concerned about your later years, it may well be a worthwhile alternative to alimony.

Another insurance policy he might suggest and you may want to consider is an endowment policy or an annuity contract. These premium payments are not deductible by your husband, but *are* taxable to you.

Weigh all these various forms of alimony and nonalimony payments to be received by you and decide on the best for you before you get into determining the child support you must receive. Keep in mind that it is unlikely that a judge will allow you to receive more than half of your husband's income, so decide judiciously the ways to receive the maximum amount possible if you know you are going to need it for yourself or your children.

In rare cases, when the wife's income far exceeds that of her husband, alimony may be awarded to the man, but those cases are the exceptions, as are cases in which the judge awards custody of the children to the father, so you can reasonably expect to have the responsibility and expense of raising your children. You will need all the money available— now and as the children grow older and enter college.

CHILD SUPPORT PAYMENTS

Child support payments are the most misunderstood payments of all. Except in one important case, they are *not* considered alimony, and I feel that even the most ardent feminist should ask for and expect to receive the largest amount possible. She will be raising her husband's children and he should certainly help to support them. These payments have an additional bonus; they are not taxable to you, and they aren't deductible by your husband, either. A vital point to remember, though, is that the payments may be considered in determining which parent will be entitled to a dependency exemption for the child or children.

There is that one important exception, and you must be sure that this is covered in the decree: If the decree or agreement does not specify an amount as child support, the payment will be considered to be alimony and will be taxable to you. Be certain that a definite amount is specified for child support. If you will be receiving both alimony and child support, have it spelled out in dollars and cents just which portion is for what. If your husband fails to pay the total amount per payment, the payments apply first to child support and then to alimony.

To determine which of you will be entitled to claim the children as dependents, you will have to decide who furnished more than half of the total support. This is assuming that the other four dependency tests stipulated by the IRS have been satisfied. These are:

1. The gross income test of the child—he/she must have gross income of less than $750 per year unless under the age of 19 or a full-time student for at least nine months of the year
2. The relationship of the child to you
3. The child's U.S. citizenship or residency in the United States, Canada, Mexico, the Panama Canal Zone, or the Republic of Panama
4. The child must not file a joint return if married, if there is a tax liability

The support test can be relatively simple if you will keep accurate records of your expenses. The IRS has worked out a formula that will help; divide the amount you furnished during the year by the total amount of support. Include in this the amounts you spent for food, clothing, shelter, medical and dental care, education, recreation, operating expenses, transportation, and other similar necessities. If you don't have accurate records, you may determine a pro rata share for each child by dividing the total by the number in the household. Other items included in total support are tax-exempt income, savings, and money borrowed to support the dependent. Add all these amounts plus those listed above, put them in the denominator of your fraction, and divide them into the amount furnished by you alone. (Some of the amounts will be in both the numerator and the denominator.) An example: Your husband contributes $50 per month toward child support, for a total of $600 for the year. You have had to pay living expenses for your child in the amount of $2,000 for the year. Divide this amount by the *total* support, $2,000 plus $600, and you will find that you have contributed 76 percent of the child's support and are entitled to claim him as a dependent.

Generally the parent having custody of the child for the greater part of the year may claim that child as a dependent, but there are two important exceptions, and you must be certain that they are considered when the divorce decree is being drawn. The first exception states that the noncustodial parent may claim the child as a dependent if that parent provides at least $600 per year for the child *and* the decree of divorce, separate maintenance, or written agreement between the parents specifies that the noncustodial parent is entitled to claim the exemption. The second exception states that if the noncustodial parent provides $1,200 per year for the child, nothing is stated in the decree, and the custodial parent cannot clearly establish having provided greater support, the noncustodial parent may claim the exemption. Note this carefully; it could make a great deal of difference in your income tax liability if you are not entitled to the exemption for each child.

Be sure that all these considerations are taken into account before the divorce decree is written—it will be too late afterward. Ask that both alimony and child support agreements include an "escalator clause," whereby you would receive a percentage of any increase in your former husband's salary, and that would reflect a cost-of-living increase, and ask that the decree stipulate that he will pay at least half of the reasonable cost of your child's college education.

Another vitally important item you must agree upon before the decree is written is visitation rights for the noncustodial parent. He (it's usually the father) is generally awarded visitation rights, meaning that he has a legal right to be with his children at regular intervals. This is such a personal matter that it must be agreed upon by each individual couple, taking into account where the father lives, the wife's schedule, and the best arrangement for the children. If your husband lives close, perhaps you can arrange for him to have the children on alternate weekends; if he lives a long distance away, probably vacation visits would have to be planned. This is important to your children, and unless their father abused them and circumstances do not warrant their being with him, it is best to avoid anything that would put them in the middle of a disagreement. They have been through enough, and should not have their affections used as weapons by their warring parents.

What if you have managed to obtain the terms you want and need and your former husband fails to abide by the court's order and either refuses to pay or becomes delinquent in the payments? There are several avenues open to you. You can have his salary garnisheed, so that his employer will withhold payment until there is a court order to have part of it paid to you. If your husband defaults on payments on a court-arranged settlement, you can ask the court to issue a contempt citation. Many men erroneously think that they can avoid all payments by moving to another state. Again, the law will move to protect the rights of the divorced wife and her children. By going to court in your own state and invoking the Uniform Reciprocal Enforcement of Support Act—in effect in some form in all the states—you can be assured of legal action in your behalf. The court will contact officials in the state to which the husband has moved; they will locate him. If he does not comply with the agreement and fails to send the sum due his former wife, he will then be considered by that state to be in contempt of its court, a punishable offense.

DIVORCE INSURANCE

The threat of punishment, however, does not deter a former husband who is determined to avoid paying child support and alimony. A really resolute man can feel fairly safe after five years; the majority of delinquent former husbands rarely comply with court orders after this amount of time has lapsed. It is for this reason that NOISE (National Organization to Improve Support Enforcement, a nonprofit group) has been formed. The founder is Mrs. Diana Du Broff, a lawyer specializing in divorce cases who hopes to help those women left with no money, no job, no skills, and usually children to support. The nation's welfare rolls are being increased annually by these women, and a solution offered by Mrs. Du Broff is no-fault divorce insurance. The insurance would cover child support payments or would pay for job training for the wife. The idea is simple; the couple, either before or during marriage, would buy a policy to be used for child support, or if there are no children, the insurance proceeds would be divided equally between the divorcing partners. It is called "no-fault" insurance because it would be payable regardless of which party was at fault.

Although bills establishing commissions to study the feasibility of such insurance have been introduced in at least a dozen state legislatures, no insurance company has yet decided to offer the policy. However, Mrs. Du Broff has written a rider clause that you may have attached to any standard life insurance policy. The rider would provide that the policy would have a cash surrender value during the three years following a divorce, the money to be used for child support. If you would like further information about the rider, write to NOISE, Abused Children of America, Inc., 12 West 72nd Street, New York, N. Y. 10023.

DO-IT-YOURSELF DIVORCE

Divorce is expensive—remember that there are two lawyers involved—and it would be ideal if we could adopt the custom of saying three times, "I divorce thee" and go on about our business. Unfortunately, it isn't that simple, and in a nation of laws we must abide by those governing divorce, as we obey all the others—especially if children are involved. If there are no children it is possible to have a do-it-yourself divorce, but in this, as in handling the probate of a will, extreme care must be taken to guarantee that all laws are meticulously observed. If the state in which you live accepts no-fault grounds (neither party was at fault) or abandonment is acceptable as grounds for the dissolution of the marriage, you may want to weigh saving the lawyer's fee against the time and the trouble you will have to expend on going it alone. Consider this alternative *only* if the suit will be uncontested by your husband. Check with a lawyer before you decide to proceed to see if you have grounds that are valid in your state. Be prepared to learn the necessary legal terms and to spend time at the library searching out all the fine points of a legal action. You'll have to prepare and file all the proper forms, and you'll have to find out if there are any deadlines for filing and when you should appear before the judge. Proceed on this course with caution, and if you have any doubts, retain a good lawyer at the outset and turn the entire case over to him. If you don't have a lawyer, contact your local bar association for a list of names of attorneys specializing in divorce. Be sure to have an understanding—in writing—of the amount of his fee.

YOUR NAME

At the time of the decree you can decide if you want to retain your married name or resume your maiden name. This decision must be yours. A determining factor may be whether or not you have children; you may want your name to be the same as theirs. If not, the judge will return your maiden name to you with no trouble.

SOCIAL SECURITY BENEFITS

Remember that if you never remarry you may be entitled to receive Social Security benefits when your former husband begins collecting retirement or disability checks. Two stipulations; you must be 62 or over and must have been married to him for at least twenty years before the divorce. If your former husband dies and you have not remarried, are 60 or over (50, if you are disabled), you were married to him twenty years or more before the divorce, or if you have children entitled to benefits, you are entitled to claim survivor's benefits. This is so even if your husband has remarried. In that case, both you and his widow are entitled to the benefits.

YOUR REACTION TO DIVORCE

While you are taking care of all the financial arrangements connected with divorce, don't overlook your emotional health. Divorce ranks only slightly behind the death of a spouse on the stress chart, so be prepared for rough days and nights ahead. No matter who was at fault, or even if the marriage was dissolved through mutual agreement, there will be moments of self-accusation. You'll ask yourself what you did wrong, how you failed your husband, why the marriage collapsed. Examine the facts and decide if there actually was something you did that was the cause of the divorce. If so, make sure you don't repeat the same mistake if you remarry. (And don't do as so many divorcees do and marry a man who is a carbon copy of the first husband; you don't want to live through the same agony again.) If, however, after your soul-searching you feel that you were *not* at fault, turn your face toward the future and don't look back. Rage and bitterness are self-defeating, and you have too much living ahead to waste a moment in anger or self-pity. Your divorce in no way reflects on your womanliness; it simply means that two people were unable to live together in happiness. It doesn't mean that there will not be another man at another time. You are not diminished by the events leading to the divorce, but you are wiser, and will become increasingly more comfortable with yourself and your future life.

If you feel that you need professional counseling go to your minister or lawyer or ask him or her to suggest an individual or group that will help you adjust to your new life. Contact your state Family and Children Services for a list of organizations specializing in divorce. Join an organization of other divorced people—they, more than anyone else, know the situation you face and can sympathize with you and can help you regain your self-esteem.

A new life is just beginning for you; close the door on the past and begin to live again, with hope and optimism. Resolve that your future will be better than anything that has gone before. You'll *see* to it that it will be.

5

COPING WITH MONEY (PART I)

How to Keep It . . .

Let's talk about money.

Single, widowed or divorced, you're going to be responsible, probably for the first time in your life, for administering appreciable sums of money. You'll want to save, invest, and spend it in the wisest ways possible.

It does no good for economists to tell you that your dollar will buy half the amount it would have bought twenty-five years ago. You're not worried about twenty-five years ago—you're concerned with *now*. Nor does it help for the experts to point out that with an annual income of, say, $10,000 you're not poor but you're economically "deprived."

You *know* that the impact of inflation has diminished your dollar's buying power. What you want to know is what to do about it.

The answer lies in practicing old-fashioned frugality. That doesn't necessarily mean doing without. You can be prudent without being penurious, careful without being cheap. Your goal is to invest part of your money in the most advantageous ways available, and to spend the rest so that you will get the highest possible quality for the lowest possible cost.

Whatever your nonmarital status and other sources of income (insurance proceeds, alimony and child support, Social Security benefits), you will probably work, so let's talk about immediate savings you can make in your salary.

YOUR W-4

When you first go to work, you will be given a worksheet and instructions for completing a W-4 form. This form will determine the amount of

Form W–4 (Revised April 1975)

Employee's Withholding Allowance Certificate

(Use for wages paid after April 30, 1975, and before January 1, 1976)

The explanatory material below will help you determine your correct number of withholding allowances, and will assist you in completing the Form W–4 at the bottom of this page.

Avoid Overwithholding or Underwithholding

By claiming the proper number of withholding allowances you are entitled to, you can fit the amount of tax withheld from your wages to your tax liability. In addition to the allowances for personal exemptions to be claimed in items (a) through (g) below, be sure you claim any additional allowances you are entitled to in item (h) "Special withholding allowance," and item (i) "Allowance(s) for itemized deductions." While these allowances may be claimed on Form W–4 for withholding purposes, they are not to be claimed under "Exemptions" on your tax return Form 1040 or Form 1040A.

You may claim the special withholding allowance if you are single with only one employer, or married with only one employer and your spouse is not employed. If you have unusually large itemized deductions, you may claim the allowance(s) for itemized deductions to avoid having too much income tax withheld from your wages. On the other hand, if you and your spouse are both employed or you have more than one employer, you should take steps to assure that enough has been withheld. If you find that you need more withholding, claim fewer exemptions or ask for additional withholding. If you are currently claiming additional withholding allowances based on itemized deductions, check the table on the back to see that you are claiming the proper number of allowances.

How Many Withholding Allowances May You Claim?

Please use the schedule below to determine the number of allowances you may claim for tax withholding purposes. In determining the number, keep in mind these points: If you are single and hold more than one job, you may not claim the same allowances with more than one employer at the same time; or if you are married and both you and your spouse are employed, you may not claim the same allowances with your employers at the same time. A nonresident alien, other than a resident of Canada, Mexico, or Puerto Rico, may claim only one personal allowance.

Figure Your Total Withholding Allowances Below

(a) Allowance for yourself—enter 1 . . . . _____

(b) Allowance for your spouse—enter 1 . . . . _____

(c) Allowance for your age—if 65 or over—enter 1 . . . . _____

(d) Allowance for your spouse's age—if 65 or over—enter 1 . . . . _____

(e) Allowance for blindness (yourself)—enter 1 . . . . _____

(f) Allowance for blindness (spouse's)—enter 1 . . . . _____

(g) Allowance(s) for dependent(s)—you are entitled to claim an allowance for each dependent you will be able to claim on your Federal income tax return. Do not include yourself or your spouse ° . . . . _____

(h) Special withholding allowance—if you are single with only one employer, or married with only one employer and your spouse is not employed—enter 1°° . . . . _____

(i) Allowance(s) for itemized deductions—if you do plan to itemize deductions on your income tax return, enter the number from the table on back°° . . . . _____

(j) Total—add lines (a) through (i) above. Enter here and on line 1, Form W–4 below . . . . _____

° If you are in doubt as to whom you may claim as a dependent, see the instructions which came with your last Federal income tax return or call your local Internal Revenue Service office.

°° This allowance is used solely for purposes of figuring your withholding tax, and cannot be claimed when you file your tax return.

See Table on Back if You Plan to Itemize Your Deductions

Completing Form W–4.—If you find that you are entitled to one or more allowances in addition to those which you are now claiming, increase your number of allowances by completing the form below and filing it with your employer. If the number of allowances you previously claimed decreases, you must file a new Form W–4 within 10 days. (Should you expect to owe more tax than will be withheld, you may use the same form to increase your withholding by claiming fewer or "0" allowances on line 1, or by asking for additional withholding on line 2, or both.)

▼ **Give the bottom part of this form to your employer; keep the upper part for your records and information** ▼

-- Cut along this line --

Form **W-4** (Rev. April 1975) Department of the Treasury Internal Revenue Service	**Employee's Withholding Allowance Certificate** (This certificate is for income tax withholding purposes only; it will remain in effect until you change it.)

Type or print your full name	Your social security number
Home address (Number and street or rural route)	Marital status ☐ Single ☐ Married
City or town, State and ZIP code	(If married but legally separated, or spouse is a nonresident alien, check the single block.)

1 Total number of allowances you are claiming . . . . _____

2 Additional amount, if any, you want deducted from each pay (if your employer agrees) . . . . $ _____

· I certify that to the best of my knowledge and belief, the number of withholding allowances claimed on this certificate does not exceed the number to which I am entitled.

Signature ▶ .... Date ▶ ...., 19 ....

federal and state and local taxes that will be withheld from your paycheck. Your objective is to have as little tax withheld as possible, without having to pay an additional sum next year when you file your returns.

If you've already completed your W-4, get the bookkeeper to give you another: it can be changed at any time during the year so that more or less will be withheld. It may be a little trouble for the payroll records to be changed, but this is *your* money we're talking about, and the amount withheld each pay period can make a substantial difference in your take-home pay. Don't hesitate to make any changes necessary.

The computations on the W-4 worksheet have been carefully determined by the Internal Revenue Service to allow you the greatest benefits, and if you follow this formula it is unlikely that you will have to pay any additional tax next year. If you do, the amount will be small, and you will have had the use of your money all during the year. The decision must be yours, but I always take the maximum amount of allowances I can legally claim—I need the money *now*.

Complete your worksheet carefully. You will be able to claim one allowance for yourself, an allowance for each dependent you will be able to claim on your federal tax return, and a special allowance if you have only one job. (If you have more than one job, you may not claim the same allowances with more than one employer at the same time.) There is an additional allowance for anyone still working after age sixty-five.

Take all the allowances to which you are entitled. Remember that if you have two jobs, tax must be withheld from both, and so must Social Security. (Yes, even though you may be eligible for benefits yourself, Social Security deductions will be taken from your salary.) If more than the maximum amount of Social Security is withheld ($824.85 in 1975), you are entitled to claim the excess as a credit against your next year's income tax.

If you plan to itemize your deductions, there will be additional allowances to which you will be entitled, but you may not want to claim them. Be extremely cautious so that you will not figure too low. You don't want to have so little withheld that you will be faced with a whopping tax liability next year. Always figure generously in favor of the tax due so that you won't be unpleasantly surprised when the day of tax reckoning comes, as it will.

The itemized deduction table looks formidable, but it's quite simple if you will read and follow the instructions. You will use Part I, for single employees. Find your wages in the left-hand column, the amount of itemized deductions you'll be claiming (in one of the columns to the right) and the number above will show the number of allowances to which you will be entitled. If your wages are under $10,000, for example, and your itemized deductions will total $2,600, you could claim one extra allowance.

Table for Determining Number of Withholding Allowances Based on Itemized Deductions

Estimated salaries and wages	Number of additional withholding allowances for the amount of itemized deductions shown in the appropriate column (See Line i on other side)												
	0	**1**		**2**		**3**		**4**		**5**		**6***	

Part I   Single Employees

	Under	At least	But less than	At least	But less than	At least	But less than	At least	But less than	At least	But less than	At least	But less than
Under $10,000........	$2,200	$2,200–$2,950		$2,950–$3,700		$3,700–$4,450		$4,450–$5,200		$5,200–$5,950		$5,950–$6,700	
10,000–15,000........	2,500	2,500– 3,250		3,250– 4,000		4,000– 4,750		4,750– 5,500		5,500– 6,250		6,250– 7,000	
15,000–25,000........	2,800	2,800– 3,550		3,550– 4,300		4,300– 5,050		5,050– 5,800		5,800– 6,550		6,550– 7,300	
25,000–30,000........	3,200	3,200– 3,950		3,950– 4,700		4,700– 5,450		5,450– 6,200		6,200– 6,950		6,950– 7,700	
30,000–35,000........	4,000	4,000– 4,750		4,750– 5,500		5,500– 6,250		6,250– 7,000		7,000– 7,750		7,750– 8,500	
35,000–40,000........	5,000	5,000– 5,750		5,750– 6,500		6,500– 7,250		7,250– 8,000		8,000– 8,750		8,750– 9,500	
40,000–45,000........	6,500	6,500– 7,250		7,250– 8,000		8,000– 8,750		8,750– 9,500		9,500–10,250		10,250–11,000	
45,000–50,000**....	8,000	8,000– 8,750		8,750– 9,500		9,500–10,250		10,250–11,000		11,000–11,750		11,750–12,500	

Part II   Married Employees (When Spouse Is Not Employed)

	Under	At least	But less than	At least	But less than	At least	But less than	At least	But less than	At least	But less than	At least	But less than
Under $15,000........	2,900	2,900– 3,650		3,650– 4,400		4,400– 5,150		5,150– 5,900		5,900– 6,650		6,650– 7,400	
15,000–35,000........	3,400	3,400– 4,150		4,150– 4,900		4,900– 5,650		5,650– 6,400		6,400– 7,150		7,150– 7,900	
35,000–40,000........	3,700	3,700– 4,450		4,450– 5,200		5,200– 5,950		5,950– 6,700		6,700– 7,450		7,450– 8,200	
40,000–45,000........	4,300	4,300– 5,050		5,050– 5,800		5,800– 6,550		6,550– 7,300		7,300– 8,050		8,050– 8,800	
45,000–50,000**....	5,200	5,200– 5,950		5,950– 6,700		6,700– 7,450		7,450– 8,200		8,200– 8,950		8,950– 9,700	

Part III   Married Employees (When Both Spouses Are Employed), and other employees who are holding more than one job

	Under	At least	But less than	At least	But less than	At least	But less than	At least	But less than	At least	But less than	At least	But less than
Under $10,000........	3,200	3,200– 3,950		3,950– 4,700		4,700– 5,450		5,450– 6,200		6,200– 6,950		6,950– 7,700	
10,000–12,000........	3,700	3,700– 4,450		4,450– 5,200		5,200– 5,950		5,950– 6,700		6,700– 7,450		7,450– 8,200	
12,000–15,000........	4,200	4,200– 4,950		4,950– 5,700		5,700– 6,450		6,450– 7,200		7,200– 7,950		7,950– 8,700	
15,000–20,000........	5,000	5,000– 5,750		5,750– 6,500		6,500– 7,250		7,250– 8,000		8,000– 8,750		8,750– 9,500	
20,000–25,000........	5,600	5,600– 6,350		6,350– 7,100		7,100– 7,850		7,850– 8,600		8,600– 9,350		9,350–10,100	
25,000–30,000........	6,200	6,200– 6,950		6,950– 7,700		7,700– 8,450		8,450– 9,200		9,200– 9,950		9,950–10,700	
30,000–35,000........	7,100	7,100– 7,850		7,850– 8,600		8,600– 9,350		9,350–10,100		10,100–10,850		10,850–11,600	
35,000–40,000........	7,900	7,900– 8,650		8,650– 9,400		9,400–10,150		10,150–10,900		10,900–11,650		11,650–12,400	
40,000–45,000........	8,900	8,900– 9,650		9,650–10,400		10,400–11,150		11,150–11,900		11,900–12,650		12,650–13,400	
45,000–50,000**....	10,200	10,200–10,950		10,950–11,700		11,700–12,450		12,450–13,200		13,200–13,950		13,950–14,700	

*7 or More Allowances: If your itemized deductions exceed the amount shown in Column 6 (above), you may claim 6 allowances plus one more for each $750 or fraction thereof of itemized deductions in excess of the amounts shown in Column 6 for your salary and wage bracket.

**When annual salary or wage exceeds $50,000, "0" column amounts may be determined as follows: for single employees (Part I)—22% of their annual salary; for married employees whose spouse is not employed (Part II)—15% of their annual salary; and for married employees when both spouses are employed and other employees who are holding more than one job (Part III)—24% of their combined annual salary. An additional withholding allowance may be claimed for each $750 or fraction thereof by which itemized deductions exceed the "0" column amount determined in this manner.

HOW TO USE THE TABLE

If you expect to itemize deductions for the current year, you may be entitled to claim additional withholding allowances (line i) and thus avoid having too much tax withheld. Your employer will treat each such allowance as a withholding exemption. The amount of itemized deductions for the current year cannot exceed the amount of itemized deductions (or standard deduction) claimed on your return for the preceding year (or 2nd preceding year if you have not yet filed your return for the preceding year), plus additional determinable deductible amounts.

These additional allowances will remain in effect until you file a new W-4 with your employer. For detailed information on allowable itemized deductions, see Form 1040 instructions.

1. Find the line in the table that includes your estimated salary and wage amount and that shows your status as either a single employee (Part I), a married employee whose spouse is not employed (Part II), or a married employee whose spouse is also employed (Part III). Also, use Part III if you are an employee who is holding more than one job concurrently.

2. Read across that line until you find the column that includes the amount of your estimated itemized deductions.

3. Note the number of allowances shown at the top of the column. This is the maximum number of additional withholding allowances you may claim on line i.

Married Couples.—If you and your spouse are both employed and file a joint return, determine your withholding allowances based on your combined wages and deductions. If you file a joint return and your spouse is not employed, use Part II. If you are filing a joint return and both are employed, use Part III to determine the total number of withholding allowances to which you are jointly entitled (you may allocate such withholding allowances between yourselves). However, if in your last filing you took separate returns, and if you expect to file separately this year, each of you must make your determination on the basis of your own wages and deductions and determine the number of withholding allowances for each from Part III.

In determining the amount of your itemized deductions, use last year's return as a guide. If you will be filing your first return next year and have not previously kept records, make a quick calculation of the expenses you can legitimately deduct. Claim everything to which you are legally entitled, but remember: it never totals as much as you think it will, so figure low. When you're paying those finance charges and hospitalization insurance premiums and deductible taxes during the year, they seem high. Yet when you total them, it's frequently less than the amount already calculated in the tax tables.

You can take medical expenses, for instance, but only if they exceed 3 percent of your gross income. You can deduct all taxes except federal (you can deduct those on your state return as a rule); you can deduct interest expenses, contributions, casualty and theft losses not reimbursed by insurance, and a few miscellaneous items such as union dues and certain expenses for child and dependent care.

I think that you will find the allowances from the first part of the worksheet ample, and you may wind up next year having a refund. We'll discuss in greater detail the intricacies of preparing and filing your income tax return in the final chapter, but you've just learned your most important lesson: Keep records, claim everything to which you are entitled, but always give yourself leeway for error.

Today many women are self-employed; as a result they will find themselves in a different tax situation. This is explained in Chapter 10.

SOCIAL SECURITY BENEFITS

Although your salary will probably be your primary source of income, you may be receiving other income as well. Social Security benefits, for example. Contrary to popular belief, these benefits are not the sole province of the widow.

You may be a single woman receiving survivor's benefits. If so, you may still receive them while furthering your education at a recognized high school, vocational or trade school, college or university. You must carry a subject load considered full time for day students at the particular institution. The course must last 13 weeks. In addition, with high schools and trade schools, attendance must be for at least 20 hours a week. A bonus—you may work while you are a student and still receive your full benefits if you do not earn over the 1975 ceiling of $2,520 per year. After you have reached that amount, the Social Security Administration will withhold $1 in benefits for every $2 you earn.

For example, if you earn $720 more than the allowable $2,520, $360 would be withheld from your benefits during the year, but no matter how much you earn, according to the Department of Health, Education and Welfare, which administers Social Security, you can receive a check for any month in which you earned less than $210. (Note: These amounts increase almost every year, so check with your local Social Security or IRS office for the latest figures.)

As I mentioned earlier, certain divorcees are also entitled, surprisingly, to Social Security benefits on their ex-husband's accounts. If your former husband starts collecting his retirement or disability checks you may receive benefits, too, if you are over 62 and were married to him for twenty years. If he dies, and you haven't remarried, are over 60, were married to him at least twenty years, or have minor children entitled to benefits, you may claim them, too. Check with your local office to see if you qualify.

If you are a widow, the Social Security payments, either with or without your salary, may well be the only means by which you will be able to maintain a home for yourself or your minor children.

You will receive, besides the ordinary monthly payments, a lump-sum amount when your husband dies, to help with the funeral expenses. The amount in 1975 of $255 will probably be steadily increased as Congress increases the other benefits, but it doesn't rise as rapidly as do the others.

The monthly Social Security checks you will receive will depend on many factors: your husband's age at death, your age, your husband's earnings credits, whether you are disabled, whether you have minor children, whether you work. If you remarry before age 60 your checks may stop unless you marry another beneficiary.

Remember: To apply for your benefits, you will need your husband's death certificate, your marriage license, his Social Security number, and the children's birth certificates. (The rules are the same when applying for Veterans Administration benefits, except that you will need his discharge paper, too.) It will take from three to four months for the checks to start—however, they will be retroactive—so file as soon as possible after your husband's death.

When you receive notice of the amount you will be receiving (your check will come separately from the children's so that your earnings will not affect their payments), you will be given a booklet concerning your duties and responsibilities in administering these funds. Study it carefully and keep meticulous records. It is unlikely that you will ever be called to account for the way in which they were spent, but it is legally possible, so take great care with your bookkeeping. Those amounts designated for the support and education of your children must be spent for them. This is not as stringent as it sounds; maintaining your home for them is part of their support, so the rules are flexible.

A word of caution if you are receiving Social Security benefits of any type: The Administration's record-keeping system is atrocious, and if you are ever overpaid, through no fault of your own, *you* are liable for the error, and every penny you owe will be deducted from future checks. If you ever receive a check that doesn't seem to be the correct amount, contact your local office and notify it of the error. If at all possible, do not use the check, but deposit it in your savings account (where it can be earning interest for you) until you hear from the office. It will either want the overpayment sent back immediately or it will choose to deduct it from your next check.

Remember—all Social Security and Veterans Administration benefits are tax-exempt, whether received because of age, disability, or death.

If you are a widow and are afraid that you may overlook some benefits to which you may be entitled, good news! There is a free service provided by 381 banks in 30 states that will help you search out and claim all financial benefits that may be due you. These could be through retirement funds, union and other pensions, profit-sharing plans, credit life insurance, workman's compensation, and others. You don't have to be a customer of one of the member banks to avail yourself of this service; write for a national directory of the banks to Special Organizational Services, P.O. Box S.O.S., Athens, Texas 75751. It will certainly be well worth the price of a stamp.

We've discussed, in depth, alimony and child support payments in the chapter on divorce, but I want to urge you, if you are receiving either or both, to follow the advice given relating to government benefits. Keep accurate records, and abide by any rules laid down by the court. A reminder: The alimony payments you receive are taxable to *you,* but the child support amounts are exempt.

All the above—salary, alimony, survivor's benefits—will be regular and budgetable; use them for everyday living expenses. Now let's discuss savings and investments.

Insurance proceeds that you are receiving, either as a widow or as the beneficiary of a relative's policy, will probably constitute the largest amount of money with which you will be concerned, and anything over and above the amount necessary for daily expenses should be put to work for you.

With that excess money you will be able to lay a solid financial foundation. With it you will have a sum of money you can call upon in case of an emergency (experts say that it is wise to set aside the equivalent of three months' take-home pay for ready access). You will be able to purchase the types of insurance policies—life, health, home, car—that will give you the maximum protection for the money you can spend. You will be able to save, invest, and have a fund you will feel free to tap for extras such as major appliances, a new wardrobe, a trip.

SAVINGS

A savings account is in most cases the best place for your money, and the kinds are as varied as the requirements of the investor. That works to your advantage, but whatever type you select will have several items in common with all the rest.

Why am I so enthusiastic about savings accounts, and particularly about savings and loan associations? Because the average female investor is governed by two factors: limited funds and a fear of risk investments such as stocks and shares in acceptance and land group companies. Government securities, while not risk investments, pay only simple interest. I contend that most women are not gamblers by nature and want their funds to be safe (insured), accessible and profitable. The ideal for the woman investor would be diversified investments such as insured savings with interest compounded to increase the principal and investment in land that has an assured growth value.

With savings accounts your capital is safe, accessible, and profitable. It is insured up to $40,000 per account by either the Federal Deposit Insurance Corporation (banks) or the Federal Savings and Loan Insurance Corporation, and in most cases you can get to your money immediately. In cases when you cannot withdraw, you can borrow, with the savings themselves as collateral. If you withdraw before the date of maturity, you will probably forfeit the interest (which is taxable as income), but the point is that if an emergency arises, you *can* get your money.

The interest on your savings will range from 5 to 7½%, depending on where you save and how much is in your account. Generally, the lowest rates are paid by commercial banks on passbook accounts. The advantage of saving at a commercial bank, even though the interest is lower than that offered by a savings and loan association (there is usually a quarter to a half percent difference), is that you can have a checking account there, and can arrange to have a specified amount regularly transferred to the savings account each month. This is a good way to save.

The highest interest offered by banks or savings and loan associations is paid on the certificates of deposit. The standard four-year certificate is sold in increments of $1,000, and the interest ceiling is set by law at 7¼% paid by banks and 7½% paid by the savings and loans. Many banks also offer their own certificates in varying amounts, ranging from $25 to $100,000, for different interest rates (6½ to 7½%), and maturity dates of from one to six years.

Another kind of note commonly called a certificate of deposit is commercial paper such as that offered by commercial banks. For example, in Atlanta the Citizens and Southern Holding Company offered, in May 1975, a $100,000 note at 5¾%, with interest amounting to $481.47 payable after only thirty days.

No matter which type you may select, your money earns interest from the day it is deposited, and no matter how the interest is compounded, it will add a sizable sum to your balance. (You can request that the interest be mailed to you so that you can deposit it in your checking account for spending.)

Let's look at some figures compiled by the Union Trust Company of Connecticut. Suppose you deposited $100 in a savings account on the first of each month for five years at 6% interest. The amount you would receive at the end of the five-year period would depend on the way your interest had been compounded. For example, if the interest had *not* been compounded (straight interest), your total investment would have increased by only $750. However, if the interest had been compounded annually, the total increase would have been $798.32; if compounded semi-annually, $912.70; if compounded quarterly, $971.74; monthly, $1,011.76; daily, $1,013.69. If it had been compounded continuously, it would have earned a very respectable $1,030.25. So check to see what alternatives your local institutions offer, and select the most advantageous.

Don't be frightened that your money will be tied up in a four-year certificate and you won't be able to use it if you need it. At a savings and loan association, for instance, you can borrow up to 90% of the total at any time, and, according to the law, can only be charged 1 percent more than the interest you receive. In other words, your money will still be in your account earning money for you at, let's say 7½% interest. Your loan interest (deductible) will be only 8½%, far lower than any other kind of loan you could get, and you are, in effect, getting a loan for only 1 percent. This may seem as if you are taking money from one pocket and putting it into another, but behind it is the theory used by astute financial manipulators the world over: Never touch your capital.

Other good savings institutions are credit unions, savings banks, and the government (United States Savings Bonds). Credit unions' interest payments (they call it dividends, but it is taxable as interest) vary from state to state, but the interest can go as high as 7% in a federally-chartered union and 8% in a state-chartered one. Savings banks are primarily found in the Northeast, and their rates and time requirements are identical to those of savings and loan associations. Both U.S. Series E and Series H bonds pay 6% interest if the bonds are held to maturity—five years and ten months from the date of purchase—and both are exempt from state and local taxes, but not from federal. The smallest Series E bond you can buy has a face value of $25, with a purchase price of $18.75, while the

Series H minimum investment is $500. You will have to declare the Series H interest annually on your tax return, but you may defer payment on the E's interest until you cash it in or when it matures.

A good idea, if you put your money into savings certificates or in anything else that does not pay interest quarterly, is to stagger your purchases so that you will receive your interest payments scattered throughout the year.

In any event, and whatever method you use, save regularly. Treat your savings account deposit exactly as you would an installment payment, and be just as faithful about honoring it. Set a goal. If you want to have $5,000 on hand in five years for a trip to Europe, start saving now. For instance: In an account with comparatively low rates (5½%), compounded monthly, you would need to deposit $72.59 each month to realize your ambition. If you wanted to wait ten years, you would only need to deposit $31.35 monthly. Naturally, at higher rates, it wouldn't take you as long to achieve your objective. The important thing is to save.

A final word about your savings account, and anything else in which you invest. Be sure to have the name of someone you trust on the account with you. One of your children would be best. In that way, the account will not enter into your estate (remember?) and no taxes will have to be paid on it when you die. Usually all that is necessary is for you and the other owner to sign a card showing both names. Remember, too, that joint and co-ownership can be tricky, so ask each institution involved for the best way to word the ownership. Sometimes the word "or" can make a tremendous difference. This is a highly technical legal matter and can vary from state to state and institution to institution, so make sure you are safe.

If there is no one individual you wish as your co-owner (I'm using the term for the sake of convenience), or if your children are too young, have the name of the executor of your will, whether a person or a bank, on the account with yours.

Now that you have set aside your salary and/or payments from Social Security and alimony for your operating expenses and the insurance money and anything extra to put into savings, if there *is* anything left over, there are other ways to have your money work for you.

INVESTMENTS

Now we're talking about money that you will not need to call on for an appreciable period of time. In other words, if you can afford to forget that you have several thousand dollars for a few years, it can start earning some substantial amounts for you.

Primary big earners are municipal bonds. They will pay you about 10%

interest that is not taxable, and even though they are issued for predetermined periods of time, you can cash them in before maturity. They are issued by any form of municipal government, and are usually sold as $1,000 bonds.

Interested in silver? Buy either silver coins of high numismatic value, in choice condition, or silver bars. But *not* from brokers or mail-order houses. You'll get a better deal buying directly from metal refiners. You can buy from Engelhard Industries (430 Mountain Avenue, Murray Hill, N.J. 07974) or from American Smelting and Refining (150 St. Charles Street, Newark, N.J. 07101). The former requires a minimum order of one hundred ounces and will buy back if you decide to sell; the latter requires a minimum order of fifty ounces but will not rebuy from you.

How about gold? The mere word conjures up visions of wealth and opulence, doesn't it? Well, wait before rushing out to buy some, now that Congress has made the sale legal again. It pays no interest, and its storage can end up costing you money.

Diamonds are a good investment, but you really have to know gems in order to get first-rate jewels that are well-cut and well-faceted. They do appreciate in value, so rely on the advice of an expert at one of the better houses.

If you are exceptionally brave, you can dabble in the stock market, but expect losses as well as gains, and expect a hefty outlay at the beginning. Don't even consider investing in stocks and bonds unless you have a reputable broker, then rely on his judgment. He's the expert; you're paying him to advise you, after all. If there are any bargains around, he'll find them.

If you want to find out about the quality of any bonds, consult with independent services such as Moody's or Standard and Poor's. You can find copies of their ratings at the library or at your broker's. These services rate the quality of bonds from the very highest (AAA or Aaa, depending on the service consulted) to the riskiest (C). If you don't want to take a chance on a loser, don't buy any securities rated lower than A.

If you invest in mutual funds you are, in effect, playing the market, but with less risk. There are several points you should remember before you invest. The advantages: High interest rates, up to 10% on some plans; instant liquidity—you can withdraw all your money at any time on instant notice without suffering a penalty; and your money is invested by experts in the highest rated securities and government notes. They can buy judiciously because you and the thousands of other investors have given them millions of dollars to invest in stocks that would otherwise be out of reach for the small private purchaser, who would have a lot of trouble buying, say 40 or 50 shares of AT&T. Mutual funds investors can buy them using money from *all* the small investors, spreading any gains among all of them, according to their individual investment. The disadvantages: your cash is not insured; there are sales and handling fees, sometimes as high as 8½ %; and the interest rate is neither fixed nor guaranteed.

If you are interested in investing, contact several mutual funds directly. There will be no obligation, and you will have the facts and figures on hand to help you decide if they are for you. For information on "no-load" funds (no salesman or sales fee involved), write to Dreyfus Liquid Assets (600 Madison Avenue, New York, N.Y. 10022), Reserve Fund (1301 Avenue of the Americas, New York, N.Y. 10019) or Money Market Management (421 7th Avenue, Pittsburgh, Pa. 15219). For "load" funds information, write to Anchor Reserve (Westminster at Parker, Elizabeth, N.J. 07207) or Oppenheimer Monetary Bridge (1 New York Plaza, New York, N.Y. 10004). Carefully read the prospectus each organization will send you before you decide to invest.

Invest in your company's pension plan cautiously, if at all. Congress has seen to it that the investors will be assured of some return on their money if the company should fail. Pension plans now have to guarantee minimum pensions to workers in one of the following ways: Twenty-five percent of full pension rights after five years' employment, increasing to a full one hundred percent after fifteen years; or full pension rights after ten years; or fifty percent when an employee's age and years of employment total forty-five, but only after an initial five years of service, and full pension after fifteen years regardless of age. The law says that a fully vested worker will receive his pension even if he quits or is laid off before retirement or the company goes bankrupt. What constitutes a fully vested worker varies according to each plan's vesting schedule. For example, if a certain plan has a 10-year schedule, the employee's share would be 10% per year, 50% after 5 years, and he would be fully vested after 10. If he leaves the job and comes back to it within a specified time, he will get credit for the total time spent with the company.

If the company for which you work has a plan, investigate it carefully. See if there are any safeguards—if the money is being invested, if it is insured. If there is a profit-sharing plan, check it out, too. On the face of it, it will appear to be a good deal: The company promises, in effect, to share its profits with its employees. See what provisions are made if you leave the company either voluntarily or not. See if there are any promises you must make as to future employment with a competitor. There are all kinds of loopholes in such plans, and they work against the employee. If the plan in operation permits you to invest in it—don't. Such investment is too risky. There are other, more secure ways in which you can invest your money. Don't let anyone high-pressure you or threaten you; it's *your* money to do with as *you* wish.

Now that you have invested your surplus money wisely and well, you will want to assure yourself that it will be used to the greatest advantage by your heirs, if you should die before you can enjoy it yourself.

YOUR WILL

Here we come to that most vital of documents, your will. No matter how much or how little you have, you will want to leave it to some person or institution, so put serious thought into the terms you will want included in the will. If you die intestate, the money will go to the state in which you live, so have a will drawn *now*.

First, find a lawyer. Shop around. Lawyers specialize just as doctors do, and they are not all experts in laws pertaining to wills and legacies. Their fees are usually set by the local bar association, so it will be wise to check in advance with the association to see what the going rate should be. You don't have to pay the highest fee to retain the most capable attorney. If you need help selecting one, write to Consumer Insurance (813 National Press Building, Washington, D.C. 20004) and ask for the twenty-page *A Shopper's Guide to Lawyers,* by Herbert S. Denenberg, lawyer and former Insurance Commissioner of Pennsylvania. The booklet is $1.00 for nonresidents of Pennsylvania; those of you who live in the state can get a free copy by sending a self-addressed envelope, stamped with two first-class stamps, to *Shopper's Guide* (Pennsylvania Insurance Department, Harrisburg 17120).

About your will. I cannot stress too often the fact that even people of modest means have "estates," and if provision is not made for the proper distribution of its assets, the total may be eaten away by taxes and legal charges that could be avoided. Your will guarantees that your heirs will realize the proceeds instead of letting the money be lost through poor— or no—planning.

A will is nothing to be afraid of or to avoid. It is simply a legal document specifying what should be done with your worldly possessions after you die. You *will* need a lawyer. I advise against a do-it-yourself will. The will must be duly and legally drawn so that it will stand up in probate court. (An unclear or wantonly illegal will can be canceled by the court.) The importance of a will cannot be overemphasized. In Georgia, for instance, if a widow dies leaving children but no will, the estate would be divided equally among the children, and the state would appoint a guardian for the children. If a widow, or any other single woman, dies leaving no will and no children, her estate would be divided equally among her parents, brothers, and sisters. If any of the brothers or sisters are deceased, their share would be divided equally among their children and grandchildren. Let me point out that Georgia has some of the fairest and most equitable laws governing the distribution of property and money left by someone who dies intestate (without a will). Some states' laws are archaic so it's best to leave nothing to chance.

In Chapter 2 I discussed the kind of will a husband should leave for his wife. The same ground rules apply in your case: the duties of the executor; the correct executor; the amount of savings your heirs will be able to realize through proper advance planning; the proper guardian for minor children. I won't repeat the rules as outlined in the earlier chapter; instead, let's go through a checklist of items you will want to consider in making your own will.

Who is to receive your property? This includes everything you own, even your clothes. We're going to keep your insurance out of the estate, though; more about that later. Who is to be the executor of your estate? If you operate your own business, do you want it continued or sold? If you have a partner, what arrangements have the two of you made about the business? Who is to be the guardian of your children? What plans do you want for your funeral or cremation/burial? Do you own property in other states? Because laws in each state control property within its boundaries, you will have to make a provision in your will that will be effective in your particular state. All of these are subjects requiring the most careful thought, and you must instruct your lawyer to state each item so that your wishes will be carried out in every respect.

If you have minor children and do not have a relative you wish to act as their guardian, select someone else as soon as possible. Otherwise, the court would have to appoint one. The selection of a guardian is the single most important step for the mother alone when she is deciding on the terms of her will. The next most important step—for all women—is the selection of a competent executor.

Someone has to see that the terms of your will are satisfied, and that individual or institution is the executor. He, she or it executes the provisions of the will, and sees that everything is done legally, properly, and at the right time. If you don't know someone to select, ask your local bank about their services. They have a department that specializes in executing wills, but there will be a fee, as there will be for anyone who is not a member of the family or a close personal friend.

Give some thought to your funeral. Today there are several options. It is not macabre to make these plans carefully; plans made now will certainly make the situation easier for your executor and family in the future. Here, as in every other area, it is foolish to spend money needlessly, and funeral directors agree. According to the Continental Association of Funeral and Memorial Societies (1828 L Street, N.W., Washington,

D.C. 20036), a nonprofit consumer organization, it is possible to have—with advance planning—a dignified funeral that is economical as well. The association offers a free pamphlet, "Funeral and Memorial Societies," and a booklet, costing $1.50, that includes a checklist of things to be done when there is a death in the family. It explains why cremation and donation of bodies to medical schools are less costly than a standard funeral and burial. (Most medical colleges will arrange and pay transportation costs within a given radius—usually from 100 to 200 miles.) You might want to donate parts of your body to medical banks for transplants. This can be included in your will, but it is imperative that the eyes and heart, for instance, are donated immediately after death, so it will be best to make these advance arrangements with the proper agencies.

If you have some sort of major change in your life—marriage, birth, death—that could alter the terms of your will, have your lawyer execute a codicil (change) and have it duly witnessed and added to your will. If you have several changes, you may need a new will revoking (canceling) the old.

Although I am a great believer in doing as much as possible for myself—to save expenses, if nothing else—I recognize my limitations, and in anything as complicated as having a proper will drawn, I bow to necessity and seek the most competent (and reasonably priced) attorney available. I don't want any future problems with my estate, and I want to do whatever I can to prevent future headaches—and costs—for my children. I urge you to retain an attorney who can guide and advise you. And, as I said earlier, laws vary from state to state, so make sure, if you move, to have your will checked by a lawyer in your new state for any violations or invalidations.

You know by now how I feel about cutting costs, so you may be surprised when I say that, except in rare cases, I think it is best to have a lawyer handle the probate of a will. Not that there is anything so complicated about it. The procedure is simply a mechanical one whereby your executor receives permission from the court to begin administering your estate. There are certain steps that must be followed, however, to insure the legality of the proceedings: letters must be written to all debtors and creditors and to anyone else who may make a claim against the estate. (Note: Write to the legal department of any company or store to avoid having the account carried as delinquent.) Minor children may have to be served legal papers notifying them of the will. And all witnesses to the will must be located and notified that they must go to the courthouse to verify their signatures. Only then will the executor be given "letters testamentary," authorizing him to proceed with the business of the estate.

Have your lawyer tell you if he thinks that saving the fee paid to the probate court will be worth your trying to bypass the usual steps; he will give you the best advice.

TRUSTS

Discuss with him, also, the feasibility of your setting up a trust, possibly for minor children. There are two types of trusts: "testamentary," which goes into effect after your death, and "living," into which you may place assets while you are alive. If the trust is revokable you will retain control of the funds during your life; the simplest kind is a bank account with you as the trustee, and listing someone else as the beneficiary.

A tax-free, as well as a probate-free trust, must be irrevocable. Here again there are various types, some tying up the money permanently, some giving you control over the administration, some allowing you to cancel, with the consent of the beneficiary.

The basic principle of a trust is simple; you turn over an amount of money or property to an individual or institution, to be held "in trust" and administered by "trustees" for the benefit of the "beneficiary." The principle may be simple, but the setting up and administration of a trust can be extremely complicated. Any bank can give you complete information as to its services and charges, which are usually a percentage of the total value of the estate or a flat percentage rate. The charges can be steep. Don't sign anything unless you know that a trust is the best way in which your estate should be administered.

Now that we've taken care of whatever you will leave after death, let's talk about the possibility that you might run short of funds now, while you're alive and the bills are coming in faster than your income. Don't panic—there are several avenues open to you.

LOANS

We've already discussed the ideal way to borrow—against your savings account—but suppose you've borrowed to the limit allowed? Understand —I don't recommend borrowing as the panacea for all your problems. It is expensive, with costs ranging from 7 to 43%, depending on where the loan is offered, the interest rate, and how it is repaid. But there *are* times when borrowing is an absolute necessity, so you'd better know some facts.

The easiest way to borrow is against your home. If you already have a mortgage, it is usually quite simple to place a second one. It will run for about seven to ten years, at about 6% interest. Or you can get a home improvement loan for twelve months at 6% add-on interest, which makes it come to about 10.89% for the year. We will explore both types of mortgages in Chapter 7, but a rule-of-thumb ratio governing the amount that should be borrowed is, according to the Equity Loan Division of the Citizens and Southern Mortgage Company, "the principal amount of the first mortgage plus the proposed amount of the second mortgage, not to exceed ninety percent of our appraised value, or the sales price of the home, whichever is less."

The second-mortgage loan can see your children through college, and can be repaid with the Social Security benefits, so it is a godsend to a woman who owns her own home and can borrow against it.

Banks offer education loans at about 12% annually, and you can get a loan from a consumer finance company for any purpose, but the interest rates are steep, and can run up to 43%. Most of their loans to employed persons run at 22.042% on a $1,000 loan that will cover two years. Their rates are high because they loan to people without collateral, and often without credit ratings or jobs.

If you don't own your home, you can always borrow against your life insurance policy up to the maximum amount shown on each individual policy. The amount will depend, of course, on the value of the policy and how long you have had it, so don't take it out today and expect to borrow against it tomorrow. The interest will vary, but usually runs a little lower than standard bank loans, generally from 5 to 6%.

Don't overlook borrowing from your credit union. Although state and federal laws limit the amount you may borrow, as well as the things for which the money may be used, credit unions are especially good sources for loans for cars, appliances, and moderate "signature" loans that require no collateral. The current average charge on a short-term loan is 12% per year.

You may want to take out a bank installment loan, either on your signature or with collateral. Remember that you will be charged not only interest but a finance charge, as well. This isn't large, usually about 50¢ per monthly payment plus an initial fee of a few dollars, but it is an additional expense of which you should be aware.

CREDIT LIFE INSURANCE

On all your loans, be sure to take out a credit life insurance policy wherever it is offered. The payment is small, but is well worth the money in case you die before the loan is repaid. With the insurance, the balance due is automatically paid, relieving your heirs of that problem, at least. If you choose to take the credit life insurance, disability insurance will also be available to you. It is for *your* benefit (as opposed to your heirs'), in case you are disabled—generally for a period of thirty days—and are unable to make your payments. The policy will make the monthly payments until you are able to do so. Both of these policies are good, in-expensive investments that should not be overlooked. (I wish it were possible to get a credit policy on the loan against your insurance, but it isn't; the amount still due would be subtracted from the total due your heirs.)

TAX-FREE GIFTS

One last word about your estate. If you feel that the estate will be large, the tax will be high, and there is no other way for you to lessen it, con-sider making gifts—during your life—to your heirs. The gifts are de-ductible to the extent of $3,000 per person per year, plus an allowable lifetime exclusion, $30,000, so this is well worth investigating. For the most accurate information, contact your local Internal Revenue Service office and ask for the estate and gift division. They will do everything possible to help you avoid paying unnecessary taxes, both before and after death. The IRS has a toll-free number in every state, so don't hesi-tate to use this free service.

Now that you know how to keep your money, we'll discuss ways to spend it wisely and to your best advantage.

6

COPING WITH MONEY (PART II)

... and How to Spend It

And now about insurance.

The second part of your sound financial foundation that you are creating is your insurance program, and is as necessary as your savings. Your coverage is vitally important and essential in every area of your life. Your insurance will establish funds for your heirs in the future; it will furnish a ready source of money in the present if you need a substantial loan; your house or apartment insurance will protect everything you own (except your car, and it will have its own policy) from fire, loss, damage or theft; your medical policy will pay all or part of your expenses in case of accident or illness; and an income protection policy will take care of expenses if you are unable to meet them yourself.

Of all the men in your new life, none is more important than your insurance agent. My own maxim is, "Blessed is she who has a good insurance agent, for he shall help her mightily."

How to find the right one? In this as in everything else, shop around. It's *your* money; no one is going to pay your bills but you, and you are entitled to get the best value you can for it, in goods or services. Look through the yellow pages of your telephone book; ask an agent to come to your home or plan to meet him during your lunch hour; outline the amount and kind of coverage you want and the price you can afford to pay; check into package deals that would include all your insurance and would give you a lower rate; interview him; size him up and decide if he is the kind of man you would feel comfortable asking advice about a damaged carpet or car, a stolen purse or television set.

Most agents are usually brokers for several companies, so ask him for the best arrangements he can make. Be honest with him; tell him that you are trying to find the best policies at the best prices and you will contact him in the near future to tell him what you decide. Interview other agents; it won't be long before you will begin to see a pattern emerging as to coverage and costs, and then you can more intelligently weigh the positive points offered by each agent. You may not be able to have all your policies handled by one agent; if the one you like and select doesn't offer health insurance, for instance, ask him to recommend another agent who does.

Questions that you must answer for yourself before buying any insurance policy are: Can I pay the premiums annually, instead of monthly, to save money? What coverage do I need and what can I afford to pay? Are there any deductibles I can utilize that will lower my premiums?

LIFE INSURANCE

Your life insurance policy and your homeowner's policy are the two dealing with the largest amounts of money. In buying your life insurance policy buy what will be a generous amount for your heirs, but do not overbuy. When determining the size of the policy, consider any other benefits your heirs will receive, such as those from Social Security or the Veterans Administration. Keep in mind the "seven times your income" rule of thumb as a guide to the maximum amount you should buy. If you like, you can ask that an automatic cost-of-living adjustment be added to the policy. In that way the face value and the premiums are raised annually to keep pace with the cost of living. This is particularly necessary if you have a family income policy, as has been discussed earlier.

There are two types of life insurance policies available. They are permanent insurance and term. With permanent insurance the premiums remain the same for the duration of the policy, and it builds cash value so that you can borrow against it or so that you can sell it for the amount it is worth at the time of the sale. The cost of the premiums will vary depending on the amount of the policy and your age when you buy it—the older you are, the higher the premiums.

Term insurance is written for a specified period, either for a certain number of years or until you reach a certain age. It builds no cash value and you cannot borrow against it. It can, however, be converted at any time to permanent, either at the face value or the current value at the time of conversion. There are two kinds of term insurance—reducing term, which reduces in value over the period of the policy, and level term, which remains the same.

Why would you ever want term insurance? For a high value at comparatively lower premiums for a specified period of time. For example, when George died I knew that in the event of my death while the children were young and without income, the estate taxes on the property would take everything else I could leave them. So, on the advice of my agent, I bought a reducing term policy valued at $50,000. The value is reduced by $2,500 each year for ten years, at which time I will convert the balance ($25,000) to permanent insurance. The premiums, based on my age in 1970, were $36.25 a month, much less than I would have had to pay (if I could have afforded it) for a permanent policy of equal value. I also have a smaller policy of permanent life valued at $10,000 so that the children will have something left over from the taxes. The premiums on it are $26.38 monthly, so you can imagine how high the cost would have been on a $50,000 permanent policy.

I'm back on the estate. Be sure to make your heirs the owners of your policies—not the beneficiaries—so that it will not add to the total amount of the estate. If you ever want to change the owners, simply write to the insurance company for the appropriate form, or ask your agent to do it for you. The case is the same as when a man has named his wife the owner. If the insured wants to borrow against the policy, the owner will have to sign the forms, and any dividend check will have to be endorsed by him or her. The same is true of group life insurance offered where you work or by associations to which you belong. You may name an owner instead of a beneficiary. And any time you want to drop a policy, just stop paying the premiums.

Investigate group insurance where you work. The premiums will be lower than those of an individual policy, but be sure it can be converted to personal insurance if necessary, in case you leave the company or organization.

If you live in an area that has savings banks, check on their insurance. You must live in the state in which it is purchased, but the premiums can run as much as 10 to 15 percent lower than regular insurance.

HOMEOWNER'S INSURANCE

On your home or apartment insurance, do not falsely economize by underinsuring. Insure the house for at least 80 percent of its replacement cost, and the contents of the house or apartment at the same ratio. Many homeowners' (including apartment dwellers') policies have the same inflation-guard stipulations as offered by the life insurance policies. These provide for automatic increases in coverage and premiums every two or three years as the cost of living climbs. (If it ever drops, readjust your policies—fast!) Ask your agent if you are eligible for any premium discounts. In areas where Operation Identification, an anti-burglary program, is in effect, some companies have offered premium reductions. Whether or not you are participating in such a program, it is always a good idea to inventory your household possessions (update it as value changes), in case of fire or theft. Some companies insist on it. Be sure that you put the current replacement value on your goods: Except for antiques, your furniture has probably depreciated, but silver, as an example, appreciates in value yearly.

It is a good idea to have a liability clause in your policy in case anyone is injured in your home. And be sure that the policy covers your possessions while in your car or away from home. Homeowner's insurance is one of the best bargains in the insurance world. A policy offering complete coverage on a $60,000 house, plus the contents, costs a little over $300 per year. The policies are usually written to cover three years with the payments due the first year, and most companies will offer a budget plan for payment, spreading the premiums over a nine-month period.

CAR INSURANCE

Your car insurance is required by law in most states; those that do not demand the actual coverage require that you have a comparable amount of money to cover any damages, injuries, or lawsuits. I'm going into automobile insurance more thoroughly in Chapter 12, and will discuss buying, selling, maintaining, and repairing a car. Because there are so many factors involved in car insurance, such as age and type of car, use, ages of drivers, and so on, I want to give you all the information possible. For now, I'll just urge you to ask your agent to recommend a good automobile insurance agent if he doesn't handle such policies himself.

MEDICAL INSURANCE

I have been using the term "health insurance" to cover the entire range of medical insurance, but let's define some terms right now.

The only deductible premiums (the formula, according to the Internal Revenue Service, is one-half of the premiums, not to exceed $150, plus the balance added to your other medical expenses and subject to the 3% of gross income limitation) are those paid for *medical* insurance. This insurance must provide reimbursement, either to you, the physician, or the hospital, for hospitalization, surgical fees, and other medical expenses. Nondeductible types of insurance are accident and disability. Any policy that specifies a guaranteed amount each week in the event of hospitalization as a result of sickness or injury is not deductible.

If you work, you will probably be offered the opportunity to join a medical insurance group. Don't hesitate. Even if you have a policy of your own, it is virtually impossible to have too much medical insurance to cover today's costs. Check to be sure that neither policy forbids you to have additional coverage. If it does, get a new policy; you will need it if you ever have to go to the hospital.

When you are buying your own medical policy, be sure it can't be canceled on short notice. Check to see what it actually covers. How much are the out-of-pocket deductibles? They mean that the policy doesn't even begin paying until after you have paid the first $100 or $500 or whatever. The lower the deductible, the higher the premium—and the premiums are high enough already. But in medical insurance, you don't always profit by paying a lower premium; the coverage is the important thing to consider. If you have children, for instance, to what age are they covered? You may have to take out supplemental policies on them when they reach eighteen. Look for a plan that has good coverage for major medical expenses. In this case you may have to accept a higher deductible, but then the policy would cover everything up to very high figures in the tens of thousands. This is for prolonged, catastrophic illness and should be considered, but not to the exclusion of ordinary medical coverage. You will pay dearly for your medical insurance, but the cost of paying hospital and medical bills out of your own pocket is incredible.

If you do not work, it is possible for you to have a group policy for you and your children, to pay the hospital bills before the patient leaves the hospital. Ask your agent about it; he probably will not carry it, but he can help you apply for it.

Disability insurance is worth investigating, and if you can afford a policy I suggest you purchase one. Benefits for women are more limited than those offered men, but it is possible to obtain an adequate policy that will guarantee an income if you are disabled. (Make sure that your life policy includes a "waiver of premiums" provision whereby the insurance company will pay the premiums for as long as the disabling condition continues.)

A point to remember—if you have a mentally retarded child or dependent, you will be able to include him or her on your private medical policy, and possibly on your group plan.

There are a few miscellaneous policies you will want to consider.

MISCELLANEOUS INSURANCE

Travel insurance for a specified trip for a specified time is a good investment, and is not restricted to air travel. The cost is relatively low for the amount of proceeds your heirs would receive. For example, the Georgia Motor Club, an affiliate of the American Automobile Association, offers a fourteen-day $5,000 accident and illness policy for $4.40, and a separate one for baggage loss, for $4.80, covering 300 pounds of luggage. An accident policy for $10,000 costs $8, and one offering $15,000 coverage costs only $10.50. This is good one-time-only insurance at a reasonable price, and is especially recommended for long automobile trips.

If you have children—or any other dependents—do take out a small policy insuring their lives. Let's be brutally practical—it will cover the cost of a funeral in case one of them dies. If their father was a veteran, they (and you) can be buried in a national cemetery free. Contact your Veterans Administration office for details.

Concerning the children, most schools offer an accident policy that is well worth the price, about $3 for the entire school year. The policy covers accidents that occur on school property during school hours, and the coverage is good.

If you and/or your children have bicycles, you might want to consider a policy against theft or damage. Although most homeowners' policies cover such things as bikes, there is usually a $50 to $100 deductible clause. You can get a small policy on the bikes for about $12 for each $100 covered, and it's a good investment. It's on sale at most bicycle stores.

You're going to find yourself with quite a few policies on hand; what should you do with them? The Institute of Life Insurance recommends that you keep a small, fire-resistant, watertight metal file box in your home. Keep the policies and will in that. Keep in a separate place, perhaps your safe deposit box, a rundown of each policy, its coverage, its costs, and its beneficiaries or owners. Don't keep the list a secret; tell your heirs and executor where the list and the policies are. If you ever lose or damage a policy, the insurance company will replace it, usually at no cost, but it will take a month or two. Keep your policies in a safe place to avoid the possibility of loss.

In your safe deposit box keep your lease or title, car title, all legal documents, but not your will. In some states the law requires that a safe deposit box be sealed immediately upon the death of the owner. It can't be opened except under court supervision. It may take several days, and during that time nothing can be done to process the will.

Of course you're never going to leave money around the house, in a metal box or whatever, but you'll have to have operating capital for your day-to-day expenses. The answer, of course, is a checking account, but what kind?

CHECKING ACCOUNTS

It seems that every banking institution in the country is after your account, but they don't all offer the same services, so you must weigh your own needs carefully.

There are two types of accounts: regular and special. The regular accounts require that you maintain a minimum balance to avoid any service charges; the special accounts charge you so much per check written. There are some banks, but only 13 percent of the total number in the United States, that offer a no-minimum-balance, no per-check fee, no service charge account. Usually you are required to open a savings account with them, but the initial deposit can be as low as $5. See what is available in your area. If there are none of the banks offering this service, you will have to weigh the advantages and disadvantages of the regular and special accounts.

If you don't plan to write many checks, the special account will be for you. There will be a 5 to 25 cents charge for each check written (remember to deduct the amount with each check), but you will always know exactly how much you have in your account. Not true of the regular account if you let your balance slip below the minimum amount required by the bank. Depending on their charges and the number of checks you have written, the charge can run from $5 to $10 a month. They don't charge a flat fee for each check written after your balance went below the minimum, either. They charge for each check on that month's statement, so beware. The minimum balance is usually $250 to $300; you are the best judge as to whether you can maintain that balance without penalty. You won't know what it is until your statement arrives, so you run the risk of being overdrawn without knowing it. (And there's a charge, usually $4, for each check written after you reach that point.)

If there is a bank offering a package deal, you might want to see if it is right for you. There is usually a $2.50 to $3 fee per month, and it covers a variety of services such as no-minimum-balance checking accounts, overdraft privileges (no penalty if you are overdrawn), traveler's checks (usual fee is $1 per $100), safe deposit boxes, bank credit cards, and, sometimes, discounts on loans. A very few banks, including one in Connecticut and one in Illinois, offer the entire package free of charge, but if you're not fortunate enough to be able to use their services, you'll have to decide if the $30 to $36 annual fee will be worth the cost. Add up your projected bank charges for the year, your safe deposit box rental, the cost of having your checks printed, the penalty if you are overdrawn, and the amount of traveler's checks you may use during the year, and see which way will be most advantageous for you.

Check to see if your bank offers automatic, guaranteed deposit of your paycheck, Social Security payments, or alimony checks if you request that they be mailed directly to the bank. The service will save a trip to the bank, the deposit date will be the same each month, and there is no charge.

Decide whether or not you will want another's name on your checking account in case of illness or death. But a word of warning: In states where joint accounts may be frozen upon the death of one of the partners, it would be an unwise move. Check local practices with your banker or lawyer.

Learn to balance your checkbook. I think it is nothing short of criminal negligence that courses are not taught in every high school on the delicate art of checkbook arithmetic. It's not all that complicated, but many people —of both sexes—find it beyond them. It's simple as long as you enter *everything* you must subtract (amount of checks, service charges, overdraft charges, cost of having checks printed) from your total deposits. Keep accurate records on each check stub—particularly if you itemize deductions on your income tax return—and maintain a correct accounting of your balance at all times. Do a little bookkeeping daily and it won't be so formidable when your statement comes from the bank each month.

A few rules to remember: Make sure that your deposit slips are filled out correctly so that your account is credited as it should be. Fill out your checks with care; never leave space for anyone to add numbers to the amount you've written. *Never* sign a blank check, and never make a check out to "cash" unless you are at the teller's window; anyone else could cash your check without identification, although most banks ask for an endorsement on the reverse side of the check. Don't cross out mistakes when you write a check; write a new one to avoid having the check bounce when the bank refuses (for your protection) to honor it.

I find it convenient to use two checkbooks, one large one I keep to use when I pay monthly bills, and a small one I carry in my purse for on-the-spot payments such as for groceries. At least once a week I total the stubs in the small checkbook and enter it in the large, where I maintain a running record of the balance in my account. Deposits and service charges are entered promptly, with the result that I can look at the large checkbook at any time and know my correct balance. And I always note anything that is tax deductible for ease in compiling the figures when I prepare my income tax return. (The ideal method is to maintain a monthly record in a ledger, but I am rarely quite that organized.)

Of course, you will want to avoid ever being overdrawn or going below your minimum balance, so you will have to develop a way to pay your bills to escape those extra charges. The best way is to begin with a budget. There are a few basic steps to follow.

BUDGETING

First, determine your total income. This includes everything—salary, survivor's benefits, alimony and child support, insurance proceeds, interest, dividends. Keep in mind any changes or limitations, such as the cessation of some of the benefit payments after a certain time.

Next, consider how you spend your money. Divide your expenses into

A page from your checkbook might look like this:

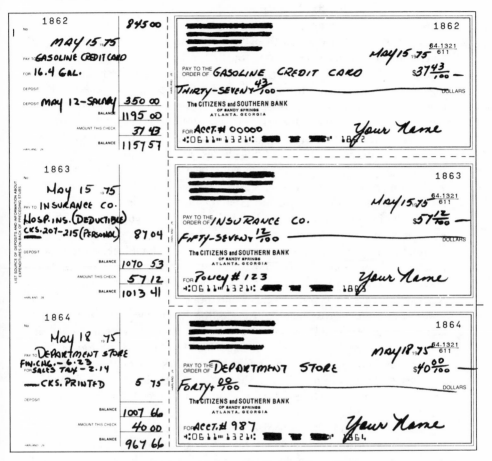

"fixed" and "flexible" expenditures. Include in the fixed payments those due monthly, quarterly or annually, such as rent or mortgage payments, insurance premiums, installment payments, utilities, your personal allowances for yourself and your children, contributions, and tuition expenses. You can reduce some of these costs by paying them annually instead of on a more frequent basis. For a monthly total of these fixed expenses, divide the quarterly payments by three and the yearly payments by twelve.

The flexible payments are harder to estimate. They will vary as to amount (groceries) and the date due or paid (home repairs, entertainment). Be expansive in your estimates—it's better to guess too high than too low.

Total all your expenses and weigh them against your total income. If the expenses are the same as or less than your income, your budget is balanced. If the expenses exceed the income, you must decide what can be trimmed from the flexible expenses first, and then try to find some way to economize on the fixed expenses.

An average spending pattern, as established by the Bureau of Labor Statistics, shows that one-fourth of your income will probably go for food (including meals eaten out), one-fourth for housing, another fourth for taxes, social security insurance, and contributions, and the rest for clothing and personal care, transportation, medical care, and miscellaneous items. Notice that nothing is specifically designated as savings. Perhaps that's included in miscellaneous, but wherever you put it, be sure that your own budget includes a healthy amount set aside for savings.

Nor is anything mentioned about charge accounts and installment buying. Be sure to account for them in your own budget, and be careful that you're not spending too much on either. You can founder on the seductive shoals of buying now and paying later if you're not cautious. I'll discuss the subject in depth in Chapter 11, but I want to give you a few guidelines about how much you should owe while you're setting up your budget.

Most authorities say, for instance, that renters should keep the cost of rent at no more than 25 to 35 percent of monthly income before taxes (not take-home pay). For anyone buying a house, the American Bankers Association says that you should spend no more than one and one-half times your annual gross income. In addition to mortgage payments, other credit payments should be no more than 20 percent of your annual income *after* taxes. If you are on a fixed income this may be too high, as inflation continues to take bigger and bigger bites out of the amount you have set aside for the necessities. Short-term debts (loans or credit-buying that will be repaid within a year) should not exceed one and one-half times your monthly income.

Stick to your budget. Recognize your weaknesses and avoid the temptation to cater to them. It's a lovely feeling to spend money, particularly on a luxury item, and you can do it—as long as you don't violate your budget. Don't buy things you don't really need; don't shop if you're tired or hungry; don't go into stores that are irresistible; don't shop with friends who may urge you to buy more than necessary; be strong—learn to say "No" to beguiling salespeople; don't *ever* let your spending get out of hand.

If you have fallen prey to the wiles of a door-to-door salesperson and later realize that you neither want nor need the product you've agreed to buy, you have a three-day grace period to catch your breath. The Federal Trade Commission's regulation states that you may cancel the contract, for a full refund, at any time during the three days following the date of purchase. This is true if the sale took place in your home or someone else's (through a party plan), and the expense exceeded $25. It's a good law, and one every consumer should remember.

PAYING BILLS

In my personal fight against inflation, I have devised my own method for paying my bills and still maintaining a reasonable balance in my checking account. Instead of setting aside one day a month for bill-paying, as I used to do when money was no problem, I now stagger my payments according to three criteria. First, I make a note each month of the days on which I will receive income. For example, when I work I am paid bi-weekly (every two weeks), so that my paydays fall on different dates each month. My insurance check comes on the thirtieth; a Veterans Administration check comes on the first and a Social Security check comes on the third. My quarterly interest checks from my savings accounts come on the first.

Second, I am careful to pay, before the billing date, any bills carrying a service charge for late payments, and I hold any unusually large checks I have written until after the closing date of my bank statement; in that way I will not run the risk of going below my minimum balance and so incur a penalty. This is especially helpful during a month when the flexible payments have exceeded my budgeted limit. (It does happen—there are always unforeseen expenses such as emergency plumbing—when you will have to write a check for an amount greater than anticipated.) I try not to let this happen too often, but sometimes it is unavoidable. The third step in my system of paying bills is selective payment. When the money situation is particularly tight one month, I will pay those bills carrying finance charges before those that do not, but even so, I try to pay at least a small amount on everything, to show my good faith.

It's always a good practice to let your creditors know that your intentions are honorable. If you do fall behind in your payments for several months, they will be turned over to a collection agency. Don't allow yourself to be harassed by the unscrupulous tactics of some collectors. Report any threats (other than of legal action, and if the bill is less than $250 that's unlikely, anyway), foul language, or late calls to your state collection agency licensing board. Ask the operator for the number if it isn't listed under your state's Department of Consumer Affairs. If your state does not license these agencies (I was shocked to learn that Georgia does not) they are usually licensed locally. In that case, there is probably no regulatory body governing them, but you can report any abusive behavior to the county solicitor's office or the city court clerk. Report the circumstances to the Better Business Bureau, the president of the company for whom the agent is collecting, and to your state representative and senator. Urge them to introduce legislation that will ensure regulations controlling these agencies' actions.

If your debt is really large and you have shown no willingness to make regular payments until it is dissolved, your employer may be contacted by your creditor and asked to withhold a certain amount from your wages. This is known as "wage garnishment," and is entirely legal. There are federal and state rules as to how much can be withheld, so contact the Wage and Hour Division of the United States Department of Labor if you suspect that too much is being taken out of your check. The basic federal guideline is that the lesser of either 25 percent of your weekly paycheck or your after-tax earnings above thirty times the federal minimum hourly wage may be withheld, but, if the state law provides you more protection, it will supersede the national rule. Check with your state Department of Labor, and for more complete information, write to Consumer Information, Public Documents Distribution Center, (Pueblo, Col. 81009) and ask for the free government booklet, 066B, on the Federal Wage Garnishment Law. The booklet has good basic information and tells you how to find out more.

One way to make sure this never happens to you is to play it safe at all times. Never overextend your spending. Be especially careful not to overload yourself with installment debts while you are working: You may not be able to carry the payments if you lose your job.

Caution and care are the watchwords for financial health, but if you ever feel that you are in over your head, don't hesitate to use some of the various counseling services available. Most banks have a counseling department; all major cities have a community service dealing with money management; and most states maintain a toll-free telephone service that deals specifically with money problems. There are courses offered at most urban colleges; there are magazines published for the sole purpose of helping you manage your money; and for $20 you can take a course offered by some banks to help you analyze and solve your problems. For more specifics, about the course and the names of the banks offering it, write to Personal Financial Planning Course (430 Lexington Street, Newton, Mass. 02166).

SHOPPING FOR GROCERIES

Nowhere will you need more expertise in money management than at the grocery store! You will have to know where, when, and how to shop for the best quality at the lowest prices.

Always considering convenience as a factor (you don't want to travel across town just because a certain store sells an item for 10¢ less than your neighborhood market), select your supermarket with great care. You'll want one that is planned well and that is pleasant and clean, but you'll also want one that is as cheap as is possible at today's inflated prices. Shop at discount stores; the savings on nationally sold brands can be as great as 20 percent, depending on the item.

Most discount department stores have a supermarket attached—their prices are as low as you will find. Use the discount supermarket as your regular store, but don't hesitate to go somewhere else for a bargain if the store is within reasonable distance. By comparison shopping in this way you will be able to save as much as $500 a year on a weekly $50 food budget. Watch the newspapers for announcements of sales. The Thursday paper generally runs ads for the coming week and there are usually recipes and free coupons as well.

When you shop is important. (You already know you shouldn't go grocery shopping when you're hungry.) Shop once a week, Wednesday or Thursday, if possible, either during the day or at night; the stores are less crowded and the produce is fresher. Check with your produce manager to see when most of his items are delivered.

Make a list. Otherwise, you'll be picking up things you don't really need. Plan a week's meals in advance and shop accordingly. You'll get out of the store much faster if the grocery list is written with the items in the order in which you will come to them in the store. Statistically, you'll spend more money than anticipated if your shopping takes longer than half an hour, so hurry! (And if you're watching your weight, don't buy or keep in the house anything that will tempt you to go off your diet.)

The only time you should deviate from your list is when you come upon an unexpected sale or bargain. Buy as much as you can afford and store. The same is true of economy sizes of such items as detergents. The law states that the economy size of any non-food item must save you at least 5 percent over other sizes of the same brand, so the larger sizes are a bargain at any time. If they are too bulky to handle, pour a smaller amount into a more manageable container and store the rest. In the case of food items, bigger is not necessarily cheaper. Unit price everything; divide the size into the price for the per-ounce cost.

Don't overlook house brands as a real source of savings. The quality is the same as that of nationally known brands; you're just not having to pay for the advertising done by the better-known product. These items include such things as salt, pepper, all flavorings and spices, canned and frozen vegetables, milk, cottage cheese, most other types of cheeses, frozen orange juice, bread, ice cream, all paper products, and aluminum foil. By buying store brands you can save as much as 20 percent on your weekly bill.

Check the "reduced-for-quick-sale" counter. Most stores, particularly late Saturday, throw out good fruits and vegetables that won't make it in the store over the weekend. Buy day-old bread; you can freeze it and keep it up to three months.

Turn to substitutes for good quality at reduced prices. The recommended adult daily requirement of two two-ounce servings of lean cooked meat, for example, can be met by substituting two eggs, or two one-ounce slices of cheese, or one-half cup of cottage cheese, or one cup cooked dry beans, or one-fourth cup of peanut butter.

Substitute nonfat dry milk for whole milk; or use evaporated milk for cooking. Use frozen orange juice instead of bottled or fresh. Use grade B eggs for cooking and baking and use large eggs instead of medium for individual servings or for scrambled eggs—you'll use fewer. Substitute less expensive cuts of meats; use chuck instead of roast, country-style ribs instead of spareribs. Use mackerel instead of salmon or tuna, pink or chum varieties of salmon instead of silver, king, or sockeye. In none of these cases is there any sacrifice of nutritive value.

Compare the costs of convenience foods with those made from scratch; often the already prepared food will offer the best bargain. Likewise, some frozen fruits and vegetables are better bargains than fresh. Compare per-serving price. For example, boneless lean meat, fish, or poultry will give three to four servings per pound, whereas steaks and chops, fish steaks, or cut-up chicken parts will give only two to three.

As a substitute for meat, economize by using more vegetables. For example, the following quantities and 1975 in-season prices (from my research and the U.S. Department of Agriculture's Bulletin #183) offer the following comparative servings per pound, and the price per 4-ounce serving of a variety of vegetables:

	Cost Per Pound	Number of Servings	Cost Per 4-ounce Serving
Asparagus	.78	4	.195
Beets	.38	4	.095
Broccoli	.68	4	.17
Cabbage	.14	4	.035
Cauliflower	.68	7	.097
Snap Beans	.48	6	.08
Sweet Potatoes	.18	3	.06
Turnips	.28	4	.07
White Potatoes	.28	3	.093

You may want to order the 35¢ USDA pamphlet HERR 37, *Family Food Buying: A Guide for Calculating Amounts To Buy and Comparing Costs.* (Send the money and your request to the Superintendent of Documents, U.S. Government Printing Office, Washington, D.C. 20402.) On the back of the booklet you will find a list of free, informative bulletins offered by the Agriculture Department advising the best ways to buy, store, and prepare your food.

If you can plant vegetables, indoors or out, in whatever space is available, you'll realize a saving. You can grow a tomato plant or two, some leaf lettuce or some parsley and chives. See if any of your neighbors want to share a community garden with you. If you're interested and want some information, write to the nonprofit organization, "Gardens for All" (Department 42099, Charlotte, Vt. 05445).

Buy your wine and cigarettes at a discount grocery, drug, or department store for savings of as much as 20 to 40¢ a bottle or carton. Cook double portions of your favorite vegetables and meats and put them in empty TV dinner trays you have saved; freeze them for an evening when you don't have the time, energy, or inclination to prepare a meal for yourself.

Don't yield to temptation and eat all your meals out to avoid cooking, either. The cost of eating at home rose, during 1974, by 6 percent, but the cost of eating out sky-rocketed by a huge 12 percent. And don't fall into that "person alone" trap of not eating properly. Take time to prepare attractive nutritional meals for yourself. It's good health insurance.

Frozen Foods

Utilize your freezer to the fullest extent, and make sure its temperature stays at zero. Buy sales items—meats, desserts, breads, fruits and vegetables—and store them for as long as is safe. Most prepared foods will keep safely for two to three months. Breads will keep the same amount of time, while some meats (roast, steaks) will stay safe for a full year. For a detailed list of the safe life of all frozen foods, plus suggestions on the care of your freezer, write for the free U.S. Department of Agriculture Bulletin # 69 (Washington, D.C. 20250). You can save tremendously by buying foods in season and freezing them yourself. If you want detailed information about freezing meats, fish, poultry, fruits, and vegetables, write the Department of Agriculture at the above address and ask for their free Bulletins G-10, G-40, G-70 and G-93. A word of caution: Don't put more than a few containers of unfrozen food in the freezer at one time—the food won't freeze quickly enough.

Home canning is tricky and, if done improperly, dangerous. For information on methods and classes, contact your state or county home economist or county extension service.

FOOD STORAGE

It's a good idea to know just how long products will remain safe on the shelf. Here are a few of the items you will probably be able to buy on sale, with their safe shelf-life:

	How to Store	Safe Shelf Life
Bouillon cubes, envelopes	Keep covered and dry	1 year
Cake mixes	Keep cool and dry	1 year
Cereals		
ready-to-eat	Keep covered and dry	Date on boxes
ready-to-cook	Keep covered and dry	6 months
Coffee		
cans	Refrigerate on opening	1 year
instant	Keep tightly covered	6 months
Cookies, packaged	Keep box closed tight	4 months
Crackers	Keep box closed tight	3 months
Flour (all types)	Put in airtight container	1 year
Fruits		
canned	Keep in cool spot	1 year
dried	Put in airtight container	6 months
Gelatin (all types)	Keep in original packets	18 months
Honey, jams, syrups	Keep tightly covered	1 year
Macaroni and spaghetti	Keep tightly closed	1 year
Meat, fish, poultry, canned	Keep in cool spot	1 year
Milk		
canned	Keep in cool spot	1 year
nonfat dry	Put in airtight container	6 months
Peanut butter	Keep in cool spot	6 months
Rice, white	Keep tightly closed	2 years
Salad oils	Keep in cool spot	1–3 months
Shortening, solid	Keep in cool spot	8 months
Soup		
canned	Keep in cool spot	1 year
mixes	Keep in original packets	6 months
Sugar, granulated	Keep tightly covered	2 years
Toaster pop-ups	Keep in original packets	3 months

It's a good idea to date all food and to put the newer purchase in the back of the shelf.

If your veterinarian approves, buy dry pet foods instead of canned—it's cheaper, but do check the label for the nutritional value. That is a good habit to get into for any food product, because the importance of good nutrition cannot be overemphasized. For example, research has proven that people who eat a nutritionally balanced breakfast are more alert and productive, and the National Safety Council says they are less prone to accidents.

For information about nutrition and other subjects of concern to the shopper you can write for many excellent free government booklets to Consumer Information (Public Documents Distribution Center, Pueblo, Col. 81009). Some of the booklets you might find useful are:

Some Questions and Answers about Canned Foods 089B
The Food-Labeling Revolution 288B
Dishing up the Dog Food 205B
Keys to Quality 112B
Nutrition Labeling—Terms You Should Know 230B

YOUR FOOD BUDGET

If you'd like to know where your food dollar is going, the Agriculture Department, in late 1974, broke down the costs of food bought by the "average" household and showed that meat took about one-third of the total food budget. Dairy and bakery and cereal products split another third, and the balance was divided among processed and fresh fruits and vegetables, eggs, poultry, fats, oils, and miscellaneous. Children cost more to feed than adults, as you probably know. Courtesy of the 1970 Agriculture Department figures again, we have statistics showing that a woman between ages 20 and 30, on a moderate weekly food plan, spends $13; if she is 35 to 55, she'll spend $12.60; 55 to 75, $10.80; and 75 and older, $9.60. Children 6 to 9 will cost $11.10 to feed weekly; girls 12-15 will cost $14.10; and those 15 to 20, $14. Boys are even more expensive to feed (as if you didn't know!), with a boy aged 12 to 15 costing $15.60, and those between 15 and 20 costing a whopping $17.40 each. So the ages and sexes of the family *will* make a considerable difference in your food budget and must be taken into account when you shop.

SHOPPING FOR CLOTHES

You will have to use the same caution when buying clothes. Although your clothing expenses won't come anywhere close to your food costs, they will take a big chunk out of the budget, and any measures you can take to cut the total costs are a necessity.

In 1973, the latest year for which figures are available, the average expenditure in this country on clothes was $300 per person, nearly double the amount spent five years earlier. And no one needs to tell you that the prices are still rising alarmingly.

If you sew you can eliminate some of this expense; the dress you make will cost you half the amount you would pay for a comparable ready-made garment.

Even if you do sew, there are still some items of clothing you will have to buy, and you'll have to join the rest of us in our relentless search for bargains—good quality at a reasonable price.

An especially good place to find those bargains is at factory outlet stores, which are usually located in small towns as well as in large cities. Unlike other discount stores, they sell goods that are seconds, irregulars, discontinued merchandise, odd sizes, designer samples, mill ends, and remnants. This kind of store is a bargain-hunter's paradise for almost any item you need, but particularly for clothes.

In some outlets you will find clothing designed by the finest couturier houses, or clothes (without the label) usually found in the most expensive specialty shops. These finds can be purchased for about one-third the price you would expect to pay at a retail outlet. Why are the prices so low? The clue is in the name of these stores—they *look* like factories. They have no decorating expenses, so are able to maintain a low overhead. They are generally in low-rent locations, and sales are usually on a cash, no-return basis, so shop carefully. Don't be put off by the fact that some of the items are seconds or irregulars; the article may simply have an irregular stitching or other barely visible defect which, while eliminating it from sale in the retail market, in no way impairs its beauty or quality. At a factory outlet or at any other kind of store, look for the signs of a well-made garment: firmly attached buttons; buttonholes without loose threads; seams wide enough to be let out and neatly finished to prevent fraying; firmly sewed hems that are invisible on the outside; fabric cut with the grain of the material; and checks and patterns that match.

Before you go shopping for clothes, make sure you know exactly what you want and how much you can spend. Avoid impulse buying, unless you see a bargain item that you will wear many times. Avoid extreme or one-occasion clothing. Try to buy items that can be worn during different seasons. Comparison shop among the traditional department stores, the discount houses, and the large chains. Look for sales. Make note on your calendar of sales and try to get such basics as lingerie and coats during one of these. Buy stockings of the same color by the half dozen, so you can add a new one in case of a run in half a pair. (The same applies to children's socks.) Update some of your last year's clothes. Try the thrift shops for good clothes at a low price; the garments are cleaned before being put on sale. Have a clothes "pool" with your friends, especially with children's clothes. Swap and share, so that none of you will be duplicating occasionally used items. Check the men's and junior departments for items you can wear and that are cheaper than similar items in the women's department. Avoid clothing that needs extensive alterations, and whenever possible, don't buy anything requiring dry cleaning. Make sure that whatever you buy (including most yard goods) has a care label.

Proper care of any garment will appreciably prolong its life and guarantee its good appearance. For more about the subject, write for the free booklet, *Care Labels Can Save You Money and Trouble,* FTC Buyers' Guide #10 (Federal Trade Commission, 6th and Pennsylvania Avenue, N.W., Washington, D.C. 20580). In no other area is labeling more important than in the purchasing of flame-retardant sleepwear for children. New rules, issued in May 1975 by the Consumer Product Safety Commission—the federal agency in charge of investigating potentially dangerous products—now covers sleepwear up to size 14.

Whether you are buying food, clothes, furniture, appliances, a car, or a house, don't be ashamed of trying to cut costs and of insisting on getting the best quality for the lowest possible price. Look on it as a challenge. It's *your* money to save, to spend, and to enjoy, in the best and wisest ways possible!

7

COPING WITH LIFE ALONE

The Key Word Is "Change"

The most important decision you will have to make as you begin your life alone is a basic one—where to live?

This decision, more than any other, will underscore your changing pattern of life. It will be governed by three criteria—location, cost, and safety.

You'll have to decide *where* you want to live. You'll have to determine whether you will want a house, apartment, or mobile home; whether you'll want to sell or stay, if you already own a house; whether you'll want to stay in the same part of the city, the same city, the same part of the country, the same country! You'll have to weigh the costs involved and decide, among other things, if you will rent or buy, if you'll have roommates or will live alone, if you will need extensive outlays of money for furniture, equipment, and appliances. You'll have to consider accessibility to your job, shopping, doctors, entertainment, public transportation, and, if you have children, to schools.

And as you make these decisions, you will have to keep in mind safety and security for yourself and your children.

LIVING ABROAD

Let's first consider the most drastic change you could possibly make—the decision to live abroad. You may decide to take all the money you now have and blow it on a grand fling overseas; not a journey, but a residence of a year or two. Or you may decide on a complete change of pace by seeking overseas employment, with the United States government, a domestically owned company, or a foreign corporation. Before you decide, learn all you can about such things as the job security offered, the length of employment guaranteed, the salary, and the provisions for schools and living quarters for dependents.

The living costs of some foreign countries are astronomically high; of others, reasonable to cheap. According to American Express, probably the highest-priced places abroad are Paris, the Scandinavian countries, and Israel. (The cost of living for Israelis increased more than 56 percent in 1974, with a possible world's record jump in food prices of 82.6 percent.) Among the least expensive countries are Greece, Spain, Portugal, and India. For an example of how far your dollar will go in another country, check the rate of exchange with a travel agency or the international division of your local bank. In mid-1975, $1 was worth 2.318 pound sterling in England, .434 per German mark, .413 per Swiss franc, and only .254 per French franc.

If you work for the government—and there are very attractive overseas posts open with embassies and various other branches—your income will be taxable, just as if it were earned in this country; however, there are exceptions under which your income would be tax-exempt. The Internal Revenue Service sends teams of representatives to selected foreign countries to assist U.S. citizens during the filing period (Jan. 1 to April 15), so you could receive help on the spot, if you need it. Before you consider such a move, however, it would be wise to learn everything possible about your tax situation, so you will know just how much you can expect to have to spend and to save. You can get comprehensive information by writing to the Office of International Operations (Internal Revenue Service, Washington, D.C. 20225) and asking for Publication 54, *Tax Guide for U.S. Citizens Abroad,* and Publication 570, *Tax Guide for U.S. Citizens Employed in U.S. Possessions.*

As important as it is to determine your tax liability before going abroad, it is even more vital that you consider every facet of such a move: Will you need a foreign language? Will it be a country in which women have the freedom to which you are accustomed? (Some of the Moslem countries are still very restrictive in this respect.) Will you be satisfied away from relatives and friends for long periods of time? Travel back to the States will not be cheap, so you won't be able to come back whenever the mood hits you. Study the country and its customs. Know what its weather is like —you might need an entirely different wardrobe, which is an additional expense. Study its religion, its people, before you decide. If you do decide to go, make the most of the experience. Don't restrict yourself to your American friends; meet people of the country, savor their differences; learn about their culture and history. You may like it so much that you will decide to try other countries or you may decide to make your permanent home there. Hang onto your American citizenship, however; don't relinquish it lightly, if at all, unless you marry a foreign citizen, for instance, and know that you will spend the rest of your life in his country.

If you don't anticipate a change as extreme as moving to another country, let's examine your options regarding moving to a new location within our own borders.

STAYING WHERE YOU ARE

I would offer one word of caution: *delay*. Don't make so important a decision hastily. I urge widows, particularly, to try to postpone any change in living conditions for at least a year, when you will be more in control mentally and emotionally, can make a rational decision, and will avoid further psychological stress.

Too many widows think that an immediate change of scene will decrease the agony of their loss. It won't. Usually a permanent change at this time is not only detrimental, it is diametrically opposed to the one thing the widow needs most—stability.

You've had enough to contend with—your loss, the demanding decisions you've been forced to make, the realization that your entire life has changed. Give yourself a break and don't plunge into anything else new. It will be difficult enough for you to adapt to your new situation without having to adapt to new surroundings and new acquaintances as well. So if you can afford to stay where you are for a while, do so; if you need a temporary change of scenery, go on a trip, visit friends or relatives, move your bedroom to a different room—just don't decide anything so quickly that you may be sorry.

The divorcee suffers stress from her suddenly altered lifestyle, too, as does any woman entering a new situation, so be kind to yourself and take one step at a time, delaying drastic changes until you can cope with them. Widowed or divorced, weigh all advice from your friends and family, no matter how well-intentioned, and make your own decisions when the proper time comes.

WHERE TO LIVE

What if you can't afford to stay put and must move? Or what if, after a reasonable period, you decide that a change would be the best thing for you? As a general rule, it is best, even though you change location, not to change environment. In other words, if you are accustomed to living in the city, it would probably be unwise for you to move to the country; if you have been living in a suburban area, it is unlikely that you would be happy in an isolated coastal spot. As with every other rule, there are exceptions. If you are living in a town or neighborhood you hate—move. If you want to be closer to (or farther from) relatives —move. If you are living in a neighborhood that is falling into decay, or, conversely, one where costs and taxes will continue to rise—move. If you feel, and earnestly believe, after weighing all the alternatives, that you will be happier and more satisfied by living in another place, *move.*

Before you move to a new city, take the time to investigate everything that can be of concern in your life: work opportunities, the housing situation, the cost of living, taxes, schools, transportation, shopping and recreational facilities, crime statistics, and utility rates. Write to the Chamber of Commerce for specific information, and if possible spend a few days there to get the feel of the place. Stay at the YWCA or an inexpensive motel, and if you have children, take them to see how they like it, too.

You won't be unique if you move; our country has been geared to mobility from the days of the earliest settlers, and approximately 40 million people move every year. So wherever you decide to locate, you probably won't have any trouble finding a place to live—it's likely to have been just vacated by someone else moving on!

IF YOU OWN A HOUSE

If you are the owner of a house, either because of death or divorce, you will be confronted by problems immediately. If there is a mortgage outstanding, you must decide if you will be able to meet the payments with the money at hand. If you have a substantial amount of money, you might want to consider prepaying your mortgage. However, if you prepay, you have, in effect, merely invested your money (in your house) at the same rate at which you were paying interest on the loan. There may be prepayment penalties, and some institutions disallow prepayments entirely. If you have a VA or FHA loan there will be no penalty, although the lender who handled the loan may attach one. There is, therefore, little advantage to prepayment, and you will be better advised to use your money in other ways.

In order to reduce your current monthly payments, you might want to refinance your mortgage, either with the original lender or with another. Again, there are hazards. If you refinance your current mortgage or repay it and obtain financing for a new one, you are not actually cutting the fixed costs. Rather, you are simply exchanging one debt for another—a short one at a higher rate for a longer-term one at lower monthly costs. The only advantage, and it's a dubious one, is that you will decrease your fixed housing expenses now. But remember that you will carry the debt for a longer time, and will increase the overall cost of the mortgage because you will be paying more interest, unless you can find significantly lower financing—a distinctly unlikely possibility at today's rates.

SELLING YOUR HOUSE

If you think that the mortgage payments are more than you will be able to handle, you will want to consider selling or renting your house. Keep in mind that if you do sell and move into a less expensive house it may cost you money you hadn't considered. As far as taxes are concerned, profit you make on the sale of your house is taxable as a capital gain. If all the money you make on the sale is invested within eighteen months in a more expensive house, according to the 1975 Tax Reduction Act, or if it is used to begin building a house of equal value within eighteen months, there will be no tax liability. However, if you are buying a less expensive house or if you do not buy at all, you can expect to pay taxes on your profit.

If you plan to sell your house, expect to pay for repairs to make your property more attractive to potential buyers. Try to economize where feasible. You might want to paint the exterior and wash the interior; you may have to replace torn screens or broken tile or repair leaky faucets, but try to avoid investing in a new roof or furnace. (Of course, if they are in really bad condition, tell the buyer and give him an allowance on the price for their repair.)

There are several ways to handle the financing that will serve the best interests of both you and your buyer.

If there is already a mortgage on your house you can transfer it without any trouble. If, however, the buyer cannot come up with the total amount required for the transfer, you can, in effect, give him a second mortgage yourself. You can agree, in writing, to accept the balance (including fair interest) over a period of years. This is a good idea *only* if the buyer has a sound credit rating and you are assured of receiving the money. You can do substantially the same thing even if you don't have a mortgage on the house. You can accept a down payment (I'd insist on no less than one-fourth the total amount) and agree to extended payments for the balance. This is known as a "purchase money mortgage," and again, exercise caution before you enter into such an arrangement. An advantage that this has over the first example is that you can write into the agreement a stipulation that if the buyer becomes able to pay the mortgage earlier than the agreed time he will do so. You can charge him the same rate that a bank would charge on a first mortgage, with the interest compounded exactly as the bank would do. (On the extended second mortgage you would be able to charge more because the interest rate on a second generally runs about 1½ percent higher than on a first.)

Another way to get around the financial crunch facing buyers today is to offer your home for rent with an option to buy. Allocate an amount of the rent toward the purchase of the house; if, at the end of a time agreed upon by you and the buyer—usually no more than two years—he cannot buy, the purchase money will be forfeited to you. Again, exercise caution regarding the buyer; verify his reliability and his credit rating with his bank, employer, creditors, and the Credit Data Referral Company before you enter into *any* long-term agreement with him.

Selling the House Yourself

When you sell, you may want to save the commission that will be paid to an agent and act on your own behalf. The saving can be substantial, generally from 6 to 8 percent of the amount realized on the sale. For instance, if your house sells for $36,000, the commission would be $2,160 to $2,880. Before you enter into such an undertaking, however, remember that there will be expenses of time and money. You will have advertising costs, appraisal and legal fees, and you must be willing to show your house to prospective buyers and to have it in good condition so you will be able to make a convincing sales talk. Ask the financial institution holding your mortgage if they will undertake to refinance your house for the prospective buyer—that will be a good selling point for you to make. Ask the bank, savings and loan association, or mortgage company that has your mortgage for the name of their appraiser; hire him to appraise your house at the current market value (this amount will be used in your tax computations), and to put the evaluation in writing.

After you finally have a buyer, ask for a deposit of no less than 5 percent of the selling price; this is "earnest money" and will go toward the total cost of the house. You will probably need a lawyer to write a contract stating anything specific that you have promised (painting, siding, so on), and you will definitely need an attorney when the financial institution transfers the title and closes the deal. By the time you have finished with the entire transaction, it probably will have cost you from one-tenth to about one-fifth of the amount you have saved on the commission. The savings are appreciable, but be very sure you follow every legal step and that you rely on the advice of your lawyer and the professionals at your financial institution.

Selling through an Agent

If you don't feel that you want the bother of handling the sale yourself, go to a reputable real estate broker, also known as a realty agent. (A "realtor" refers specifically to a member of the National Association of Realtors.) Although the broker is licensed in the state in which he operates, he is not regulated by law as to the services he will offer, so you will have to shop around just as you would for a lawyer. Look at his advertising; go by the offices. Ask for the names of some of his more recent customers so that you can get their opinions of the services received. Interview several agents. Ask specific questions. Find out about his commission rate. Keep in mind that it will *usually* range from 6 to 8 percent, but that recent court rulings have stated that fixed rates are illegal, so that, theoretically, an agent can charge as much as he wishes. (When you select an agent, have him put his fee in writing.) Check to see exactly what his fee will cover; there is more to selling a house than appears on the surface, as you have seen above. Make sure that he will handle all of those things you would be doing if you were bypassing him.

Find out what kind of listing your house will have. If it is an exclusive listing, it means that if the house is sold by you or another broker during the time that the original broker represents you, you will still have to pay him his fee. The other side of the coin is that an exclusive listing generally guarantees more interest on the part of the broker, and you will probably have more say as to the hours in which the house may be shown, the types of prospects you will consider, and so on. An exclusive-agency listing is the same as exclusive, except that if you sell the house yourself you will not have to pay the agent's commission. Multiple listing means that one agent has the exclusive right to sell, but other agents in his group may sell and will receive a percentage of his commission—from him, not you. An open listing means that an agent designated by you can sell the property but that you may also, and without paying his commission.

Select the listing that best suits you; try to enforce the hours and days during which the house is to be shown, and, as much as is possible, exercise caution about allowing strangers into your house—whether or not you have an agent. Never show the house alone, put your valuables out of sight, and don't leave the prospective buyer unattended anywhere in the house.

RENTING YOUR HOUSE

If you decide that it would be best for you to move but you don't want to sell your house, it can be used as rental property and can bring in a nice income. You can leave it as it is, divide it into a duplex or apartments, or convert it into office space. But first check the local zoning ordinances to be sure it's legal in your neighborhood.

Before you rent, examine all the complexities of operating rental property to be sure you will realize a profit. Consider the expenses, responsibilities, and tax ramifications. For example, some of your expenses in maintaining the property will be deductible, some will not. Some will be deductible in whole in the year incurred, some will be added to the total value of the property. There are various items of which you should be aware: A security deposit is not included in your income unless it is forfeited, and if it is to be used as advance payment toward the rent, it must be reported when received. And, if your tenant doesn't pay the rent, you cannot deduct it unless you are on the accrual basis of accounting and have already reported it as income. If you plan to rent to a friend or relative, you must be sure to rent for the purpose of making a profit; otherwise, only certain items such as interest and taxes may be deductible in full, while other expenses may be limited to a certain extent.

Do not become a landlady without carefully examining your legal, financial, and custodial responsibilities. Among other things, you will have to maintain the premises and keep the place in good condition; be prepared to replace or repair equipment and appliances; and carry insurance to cover fire, damage, loss, and liability.

Before you do anything else, have a good lease drawn by your attorney so that both you and your tenant will be protected from misunderstandings. Spell out exactly who will be responsible for paying the utilities, for instance. If you don't want to rent to anyone with pets or children, state that explicitly.

Check with other landlords in the area to determine what is a reasonable rent, and see how often it has increased in the last few years, and by what amount. Make sure that you are in compliance with your city's housing code and that you have taken proper precautions to obey the local fire safety regulations. Weigh all the pros and cons, and if you decide to proceed, advertise, screen your applicants carefully, and try to select ones who will be good tenants. Go over the property with the one you select, making a list of all existing damages; make two copies, signed by both of you, and give one to your tenant. When the renter leaves, there will be no arguments as to whether or not he is entitled to have the security deposit returned. You might want to insist on a short-term lease, initially, in case you are not sure that you'll like the role of landlady. Try it for a time; you can always dispose of the property later if you don't like the situation.

LIVING IN THE COUNTRY

Now to get back to where to move. Unless you already have a farm, or are experienced in farm life, I urge you *not* to go into farming alone. Not only is it a herculean task under the best of circumstances, it is almost impossible, in today's economy, to earn a living on the land. But if you are determined to try the pastoral life, contact the County Agent for advice about land, crops, stock, and help. I'm afraid the picture will be terribly discouraging and I cannot, in good conscience, recommend it to a city-dweller.

LIVING IN THE CITY OR SUBURBS

When you are considering the relative merits of town, city, or suburbs, it would be wise to draw up a balance sheet with the advantages versus the disadvantages of each. For instance, if you're concerned about crime—and who isn't?—the worst place to live is a city that is designated by the Bureau of the Census as an "SMSA." Translated, that is "standard metropolitan statistical area," and is either a city of 50,000 or more inhabitants or a city of at least 25,000 that is combined with its contiguous areas for a total population of 50,000 or more. The central part of the city is the most crime-ridden, and the suburbs are the safest.

If you are debating between a smaller town or a rural area, you will have to decide which crimes seem the least desirable, because their incidence seesaws between the two locales. You will be safer from murder, rape, aggravated assault, and burglary in a small town, according to the 1973 annual *Uniform Crime Reports for the United States,* issued by the U.S. Federal Bureau of Investigation, and the rate is lower for robbery, larceny-theft, and automobile theft in a rural area.

Balanced against the crime figures would have to be job opportunity, quality of schools, accessibility to doctors, and availability of entertainment and public transportation. Wherever you live, all these criteria must be considered. If you live any distance from your job, commuting costs must also be figured into your proposed budget. Depending on your mode of transportation (your own car, car pools, or public trains and buses), the price of gasoline, the distance you will be traveling, and the cost of parking facilities at work, your daily expenses could range from $1 to $10. Total this amount for a year of working days and you can see that the choice of your living site could cost more than is readily apparent.

On the plus side of your ledger for a city would be diversity of job opportunities, the varied shopping facilities, the abundance of medical and dental services, the limitless educational, religious, entertainment, and sports offerings, and the variety of cultural backgrounds of the citizens. On the minus side you would have crime, high taxes, pollution, and overcrowding. As far as suburbs, small towns, and the country are concerned, the plus side would show security (in 1973, there were 7,372,000 crimes known to police in metropolitan areas versus 763,000 in smaller towns and 504,000 in rural areas), clean air, generally lower taxes, and in most suburban areas, better schools. On the minus side there are the limited jobs, fewer recreational facilities, and the lack of diversity offered by a large city. The favorable and unfavorable aspects of each locale must be weighed in the light of your particular needs and desires and those of your children.

Don't be hesitant about settling in the suburbs alone; more and more single people are doing it all the time, and for the same reasons married people are moving out of the cities—to search for a better life. To lure the prospective residents, builders are reclaiming land that would be unsuitable for subdivisions and are constructing apartments and condominiums. As further inducements, many are including community swimming pools, clubhouses, and tennis courts, all designed mainly for the unmarried occupant. It can be a very desirable life, and the costs are usually comparable to the rent you would pay in the city, although you'll still have those commuting costs. Living in a "singles" community is a good way to meet new people, but women generally outnumber men two to one, so don't expect to find a dating heaven. The men can pick and choose—and do—and are not especially interested in changing their ideal living situation. Why should they?

When you have chosen between city or suburbs, but before you decide whether or not you'll want to build, buy, or rent, select your specific neighborhood.

Selecting a Neighborhood

You'll already have a pretty good idea as to whether you'll buy, build, or rent and how much you can afford to spend, so your neighborhood will, to a certain degree, be determined by the availability of the necessary property. Let accessibility be as important a factor as will be cost. You don't want to be stuck in a pretty neighborhood that is miles away from shopping, schools, and so on. How close will you be to your bank, the drug store, supermarket, cleaners, and post office? Use the same criteria you used in selecting your location, and carefully investigate everything concerned with living in that particular spot.

It is very important to select the neighborhood with care. Crime is a matter of economics, so try to avoid the extremely low-income areas; crime is higher there, and you stand a better chance of being raped, robbed, mugged, or murdered. Choose a neighborhood whose occupants are compatible with your own age, family pattern, and socioeconomic background. This doesn't mean that you should select a homogeneous, insulated area—diversity is to be desired—but, realistically, a woman alone must be particularly concerned with safety and security for herself, her children, and her property. For specific information about the area that interests you, check with the police department; they have the facts and figures and will give you the rate of crime in that neighborhood. They will appreciate your concern; they are almost as interested in preventing your becoming a victim as you are.

Don't decide on your neighborhood impulsively. Look at it in the rain and at night; check out the storm drains (do they back up during a heavy rain?) and see if the street lighting is adequate at night. Find out about the frequency of garbage pickups and mail deliveries, learn how often the neighborhood suffers power outages, both winter and summer, and check on the adequacy of snow removal.

If at all possible, try to find out the special interests of your potential neighbors and their children, as well as the reputation of the local schools. If your children are music-oriented, for instance, and the high school is a haven for "sports jocks," there may be problems. And if you cherish your privacy, you'll be unhappy in a neighborhood of drop-in "kaffee klatchers." And if you detect a whiff of discrimination against you because of your sex or race, report it immediately to the municipality's fair housing division, or write a detailed complaint to the United States Department of Housing and Urban Development (451 Seventh Street, Washington, D.C. 20410). HUD will investigate and correct the situation if possible. For a detailed explanation of the two primary laws concerning housing discrimination, and the addresses and phone numbers of Fair Housing Assistance offices throughout the country, write to the Public Documents Distribution Center (Pueblo, Colorado 81009) and ask for the free government booklet #150B, *Fair Housing U.S.A.*

BUILDING A HOUSE

It is rather unlikely, at this particular point in the nation's economic history, that you will choose to build. It's a chancy undertaking at best, and one that I, even with the experience I have had with George's architectural practice, would hesitate to tackle. It involves too much time, money, knowledge, and determination, and I think those attributes could best be devoted to more immediately productive endeavors. If you are determined to build, however, retain a qualified, experienced architect. You'll pay him a fee that can vary from 3 to 7 percent, depending on business conditions and the locality, but he will save you money and headaches by acting as your go-between in your dealings with the builder. The architect will design the house you want (although it will be cheaper to use a plan he has already designed and can modify for you), and will see that the specified materials will be used. He can tell you, almost to the penny, the total cost, but there will always be unexpected or additional expenses, so put an extra amount in the budget. Ways to save at the outset would include having the house designed as a rectangle; every corner you add to the house adds money. For the same amount of floor space a two-story house is cheaper than a one-story, and the least expensive roof, generally, is a standard gable type. You can ask that treated wood be used in the foundation instead of brick or concrete; it is less expensive and is approved by the FHA. A fireplace is costly, but if you live in an area that frequently loses power during the winter, you might consider it a good investment. Of course, money will be a problem. In the first quarter of 1975, to quote an official in the residential loan department of Atlanta's largest bank, Citizens and Southern, "A loan, if you could get one, would be at 9% interest, but we're not making them. The building market, at this time, is dead." That could change at any time, naturally, but the building industry is always the first to suffer in a period of recession and the last to recover when the economy stabilizes.

BUYING A HOUSE

The outlook is not much brighter if you want to buy; money is scarce, rates are high, and length of time for which the loans are given is short. A second mortgage, early in 1975, was offered for no more than ten years, at an annual rate of 12¼%. First mortgages were offered for up to thirty years at a maximum rate of 9% at banks, and 8¾% at savings and loan associations. These rates are the maximum set by the Georgia usury law (the rates in other states range from 8 to 10%), but there are other costs that increase the total. By the time a loan at 8¾% has had discount points, closing costs, and origination fees added to it, the annual rate will be from 9¼ to 9½%. This is perfectly legal and understandable. All the financial institutions are offering savers inflated rates of interest; they have to recoup through the money they are lending.

Early in 1975 the federal government acted to help middle-income home buyers by reducing the interest rate of mortgages backed by the Veterans Administration and the Federal Housing Authority to a maximum of 8½%. Although that sounds impressive, the interest rate drop is not too important to builders because the FHA and VA currently make only about 7 percent of the total home loans in the U.S.

Although money is tight for conventional, FHA, and VA loans, there is some money being made available by the federal government to help professionals build houses costing less than $40,000. You might be able to find one of these. Be careful, though; in their haste to take advantage of the situation, some builders may be less than meticulous in their construction standards. For the first time, however, some builders in twenty-four states are offering the buyer a ten-year warranty covering faulty workmanship and materials. The voluntary Home Warranty Agreement, devised by the 75,000-member National Association of Home Builders, costs the home buyer $2 for every $1000 of the cost of the house. The warranty is transferable to a new buyer, and covers specific items for three periods of the warranty. For instance, it covers, during the first year, all defects attributable to faulty workmanship and defective materials. During the second year the builder (if he goes out of business the warranty is covered by insurance) is still responsible for construction problems and for the materials used in the heating, cooling, plumbing, and electrical systems. During the last eight years of the warranty, the builder would be responsible only for major construction defects. Because this term is vague, a disputed complaint by the buyer could be arbitrated by the local warranty council, and if satisfaction isn't obtained, the buyer can, for a $75 fee, appeal the decision to the American Arbitration Association. The warranty is long overdue, but it is not mandatory, and its vague wording on the section covering those last eight years can pose problems. If you're interested in finding the names of the builders in your area who offer the service, write to Home Owners Registration Corporation (15 and M Streets, N.W., Washington, D.C. 20005).

In another effort to help builders and buyers, the Tax Reduction Act of 1975 offers a credit against the buyer's tax liability. The credit, limited to 5% of the adjusted basis (cost plus fees) of the house, but not to exceed $2000 ($1000 for a married person filing separately), cannot amount to more than the actual tax liability. In other words, if your tax liability for 1975 is $1400 (the amount shown on line 12 of 1040A, line 16 of 1040) and the credit were $1200, your tax would only be $200, and taxes withheld or prepaid would be credited against that. The overpayment would be refunded to you.

To qualify for the credit, the house must have been under construction before March 26, 1975, must never have been offered at a lower price, must never have been occupied before, and must be purchased and occupied between March 12, 1975 and January 1, 1977.

Unquestionably, the credit offered an impetus to many hesitant buyers and helped those builders who had houses already under construction, but Congress will have to extend the act into 1976 if any long-range benefits are to be realized.

To help alleviate the tight money situation, the Federal Home Loan Bank Board has begun to allow its member savings and loan associations to offer "variable rate mortgages." As explained by Mr. Jerry Sewell, Vice-President of Atlanta Federal Savings and Loan Association, these rates will be determined by the cost of U.S. Treasury Bills, bonds, and government notes, and will therefore fluctuate with the economy. There would be a saving for the buyer if the rates come down; there would be an advantage to the lender if the rates go up. These adjustments are made annually or semi-annually to reflect the status of the economy. Don't count on a reduction in rates any time soon, however; variable interest mortgage loans in England climbed from 8½% to 12½% over a two-year period. The measure is intended to help the flagging building industry and to keep the lenders in business during these inflationary times; they have old loans out on which they are receiving only 4¼%, and are paying 7½% to their long-term savers.

The picture is bleak if you want to buy a mobile home. Even though the cost is much less than for a house of comparable size and accommodations, the money outlook is worse. Few institutions are offering loans, and those that are charge anywhere from 12 to 14%. Before you decide on a mobile home, use the same checklist you would use for any standard neighborhood as to cost, accessibility, safety, and so on. Remember that they are generally restricted to certain areas of town—often on the outskirts—and be sure you have in writing exactly what the mobile home park offers in its fee.

If you ever *do* buy, now or in the future, there are some general considerations you should keep in mind.

How much should you spend when you buy a house? The American Bankers Association, as I pointed out earlier, suggests that you should spend no more than one and one-half times your annual gross income for your mortgage, interest, and property taxes. Keep in mind that the latter two are deductible and that the interest payments will decline over the period of the mortgage. For example, if you are buying a house with a twenty-five-year mortgage and have already made a down payment, bringing the amount to be mortgaged to $30,000, your payments, at 8½% interest, will drop from the first year's payment of $2,931 ($381 on the principal sum, $2,550 interest), to the final year's payment of $2,931 ($2,716 on the principal and $230 on the interest). You'll have the greatest tax deductions early in the loan but, unfortunately, as they decrease your repair and maintenance costs will probably increase.

As a buyer, explore the same avenues already examined as a seller. (In either case, try to require the other person to pay the closing costs.) Perhaps the seller will offer to handle the mortgage himself; perhaps the institution holding his mortgage will extend a second mortgage to you; maybe the seller will agree to a rent-and-purchase contract. The options are varied, and if you want further information and suggestions you can write to the National Homebuyers and Homeowners Association, Dept. PW (1225 19th Street, N.W., Suite 602, Washington, D.C. 20036) for their booklet, costing $1, and titled *Home Buyer's Checklist.*

Decide before you sign the contract exactly the way you want the title to read; remember that there will be future tax advantages if at least half the value of the house can be kept out of your estate. With joint tenancy the property will automatically go to the survivor. However, you can face legal and tax problems, so consult with your attorney as to the most advantageous way this should be handled.

I wish I could tell you what the money outlook will be later this year
or the next year or the next. I can't, and no one else can, either. The
people in the front lines, those lenders who are unable now to make loans,
or are having to make them for shorter terms at higher rates, are, by profession, optimistic. They expect a reversal of the trend; they hope for an
economic upswing. Experts on Wall Street are formulating their own
charts, based on past stock market performances, showing an upturn in
years ending in the number five, or in four-year cycles, or in an esoteric
index concerning the difference between the number of rising and de-
clining stocks. But this is largely speculation, and there is no way of
knowing if we are facing the worst depression since the Thirties or a
temporary setback. In any case, after knowing the facts, only you can
decide whether or not it would be best for you to buy at this time.

The only bright part of the economic picture is that when the economy
is depressed, home prices fall. If you can find the money you can snap
up a good buy. The National Association of Home Builders have been
urged by their senior economist, Dr. Michael Sumichrast, to sell, sell, sell.
"You must sell," he said. "Take any deals. Don't turn anybody down."
NAHB members were told to sell with a minimum or no profit, to stim-
ulate the sagging building industry.

RENTING AN APARTMENT OR HOUSE

Under the circumstances, and knowing all the facts, you may decide that
renting would be best for you. If so, go into it as carefully as you would
if you were buying. Even though there will not be the extended length of
time or the large amount of money involved, you will still want to obtain
the best deal for the time and effort spent.

Determine how much you can afford to pay for rent. Most authorities
say that renters should not pay more than twenty-five to thirty-five percent
of their monthly income before taxes (your gross income, in other words).
Using this as a yardstick, you have a variety of ways to locate the apartment that is right for you. The most obvious way is to contact rental
agencies or to read the advertisements in the local newspaper. You can
also check at newsstands or bookstores for magazines or booklets covering
the rental of apartments. These magazines will tell you what is included
in the apartment (equipment, furnishings and so on), will tell you if pets
and children are allowed, and will usually give a rundown on schools,
shopping, and theaters in the area. Some cities have apartment search
agencies, with the fees paid by the owners; some of these will even help
you find roommates.

Furnished apartments are not to be found in some parts of the country.
In some locations they are cheaper than unfurnished, but these are usually

in an older part of town and the furnishings are less than desirable. In most places, unfurnished apartments are considerably less expensive and you can start housekeeping with a minimum of effort. Even unfurnished, you will generally have a completely equipped kitchen, so you needn't worry about buying appliances.

If you rent, use exactly the same standards as a tenant that you would have used if you were the landlady. Go over the apartment and note any damages. (Make an original list for yourself and a duplicate for the landlord.) Check the apartment for safety, and report any violations of the housing and fire safety codes to the proper authorities. Verify the rent, see when it was last raised, and when it will probably go up again. Know exactly to whom you will be paying rent, and get the name and address of the owner so you can contact him directly if you have any problems with the manager. Have in writing an agreement as to which of you will pay the utilities, you or the owner. Find out if you may paint or hammer nails; some apartments forbid it. Don't sign a lease without an escape or exit clause. You never know what may happen and you might need or want to move. Sign a short-term lease with an option for a longer-termed one if you and the landlord agree. Don't sign anything unless you clearly understand the terms—and the terminology. If possible, arrange to have the lease expire in the middle of the month; when you move the charges will be less.

Shun basement or first-floor apartments; they are invitations to robbers and rapists, and if the apartment is in a converted residence, you might want to request that burglar bars be installed on your windows. The safest apartments are those with doormen or security guards, but you will pay dearly for the service.

If you can find an apartment with its own laundry room, that will be an added bonus, but if you have your own washer and dryer, find out if they will increase your rent; frequently there will be a small amount added each month to cover the cost of the extra plumbing connections required.

While you are apartment-hunting, you may want to stay temporarily at the local "Y," if it has a dormitory, or in a boarding facility that is run by a religious or professional organization. The rates are low but the rooms are clean and the buildings are generally well-protected. In Atlanta, for example, a single woman between the ages of 17 and 35 can live in the Churches Home for Business Girls, Inc. for $27 a week—that includes room and board, linen services and all utilities. There is a small ($5) monthly parking fee. Most major cities offer similar boarding opportunities.

Wherever you decide to live, there are a few other points for you to consider. For safety's sake, do not use your full name on the mailbox, in the telephone book, or with the utility companies. Instead of "Mary L. Smith," have everything listed "M. L. Smith." Why the utilities? Because someone may see your mail, and the utilities are usually listed in the name of the head of the household. No matter how liberated we may be, it is still safest to let the person who may not have the most honorable intentions think that there is a man in the vicinity. Especially avoid having yourself listed in a city directory—this spells out your household situation for anyone to read.

You won't be able to keep the fact that you live alone from everyone, but the fewer who know it, the better.

ROOMMATES

You may decide to play for safety in numbers and have one or more roommates. The solution has several advantages: living costs will be cut; there really *is* less danger if the house or apartment is inhabited by more than one person; and it can ease some of the loneliness. On the other side of the argument, you will forfeit your privacy. If you decide to go the roommate route, select your living partner(s) with great care. It is ideal to have a roommate you already know and with whom you can be reasonably certain of being compatible. If you take in a stranger, get references from as many sources as possible, and set down your joint living rules immediately. You'll have to agree on schedules for the bathroom, dates, work, and so on. Divide the work right down the middle, and for variety, change around on chores such as cooking and cleaning.

Some women, with an eye to safety, are even taking in male roommates often on a strictly platonic, business basis. The advantage, of course, is that there is a male on the premises. However, it can present more problems than it solves, not the least of which is the division of housework. You don't want to find yourself saddled with all the cooking and cleaning while he sits with his feet up, so if you do have a male roommate, have an understanding about the work as well as about everything else involved with living under the same roof.

Of course, you may elect to live with a lover on a long- or short-term basis. This arrangement will demand as much thought and care as does the traditional marriage (more about this in Chapter 14), but there is more than one advantage involved in having a man you love in your home.

About living quarters again, if you think that you would prefer the spaciousness and privacy afforded by a house, consider renting one, using the same standards you would for apartment renting. You must have everything clearly spelled out about maintenance, repairs, utilities, and yard care. If the roof leaks or the fence needs mending, a step is broken or the lawn needs mowing, how much will be your responsibility? If the plumbing needs repairs and the owner can't be reached, what do you do? Will you be reimbursed for this and other out-of-pocket expenses? Investigate carefully, and read that lease.

MOVING

When you move, try to cut your moving expenses. If possible, let the mover know in advance—a month to six weeks is sufficient—and give him some choice of the best day of the week. Avoid, if you can, moving between June and September—the busiest months—and during the last ten days of the month. In fact, try to avoid moving around the first *or* the last of the month; most leases expire then, and movers are at their busiest. You will receive more efficient service by proper timing, and the rates should be lower (some carriers may offer you as much as a 15 percent saving on an out-of-season move).

FURNISHING YOUR HOME

If you're faced with an empty house or apartment, you will also be faced with immediate decisions as to what you will need to fill them, and what you can do without—at least temporarily. Conceivably, you could manage with a bed, a table, a chair, a refrigerator, and a stove, and these may be your basics for a time. But you will want to expand your furnishings and equipment, and will have to expect to spend considerable amounts of money on some items. There are, however, ways to pare the costs to a minimum, always keeping in mind the Yates Law of Economics: *Never pay full price for anything you can get reduced.*

SHOPPING FOR BARGAINS

The opportunities for bargain-shopping are almost limitless and can be looked upon as a challenge to your ingenuity and inventiveness. The obvious places to begin your hunt for bargains are the discount stores. At these outlets you will be able to purchase everything from books and records to prescription drugs (by their generic, not brand names); from clothes for the entire family to automobile and home-care products; from furniture and appliances to cosmetics and deodorants; from pet supplies to gardening equipment.

But don't stop there. Go on to unclaimed freight warehouses, estate sales, thrift and second-hand shops, and auctions held by local and federal government agencies of goods that have been confiscated or have gone unclaimed by the persons who ordered them. And the sales! You've got department store warehouse sales, sales of floor demonstration models (check for damage), garage sales, year-end sales, seconds, less-than-perfect, and irregular sales. You can get in on close-of-stock sales, when a manufacturer is changing to a new model; just verify that you will be able to get replacement parts if needed. There are remnant sales for you who sew and sales of Christmas wrappings and decorations for everyone. There are out-of-season sales and sales before, during, and following every holiday on the calendar. There are inventory and going-out-of-business or moving-to-a-new-location sales. And nothing can beat the January white sales for savings on towels, sheets, and table linens.

Watch the newspaper ads for these sales; you will be able to realize substantial savings from timed shopping. Look for swap advertisements; you may have something you don't want but that will constitute the price of an item that someone else wants to swap. Get together with your neighbors for the purchase of expensive items occasionally used, such as power lawn mower, large coffee urn, or snow shovel.

Another way to save in your shopping expenditures is through the use of a referral buying service. Generally, you must belong to some kind of group—union, employees' organization, professional or fraternal association, or church—that has contracted for the buying service. Or it is possible for you to be accepted as a participant if you belong to an organization with over one hundred members and if there is a service in your area. When you become a member and have selected the item you want, you call the buying service, giving all the necessary information, and it will send you a certificate entitling you to a discount at an authorized dealer's showroom. There is no fee to pay, and you are under no obligation to buy. The service makes its money from the dealers, and the dealers make their money from the thousands of members using the service.

The savings are large, ranging anywhere from 10 to 60 percent off retail price, and averaging 30 percent, depending on the item. Most buying services are members of the National Association of Buying Services (5480 Wisconsin Avenue, Chevy Chase, Md. 20015), and although most of the services are concentrated in the East, there are some located in more than twenty cities throughout the nation.

You can also write to the National Association of Catalog Showroom Merchandisers (63 E. 9th Street, New York, N.Y. 10003) for information on catalog sales showrooms near you, and to Unity Buying Service (Hicksville, N.Y. 11802) or Consumer Buyer Service (P.O. Box 3086, Rock Hill, S.C. 29730) for buying services involving membership fees. These operations offer varied services and goods, so carefully evaluate both before you agree to membership and before you buy.

You can do some attractive, inexpensive decorating with paint, remnant materials, bed sheets (one of the cheapest ways to buy good, pretty material in large quantities), and furniture bought second-hand. Don't overlook Goodwill and Salvation Army outlets, moving companies, and used furniture donated by your family. Save now, and buy better pieces later, as your tastes and savings warrant. It's fun to spend money—it's one of my favorite forms of therapy—but you're going to have heavy initial costs establishing your home, and you should try to economize as much as possible.

You will be in line with the "typical U.S. family" used by the U.S. Department of Labor as a guide to budgeting if you set aside 7 percent of your total budget for "home equipment," including furniture, appliances, and carpeting. That is the figure for an established home; your costs will run over that rate during the first year.

Furniture

When you begin to shop for furniture, you will have several ways to cut your costs.

Try to buy any department store furniture in February or August, the traditional sales months for these items, and be sure to ask about delivery charges, if any. Usually there is no charge, but if there is, you will want to figure it in the overall price. Most department stores offer free decorating services; if they *are* free, ask the decorator for advice or suggestions as to quality and choice of items available. Check out the construction of any piece of furniture—you can tell more by the soundness of construction of the drawers (they should be tight and heavy) than of anything else—and the quality of the upholstery.

If you want to use unpainted furniture, remember to add into its costs the amount you will spend on paint or varnish, and on any necessary hardware. You can try your hand at building a few pieces, using pre-cut lumber or some of the attractive shelves and spindles that form any number of storage items. You can buy a hollow-core door for a reasonable amount, add legs of the proper height, and make anything from a table to a couch. And for inexpensive floor coverings, you can get remnants and samples at low cost from a carpet mill warehouse outlet, or you can make some handsome area rugs with a latch hook kit.

Appliances

You are limited, in decorating, only by your imagination and your pocketbook; it isn't quite that simple when you begin to shop for appliances. Your choice will still be governed by your pocketbook, but you will also be under pressure caused by the very real necessity for buying the item under consideration. You can do without an extra table or chair, but when you need a stove or refrigerator, you need it *now*.

Again, check first for floor models, but be sure that they are damage-free and are covered by a warranty. You might be able to find a second-hand appliance on sale through the newspaper; find out why it is being sold, and verify that it is in good, workable condition. You won't get a warranty from a private owner unless the item is being sold because the owner is moving or is buying a newer or bigger model. In that case, get all the warranty information, and if it is still in effect, write to the dealer or manufacturer, giving your name and the date of purchase.

Decide before shopping exactly what you need. If you think they would be adequate, consider scaled-down washers, dryers, refrigerators, and freezers. Decide whether or not you really want to pay extra for some of the optionals offered by self-defrosting refrigerators and multi-cycled washing machines. Many of these luxuries use a great deal of electricity. (I can accept a simple wash, rinse, spin washer; I'd sacrifice almost anything else before I would part with my self-defrosting refrigerator-freezer. The time it saves me is well worth the extra initial cost and the extra operating expense.)

Shop around for your appliances; don't be tied to one dealer or one brand name, although good service in the past is a recommendation for good service in the future. Read *Consumer Reports* and family magazines for recommended features and prices. Carefully check appliance capacities; surprisingly, a thirty-inch stove usually has as large an oven as a forty-inch, and takes up less floor space. Make sure that the wiring in your home is adequate for the needs of the appliance, and familiarize yourself with the operation of the item before you decide to buy it. Keep in mind that a white appliance is cheaper than one in a decorator color.

Stoves. One factor that determines your selection of a stove will be whether you will want or need gas or electric energy. Gas heats more quickly, and in most areas is cheaper, but as far as service and design are concerned, the two are comparable. So your next consideration will be size, style, optionals, and construction. The size will be determined by your kitchen space and your cooking needs. Don't overbuy; a smaller model may be perfectly suitable for all necessary and party cooking. Decide on the style you want; if you want separated oven and cooking tops you will pay extra for them—a standard free-standing range will be the most economical model you will find. You will pay extra, too, for optionals such as self-cleaning ovens and smooth ceramic tops. In the case of the self-cleaning oven, as with the self-defrosting refrigerator, your time and energy must be weighed against the additional cost.

When you are weighing the merits of the construction of the stove in question, examine the outside finish; the best are porcelain, baked enamel, chrome or stainless steel. A cheap finish will bubble and crack, and will cause rusting of the body of the stove. Make sure the range has handles of heat resistant material, vents for the oven, well-sealed oven door, and rust-resistant, well-balanced oven racks that will not tip.

Refrigerators. Many of these same criteria will be used when you are selecting your refrigerator. Determine the size, style, and optionals you need and can afford, and check out the construction. Again, decide whether or not a smaller size will meet your needs and whether you will want an independent refrigerator or a combination refrigerator-freezer, and settle on the optionals you feel are worth the extra money and energy (self-defrosting unit, ice-maker, door-front water dispenser). A separate freezer should be easy to defrost and offer ease of access to the contents. Check out the construction. Here again, the finish is important, and should be porcelain or baked enamel, the doors should seal completely, and any condensation tray should be readily accessible for emptying. The best time for buying your refrigerator or freezer is July, the traditional sale month, although you might find sales at other times of the year. These appliances must be selected carefully; you can expect to get from fifteen to twenty years of service from them.

According to the U.S. Department of Agriculture, if purchased new, a freezer will last for twenty years; a refrigerator fifteen; electric clothes dryer fourteen; gas range and clothes dryer thirteen each; color TV twelve; and a dishwasher and black-and-white TV each eleven years. Appliance prices have risen only 12 percent since 1967 (most other items listed on the government's Consumer Price Index rose by 51.9 percent), and are still a good bargain. Even if you decide to buy a used appliance that is in good condition, you can expect, according to the USDA's figures, another nine years for a freezer; seven for a refrigerator, gas range, dishwasher; six for an electric range; and five for a washer, dryer, and black-and-white TV.

Washers. Before you start shopping for a washer, gather as much material from the dealers as possible. They will give you the exact specifications as to construction and performance, and you can evaluate them before you decide. Look for sturdy construction and good finishes as you did with the refrigerators and ranges. Study the variety of extras offered, such as pre-soak cycles, lint filters, multiple water and temperature controls, and dispensers for various laundry additives. Most machines clean equally well, so you must decide what extras are worth the additional expense, and what size washer you will need. Full-sized models can wash from fourteen to eighteen pounds of dry weight, so you may select the larger model if you know that you will do your own spreads, draperies, and area rugs. If you know that your washing needs will be limited, consider a smaller model or a combination washer-dryer; they are cheaper to buy and to operate, and take up a minimum of floor space. Generally these compacts don't need venting, but check the specifications carefully.

Dryers. Standard-size dryers will need a separate vent, and you may need a separate 220-volt line for your washer and dryer. You may also need new plumbing connections for both, so consider these in your costs. As a rule, if the plumbing and electrical connections have already been installed before delivery, there will be no additional installation charges, but again, check to be sure that there are no hidden costs when you pay the bill.

You might want to consider buying your appliances from your local electric or gas company; it's a painless way to pay. The bill will be added onto your monthly statement, but the carrying charges will be steep. They can run as much as 20 percent per year, and interest will be charged on the total balance each month. You will do much better with a bank loan or a loan against your savings and loan account.

Furnaces and Hot Water Heaters. When you buy a furnace or hot water heater, consult with a reputable dealer for recommended size and cost. The size will be determined by the size of the dwelling and the requirements to be met. In the case of your furnace, whether it is gas, oil, or electric check carefully into the BTUs (British Thermal Units) it will deliver, and compare features such as thermostats, filters, and blower systems. On these items I feel that you shouldn't economize too much; you will want a good, accurate thermostat to conserve energy, and the quality and effectiveness of the filter (which should be changed regularly) and the blower will determine the unit's efficiency and your operating costs.

In the case of the hot water heater, your needs will determine its size. How large is the dwelling? How many people will there be? How many baths are there? Do you have a washing machine or dishwasher? I recommend that you get one size larger than the minimum required; then you will be assured of hot water when you want it. (A good way to conserve hot water and its cost is to wash *everything* in cold water; I haven't used hot water in my washer for five years, and the savings have been tremendous. Most clothes get just as clean, there is less wear than would be received from hot water washes, and I usually add bleach to the loads of towels and sheets.) Almost all water heaters are glass-lined, but if you run across one that is not, avoid it; you'll eventually be plagued with rust every time you use hot water. It's a good idea to drain the heater once or twice a year, depending on the minerals in the water in your locale; the life of the heater will be considerably lengthened.

Dishwashers. If you buy a dishwasher, see if you really need a top-of-the-line model. Most now have pre-rinse, wash, and dry cycles, and you can save energy and expense by using the pre-rinse sparingly. Again, when you are selecting the appliance, look for good construction and ease of operation. Determine the plumbing and installation costs and add them to the price. Decide what size you want; a large size may be more economical to operate if you can manage to use it only once a day, with the entire day's load of dishes to be washed at once.

Warranties. On any appliance you buy, scrutinize the warranty carefully. Some are excellent, some are practically worthless. Most refrigerator warranties are very good, for example, guaranteeing replacement of parts and paying for the labor involved, for a full year; the refrigeration system is generally under warranty for two to five years. Some appliance warranties promise the barest minimum for the shortest possible time in the way of replacement parts and promise nothing in the way of payment of labor costs. Consider these warranties carefully; they can make a difference of several hundred dollars over the life of the appliance.

Service Contracts. Some dealers offer a service contract for a small sum; decide whether or not your appliance's warranty is adequate, then determine what the service contract offers. Does it include parts and labor? For what length of time will it run? Exactly what does it cover? Will the dealer offer servicemen or authorize you to use only those it considers acceptable? Whether or not you feel that it is necessary to buy such a contract, make sure that there are good, honest, competent servicemen who are capable of repairing your appliance.

If you buy a trade-in from a dealer, ask for a conditional warranty (you can't expect the same guarantee on a used model as on a new) that will cover major repairs, and see if a service contract is offered.

Sewing Machines. Usually one of the safest used buys is a second-hand sewing machine. Most dealers sell trade-ins and reconditioned models, and they are generally in good condition before they are offered for sale. To be sure, however, you can check out such points as the ease of thread removal, the simplicity of the controls, any unnecessary vibration, the location of the light, and the facility with which the attachments can be used. Ask for an instruction book and ascertain the availability of service and of parts.

Vacuum Cleaners. You can follow the same pattern with a vacuum cleaner; most dealers have reconditioned and trade-in models. Decide on the type you want—upright models are generally better for heavy cleaning, tank types are more versatile. Test the suction, see if it is comfortable for you to use, and find out about the service and warranty.

I don't recommend that you try to buy everything you need immediately; there are some things you will use so seldom that it will be more practical to rent them—such as carpet cleaners, power tools, and gardening equipment.

There are several more free government booklets you may want to order from the Public Documents Distribution Center (Pueblo, Col. 81009) that will answer any questions you may have about small appliances and home entertainment equipment. Write for booklet #250B, *Buying Small Appliances,* #223B, *Energy Efficiency in Room Air-Conditioners,* and # 252B, *Purchasing Hi-Fi Systems, TV and Tape Recorders.* They will cover everything from electric combs to the varieties of phonograph turntables you can buy, and will help you select the best.

ROBBERY

You may also want to ask for booklet #180B, *Protecting Your Home Against Theft.* It suggests ways to discourage thieves, and tells the best kind of locks and safety devices you can use. Police officers will tell you that a really determined burglar can break any lock and enter any office or residence; the goal is to make it as hard as possible for him to do it, so that help may be summoned, or so that he will simply pick an easier target.

You can make it harder by using a dead bolt and chains, and by securely locking everything, both when you are at home and when you are away. Burglary is on the increase, and law enforcement officers say that as the economy worsens so will this particular crime.

If, in spite of all of your precautions, you are burglarized, there are certain steps you should follow. First, of course, notify the police and give an accurate description of the items stolen. Next, notify your insurance agent or company. If your claim is denied and you don't think it should have been, write to your state insurance department giving all the details. If you receive no satisfaction from this agency on your complaint, write to the Federal Insurance Administration (P.O. Box 41033, Washington, D.C. 20014) and action will be taken against the insurance company. An Administration study shows that millions of people are being denied insurance because they live in high-risk (crime) areas. Because of this the agency created, in 1971, the Federal Crime Insurance Program. In effect presently in only fourteen states, the program offers, through authorized companies, homeowner policies from $1,000 to $10,000 coverage. The policies are easily obtained, are inexpensive, and are non-cancellable. They cover burglary, larceny, robbery and damage to the premises, as well as such off-premises losses as cash stolen during a mugging or property stolen from a car. Write to see if your state is a participant in the program, and if it isn't, write your local, state, and national legislators to see why not and when it will be.

Check to see whether or not your police or fire departments have engraving tools with which you can engrave your personal identification— your Social Security number—on anything that might be a target for a robber. And make an inventory of your goods, listing the fair market value of each item, in case of any kind of loss, whether it is by burglary, fire, or natural disaster. If you do suffer a loss, a portion of the amount that is not reimbursed by insurance is deductible on your tax return. You will have to know the value of the item when purchased and its fair market value when stolen—another argument for having a precise inventory of your goods.

Take ordinary, sensible precautions against allowing yourself to become a victim. If your apartment has an attic that connects with others, be sure the trap door is bolted, for instance. It is astounding to read that women are still allowing strangers into their homes; that they fail to lock the doors of their cars when they park and when they drive; and that they are still giving and accepting rides at the acknowledged risk of their lives and safety. They still frequent places that are isolated or unsafe, and persist in denying the danger. I agree with the feminists that we should be able to go anywhere at any time with complete safety. That is the ideal, however, and I am a realist. I think the truly liberated woman is one who works toward a better tomorrow while protecting herself against the dangers of today, whether economic or physical.

8

COPING WITH RAPE

Don't Become a Target

Rape is ugly.

The Victorians coyly termed it "a fate worse than death" because it was a violation of virtue. I don't think *anything* is worse than death, but I despise rape because it is the physical and emotional violation of one human being by another.

Every woman ever born upon this earth has been a potential victim of rape. The trouble is that until recently we have not been told enough about it. We have not been told how to avoid rape nor even what rape really means.

WHAT RAPE IS

If you still have some vague idea that rape is simply the forcible thrusting of a man's penis into a woman's vagina, you are not giving yourself the advantage of knowing just exactly how ugly rape can be. Rapists are not confined to the ordinary mode of sexual intercourse—only about one-half of rapes are committed that way. A rapist will not hesitate to force a victim to participate in anal or oral sex, and he frequently gets an additional thrill from beating his victim. Some rapists get their kicks by burning their victims, usually with lighted cigarettes. There are many deviations which they are capable of forcing on their prey, but they all add up to one conclusion: Rape is a sick and repulsive act, and you want to avoid being a victim. The physical scars will heal; the emotional wounds may never mend.

In the old movies, the rapist approached his victim with a leer on his face; she cowered in terror, and the screen darkened discreetly while we were allowed to conjecture what was happening. Moments later, the heroine appeared, a bit disheveled, her blouse photogenically torn from one shoulder. She looked only slightly more beautiful and helpless for the experience.

In the world of reality, however, unless the victim is approached while sleeping and is raped in bed, she will probably be thrown to the floor or the ground. Her clothes will be ripped and her face and body bruised, cut, and battered. She'll be lucky to escape without losing some teeth or having some bones broken, and she will suffer both physically and emotionally from the consequences of the rape for a long time to come.

She may react with bouts of nausea to the anti-pregnancy medication the doctor will give her when she is being treated for her injuries. She will probably sustain bleeding and prolonged pain if she was raped anally; and she may have vaginal discharge and distress if she was raped "normally." There is a possibility that she will be allergic to the drugs that are usually given to combat venereal disease.

As distressing as the physical results of rape are, the emotional results are worse. Women who have been raped become frightened to be out alone; they have trouble with insomnia and nightmares. Fear and distrust become constant companions, often accompanied by an underlying, smoldering anger. Some women react by withdrawing and trying to deny to themselves and the world that the assault ever occurred. They try to forget one of the most humiliating aspects of the ordeal, the fact that they were probably forced to pretend to enjoy the experience, and to beg for more. Some women are overcome with self-loathing and shame. There is no question about it; rape is *ugly*.

How likely are you to become a victim? According to FBI figures reported in the *1975 Statistical Abstract of the United States,* rape is on the increase; the rate per 100,000 inhabitants rose from 9.5 in 1960 to 24.3 in 1973, with a staggering jump of 95.8 percent during the ten-year period from 1960 to 1970, and an increase of 30.6 percent from 1970 to 1973.

THE VICTIM

And who are the victims? Contrary to a popular—and dangerous—misconception, they are not women who "ask for it." They are women of every marital status, of every age, every nationality, and of every occupation. They cross all socioeconomic lines. If there can be one composite picture of the victim, she will be shown as polite, helpful, and not particularly strong-willed. According to studies conducted by police departments from Atlanta to New York City, and by such experts as James Selkin, since 1966 director of the Center for the Study of Violence at Denver General Hospital, she probably works in a service profession, in which courtesy is part of her trade. As a teacher, nurse, waitress, social worker, or sales clerk she has been trained to put the wishes of others before her own. She may allow a stranger into her home to use the telephone; she may enter an elevator in which the only other passenger is a man; she may offer to drive, or accept a ride with, a stranger; she may approach a man's car to give him directions or help. She wants to be helpful and nice, and her reward is, too often, rape and sometimes even murder. When the rapist has sized her up, decided that she is vulnerable, and makes his move, she is typically too frightened to resist. And so another victim is added to the gruesome statistics.

In studies conducted at Denver General Hospital, the women who successfully resisted rape were those who felt competent and self-assured, not through strength, but through a sense of self-acceptance and well-being. During those first crucial moments of initial contact, they refused to be intimidated, and they refused to obey the rapist's orders. The rapists usually fled; they wanted an easy encounter and sought out more submissive prey.

THE RAPIST

There is a fairly well-defined picture of the rapist. I am speaking now of the man who goes out with the deliberate intention of finding a victim; the man who snatches an accidental opportunity to rape cannot be so easily categorized. But the intentional rapist falls into a pattern. He is usually young, employed, and apparently normal. He may be married and have children. Somewhere in his life he feels that he has failed to live up to the definition—his own, his parents', society's—of masculinity. Or he feels that he is a failure in his sexual and/or personal relations with his wife or other women. Gang rapists are suspected of having strong—but hidden—homosexual tendencies that are satisfied by watching other men have intercourse, especially anal, with a victim. Massachusetts psychologist Dr. Nicholas Groth says of gang rape, "In part, the rape is motivated by a wish among the men to have sex together and the victim becomes the vehicle for achieving this." Or the rapist may be attempting to assert his *machismo*, his virility, over a woman who symbolizes the dominance of any woman in his life.

But whatever his problem, he is a weak, sick, unstable character looking for a victim who is weaker than himself whom he can frighten, subdue, hurt, and humiliate. In an article he wrote for the January 1975 issue of *Psychology Today,* Dr. Selkin says that, "The ultimate tragedy in rape is the dehumanization of both victim and assailant." He states that the rapist's feelings of omnipotence, guilt, fear of retribution, or anger can be keys to diagnosing and treating his sickness. One rapist interviewed in jail said, "I wish no harm on anyone. If I cannot overcome my sickness I would not want to live anymore." But, as Dr. Selkin observes, "Unfortunately, most rapists can neither admit nor express the fact that they are a menace to socitey. Even convicted rapists who are serving long prison terms deny their culpability. They tenaciously insist women encourage and enjoy sexual assault. These men will tell you they are the greatest lovers in the world."

RAPE—WHERE, WHEN, WHY

Is there a pattern to rape? Is there a where, when, why to the pattern? National figures compiled in 1973 for the U.S. Department of Justice's *Source Book of Criminal Justice Statistics* do show a pattern, and a picture of the crime emerges.

Taking Atlanta as a good example of a large, multiracial city with a high per capita rape rate (and it is estimated that only one-third of all U.S. cases are reported), I consulted with Ms. Pola Eisenstein, Crime Analyst for the Atlanta Police Department, for the official figures for 1974. The pattern began to take shape.

Of the 479 reported rapes during that time, involving 556 perpetrators, about half of the victims were known to the rapists (the ratio was one to three in the multiple rapes). Seventy-five percent of the victims were between the ages of 15 and 30, although the youngest was 5 and the oldest 77. The victims and perpetrators were usually of the same race, but there were cases of black men raping white women and white men raping black women. (The latter are the least likely to be reported because of the black woman's feeling that she will not be believed.)

Where

Women are most vulnerable outside; 55 percent of the attacks occurred in cars, alleys, parks, parking lots, wooded areas. Of attacks outside, 29 percent involved cars, and in half of those incidents the victim was taken to another location—an abandoned house, her own house or apartment, or the rapist's. The victims whose initial contact with the rapist had involved cars displayed a singular lack of safety intelligence. They had hitchhiked; given rides to strange men; failed to lock their car doors while driving or when leaving the car parked; gone to a man's car to answer a question about street directions, or allowed a man to come to their own car to ask questions, for which the window had to be rolled down. They had been forced into their own cars in a parking lot; or had gone to the rapist's car to help him. Of the 45 percent of rapes occurring inside, 57 percent were in the victim's own home. Some of these cases involved break-ins, some involved guests. They happened at various times of the day or night.

When

Still citing the Atlanta Police Department figures, the rapes involving children and young teenagers usually took place on a weekday afternoon, when no adults were likely to be at home. Women over 45 were more apt to be raped between six in the evening until midnight. The most dangerous times for all women of all ages are from midnight to six A.M., every day of the week, with special danger from Friday noon to six o'clock Sunday morning. Although police officers won't be quoted, they agree, based on years of experience, that the monthly time of the full moon seems to trigger more violent crimes of every type.

As for the safest times of the year, the peak season for all violent crimes is generally the hot summer months, but using Atlanta's 1974 record as a criterion, there is no discernible pattern to the ebb and flow of incidents. The total, up by eleven reported cases from 1973, looks like this:

January	59	
February	37	Only 4 multiple rapes during the
March	47	first seven months of the year.
April	38	
May	53	
June	37	
July	37	
August	22	
September	52	Of the 171 rapes during the latter
October	35	five months, 35 were multiple, with
November	35	4 in December, 7 in August, and 19
December	27	in September.
Total	479	

I have underlined the figures for January, May, and September because of their inexplicable rise. Ms. Eisenstein and I toyed with the idea of some sort of four-month cycle, but could find no valid argument for it. We recreated Atlanta's economic and weather climate and could find nothing of substance (except for the increased number of layoffs during the last half of the year) to account for the increase of the most vicious type of crime, gang rape.

Why

Why 479 rapes in Atlanta? Perhaps it was anger and frustration that boiled over into violence. Perhaps long hours with nothing to do trigger the latent predators. Perhaps the groundswell of the women's liberation movement threatened some men's fragile feelings of masculinity. Maybe the glut of pornography gave just the needed impetus to push certain already unbalanced men beyond the edge of reason. All this is merely speculation, but whatever the cause, the rapist went out searching, and he found his victims.

Surprisingly, though, in Atlanta in 1974, he didn't murder. This bears out the accepted national picture of the rapist—he seldom commits murder.

Of course, the victim has no way of knowing whether or not the man accosting her is one of the exceptions who will kill. He will threaten her with bodily harm, and he may be armed with a gun or knife. Twenty-one percent of Atlanta's rapists in 1974 threatened their victims with guns, 10 percent with knives, and 5 percent with other weapons; the others were armed only with their own bodies. Which brings us to the vital question: "Should you fight back?"

FIGHTING BACK

Law enforcement officers across the nation make this point: *If you are going to resist, do it at once;* if you appear to be docile and obedient at first and try to fight later, you will anger the rapist and his actions will be completely unpredictable.

You will have to decide for yourself what the circumstances warrant. If the assailant is alone and unarmed, your chances are pretty good and there are some protective moves you can make immediately.

If you are approached, ignore him or tell him to leave you alone—in whatever terms you like. If he persists, *scream*—but not "Rape!"; you'll get more attention yelling "Fire!" Get the adrenalin flowing; get as mad as hell—fighting mad! React with fury, not fear. How *dare* that twisted, distorted piece of humanity expect you to subject yourself to a painful, degrading experience? Forget that you are a lady, and fight dirty. He probably won't expect it, so you'll have the advantage of taking him off guard.

If you are attacked from the front, jab at his eyes, and jab to blind. If your hand is free, make a fist (with the thumb on the *outside* of the fingers; it may be broken if you enclose it next to your palm) and smash, not into his jaw where the bone is, but into his nose. Smash *hard*—you know how much a bump on the nose hurts; imagine what a real blow will do. When he loosens his grip on you, run as fast as you can. If he has grabbed you frontally and is choking you, knee him in the groin; he can't protect it and choke you at the same time. Knee hard—you could disable him. Again, run, get away, don't wait to see the results of your actions. Chop his Adam's apple as hard as you can; he'll feel as if he's choking.

If you are seized from behind and he is choking you, don't waste time clawing at his hands; grab one of his fingers and bend it back as far as you can. Try to break it; halfway measures don't count in a situation like this. Bring your heel down hard on his instep and jab your elbow into his ribs on the same side. Try to break his ribs. He'll give on that side, and when he does you can run in the opposite direction.

Keep in mind that even though you are unarmed you have your body with which to fight; that means two feet, two knees, two hands, ten fingers, two elbows, and a mouth. Use them, and use them to hurt.

An armed man is another matter, and each woman will have to evaluate the situation and her chances to determine whether or not she will fight back. There's one point to keep in mind; if he has a weapon he's probably concentrating on it and you possibly could distract him long enough to call for help or to get away. It's impossible for any woman to say what she would do- if she were confronted by an armed assailant. I *think* I would fight, but if I have to make a choice between rape and murder I know that I would choose to live. However, there is one thing that I will never do, and that is go somewhere with an armed man, whether his aim is rape or robbery. Once in a car, a woman's chances of escaping are much slimmer. (Later, we will discuss self-defense as a way of coping with attacks on women.)

There have been cases of women trying to reason with a rapist—some have been successful and some have ended in tragedy. In one instance, a nurse was forced at gunpoint into her car after she had left work late at night. She kept her head, and calmly told the would-be rapist that he could do as he liked, but that she had an advanced case of venereal disease, so the choice was his. He left—fast! In many cases, women try to appeal to their attackers but act so frightened and hysterical that the men are goaded into violence instead of flight; sometimes victims are killed because of this. If you are going to try to reason with the rapist, don't act afraid. In deciding to talk, as in deciding to fight, each woman must use her own judgment and common sense. You're going to be frightened, but try to use your head. An unflustered, self-assured woman *seems* less a victim; and what the rapist wants is a victim. He may be deterred by a rational and calm approach, whereas a hysterical outburst may frighten him into violent behavior; but just *maybe*. Each situation is unique and requires a different response. At any rate, if you can act rationally, you may be able to take advantage of any opportunity to escape.

The Victim and the Law

What should you do if, in spite of all your precautions, you are raped?

First, call the police, of course. Ask if there is a woman on the sex crimes squad to whom you can talk, and find out if there is a rape crisis center to which you can go. Second, as much as you want to, *don't wash* and *don't change clothes.* As distasteful as it will be, the doctor must be able to find evidence of the rapist's semen; if your clothing is torn, he or the police officer must be able to testify to this fact in court. Unfortunately, in a rape case, unlike any other type of criminal case, the dice are loaded against the victim. In most states, her word is not enough; corroborating evidence is necessary. What the courts would really like is a witness—and this is highly unlikely. So be careful not to destroy any evidence of the rape.

In court, according to law, the criminal's past history may not be introduced, even though he may have had prior convictions (and most rapists are repeaters). However, incredible as it may seem, the most intimate details of your own sexual encounters may be demanded! You may be asked your age when you lost your virginity, how many men you have had as sex partners, whether you have ever had anything other than vaginal intercourse, whether you frequently visit single bars and whether or not you ever invite men to your home. The idea, of course, is to discredit your testimony and to make it appear that you encouraged and enticed the rapist. It is no wonder that only one-third of rape cases are reported!

There are glimmers of change, however. California has passed a law banning almost all disclosures of the victim's previous sex life, and New York has a law that allows semen on the victim's underclothing, or torn underpants, to be introduced as evidence of rape or force. However, the law does not go far enough; the injuries and semen must *both* be proven. Remember that rape is the only crime in which the victim's testimony is not enough; you can claim that you have been robbed without providing corroboration, but not so with rape.

There is still the archaic idea that a woman who resists can't be raped. Proof of resistance is still demanded in court, yet how can anyone judge the extent to which a person can be disabled with fright and fear for her life? Some police officers wonder aloud why a woman who is forced to perform fellatio doesn't *bite* during the act. Probably because the man has a gun or knife at her head, or has his hands around her throat. The only time he would be vulnerable would be during orgasm, but by then would the victim still have the will to fight? There is no way for any person to imagine himself in another's place or to understand the disabling fear that one usually feels at the threat of bodily harm. Most women have spent a lifetime avoiding injuries, as well as avoiding inflicting physical harm on anyone. How then can we be expected to react without fear in an ugly and unfamiliar situation? But we must remember that forewarned is forearmed —*think now* of what you would do if you were attacked. If you *are* going to fight, do it at the outset; don't wait for a better opportunity. Better still, think about the many ways you can avoid becoming a victim at all.

THE RAPIST AND THE LAW

What happens to the rapist if he *is* convicted? Laws vary throughout the nation, but Georgia is fairly typical. The rapist may be sentenced to three to seven years, and can be put on probation after serving only one-third of his sentence. Then it is highly likely that he will be out on the prowl again, looking for another victim.

The cause of the increasing number of rapes is threefold: First is a judicial system that is unable to control crime effectively; second is an inadequate or incorrectly utilized police force. The police feel helpless. They apprehend a rapist, and he is given, if convicted, a slap on the wrist (the sentence for larceny can be as much as three times longer than for rape), and is soon turned loose on society again. Third is the fact that punishment alone does not deter the rapist; what he needs is to be treated for his illness and kept out of society until he is no longer a danger.

HOW TO FIGHT RAPE

There are many strong opinions about the causes and treatment of crime. Some see a growing laxity on the part of the courts; some stress the liberal trend in society as the cause of increasing crime. Many feel that old-fashioned discipline and standards of decency are needed. Whatever our society is and does, however, it is plain that something needs to be done about rape. Ways must be found of preventing the sickness, of treating it. Fairer ways of dealing with the crime, once committed, must be brought into the police departments and courts. People must be educated as to how to prevent and avoid rape, as well as what to do when it does occur.

What can *you* do?

You can fight the causes and consequences of rape—of yourself or other women—as vigorously as you would fight the act itself.

In particular, if you are raped and do not receive the treatment that you should expect from the police, make a formal complaint to the chief of police and to the mayor. Tell in detail the time, place, and circumstances; give the name and badge numbers of any offending policemen. If this doesn't work, go to the editor of a newspaper or the manager of a radio station with the entire story of your mistreatment. Your name will be withheld (names of rape victims are rarely divulged) and action can almost be guaranteed. No police department wants a bad press, and your actions will prevent the same treatment being given to the next rape victim.

General action any woman can take, whether or not she has been raped, is to lobby to have the law altered. No woman should ever have to suffer the double indignity of physical rape and legal violation. In the forefront of this battle are the feminist groups, but any woman can organize other women to form a strong coalition for change. The laws should be changed in four ways: No longer should proof of penetration be necessary; no longer should corroboration be necessary; no longer should mention of the victim's sexual past be permitted in the courtroom; and no longer should the rapist face a negligible sentence and little or no psychiatric examination or treatment.

As necessary as changes in the law are changes in knowledge and attitudes. They are the two fundamentals of prevention. Many YWCAs, community groups, and community colleges are offering courses on safety and self-protection, teaching women how to secure themselves from attack at home and outside. Most of them offer self-defense courses of various degrees; some offer the rudiments, some go into the martial arts in depth. You can choose the course best suited to your needs and your psychological and physical capabilities. If there is not a course being offered in your area, contact the police department and request that one be given. Notify the newspaper and radio and television stations so that the course will be publicized, and get your friends to join. These courses meet with overwhelming success wherever they are offered.

The methods and weapons of self-defense are as varied as a woman's imagination can make them. You can carry Mace, hair spray, a small siren device, a squirt dispenser of lemon juice or ammonia, a ten-penny nail, or tear gas. Check to see if any of these, such as Mace or tear gas, are considered illegal in your area. It isn't necessary to carry something of potential danger to you or your children to be ready to defend yourself.

Nothing can instill fear into a would-be rapist like a large dog, inside your home or on a leash when you're walking, but don't neglect other rudimentary safety precautions. Have tamper-proof locks and bolts installed on your doors and windows. Have the locks changed so that the previous occupant's key will not fit. Have the utility meters placed outside the house. Install burglar bars or alarms on the windows. Don't live on the first floor in an urban area. Never enter your house or apartment if you notice anything suspicious. Don't allow a stranger into your home—if he wants to make a telephone call, tell him you'll make it for him, or that your "husband" is using the phone.

Reduce the rapist's opportunity. Avoid deserted places. Don't work alone in an office, especially at night. Don't go into basements alone. Don't go into any isolated area. Don't go into apartment laundry rooms alone at night—in fact, as much as is possible, don't go anywhere alone at night, and in some areas, as seldom as possible in the daytime. Don't go anywhere with a man you have just met in a bar; avoid any kind of pickups. Don't go out looking for excitement; you might find more than you expected.

Remember that a would-be rapist may watch you for weeks. Try not to leave any clues as to your living habits or your address. If you live in a state that requires you to have your car registration visible on the steering column, turn it so that it can't be read by passersby. *Never* tell a telephone caller that you are alone.

As more and more attention is being given to rape, more and more rape crisis centers are being established to deal with the injuries and trauma of rape. Women are being counseled so that they will realize that the degradation of rape is something apart from them, something they will be able to overcome. With strengthened police forces fighting sex crimes, sensibly revised laws, increased attention to prevention and treatment efforts in the area of mental health, and the concerted efforts of educated, alert women throughout this nation, we may, perhaps, hope to overcome the ugly fact and the awful act of rape.

9

COPING WITH CHILDREN

A Mixed Blessing

There is no question that children raised by a lone parent are in a unique category. There are more than 9.3 million children living with single female parents, a condition unparalleled in history—and their problems are different from those of children living within the traditional family group.

Just as our society is predicated on the "couple" theory, so is it built on the nuclear family unit, and the child from a one-parent environment has special obstacles to overcome at the same time he is attempting to cope with the normal tensions connected with growing up.

Nor are the problems his alone; his mother is having to face a two-person task by herself, one that is not easy under the best of circumstances. This is a formidable situation, and the miracle is that so many of us—mothers and children—not only survive but benefit from the experience.

Just think of it: In a two-parent household the job of child-raising, although traditionally the mother's lot, is usually shared by both parents. The father is responsible for the financial well-being of the family, shares in the disciplining of the children when he is at home, and is able to impart some of his own precepts and philosophy to his offspring. The mother's role, historically, is that of teacher, nurse, cook, comforter, and companion. While the husband works, she rears the children, cleans the house, does the shopping, and takes care of a thousand and one errands and chores. She also consults with the children's teachers, oversees her family's health, and cooks the meals. She may work to supplement her husband's income, but the family is usually not totally dependent on her salary.

The mother alone, however, knows that the family *is* dependent on her salary. The responsibility is awesome. What she needs is a "wife," but in lieu of that solution, she has to do the best she can.

If you are a widowed or divorced mother, you will find that your children are the greatest blessing you have. They will give you love and understanding, and will give the impetus you may need to become involved in life again. You simply *can't* spend your time brooding while there are children around. You have to take care of their physical needs and try to satisfy their psychological requirements. Remember that their lives have been shattered, too, and you will have to help them in their search for understanding and peace. Their emotions, too, have encountered challenges for which they were not prepared, and it will be a constant struggle for you to help them maintain their equilibrium.

THEIR PROBLEMS

There is no question that a child from a "broken" home faces more psychological adjustments than do other children, or that the remaining parent must use all her (or his) resources to raise him. We women alone must try to give our children the love and care and protection they would receive from two parents, all the while being careful not to fall into the trap of compensatory maternalism—of smothering them with two *much* love and overprotectiveness, of being super-moms.

Many children of divorce feel guilty about the breakup of their homes; they feel responsible. Many a child thinks that Dad left home because he or she was naughty or unlovable. Or the child may inadvertently stumble on a truth not recognized by either parent—that he actually *is* the cause of the divorce.* Dr. Bruno Bettelheim, distinguished child psychologist and long-time Professor of Psychology and Psychiatry at the University of Chicago, feels that this may be a strong element in many divorces. "The birth of children, particularly the birth of the first child," writes Dr. Bettelheim, "causes a great change in the family constellation. Some fathers, for example, feel that the child demands too much of their wife's time and interest. While he rarely puts the blame directly on the child, the husband no longer finds the same satisfaction in his marriage as he did before the baby's arrival."

Obviously, children of a divorce must be made to believe that they are loved and that they are in no way to blame for the separation of their parents. This assurance must be gauged according to the child's age and capability of understanding, but should be stressed, preferably by both parents, throughout his childhood and adolescence.

The child whose father has died needs different reassurance. He has

---

* Throughout the book I use the traditional masculine third-person singular to denote *a* child, either male or female. It is far less awkward than saying "he or she" —but of course I mean to refer to both boys and girls and do not want to imply any sexist leanings!

suddenly been confronted with mortality, and it frightens him. His primary fear will be that his mother will be taken, too. To control this fear he may react with rebellion against a fate over which he has no control; or he may withdraw from his mother and family. The unconscious rationale for this sort of behavior is that if he dosn't love them, he will be hurt less if they, too, die.

The child's rebellion can take any form, from misbehavior in school to running away from home to turning to drugs or alcohol, and it will force the mother to employ every ounce of her devotion and patience to deal with the situation. A wrong step at this crucial time in a child's life can have far-reaching repercussions.

COUNSELING

If your child's behavior in school has deteriorated since your divorce or your husband's death, consult again with his teachers and principal. (You should have an initial discussion of all the facts with them as soon as your family status is changed.) Among you a solution should be sought to deal with the child's new behavior pattern. The consensus may be that he needs extra counseling—or, better still, that you and he should participate together in a family counseling service. There are various agencies offering expert counseling at little or no cost. Those supported by the community or by volunteer contributions are generally free, while those under the aegis of a religious group usually set a sliding fee scale, so that you pay an amount based on your income and the size of your family. Check with your state department of family and child services to see if it offers counseling or can refer you to a good service. Contact the Family Service Association of America (44 W. 23rd St., New York, N.Y. 10010), and ask for the affiliate nearest you; the cost of such services is minimal. If there is not an office of the Catholic Social Service, the Jewish Family Service Agency, or the Urban League (which specializes in counseling with black families) in your area, write to either the American Institute of Family Relations (5287 Sunset Blvd., Los Angeles, Cal. 90027), or the American Association of Marriage and Family Counselors (225 Yale Avenue, Claremont, Cal. 91711); they both maintain nationwide referral listings of private and public agencies. The private agencies, also, use a sliding scale to determine the fee, which will probably run from nothing to $35 an hour, based on the size of your family and your ability to pay.

If the counselors think that your child's problem is severe enough, they will refer you to a psychiatrist. The fee will probably be steeper; however, your agency may be able to refer you to a service-connected psychiatrist whose fees are within your means.

If you and the counselors find that your child's problems are caused by physical as well as emotional difficulties, you can write to the National Association for Children with Learning Disabilities (5225 Grace Street, Pittsburgh, Pa. 15236) and ask for its literature, for the location of the chapter nearest you, and for the cost of its services.

Although your child's problems may not reach such serious proportions, he may become prey to nightmares and susceptible to ill health. He may appear to be adapting to his new life with ease, but masking his inner feelings in order to spare you further distress. Perhaps your son has been asked to grow up too soon, to accept responsibilities for which he is not prepared, to try to become the "man of the family." Or your daughter may feel that she should help you shoulder the burdens of motherhood. In either case, talk with the child, and try to be patient and understanding. Listen to your children; let them know that your love is unchanging, and that whenever they need you, you will be there to help. Do not burden them with more of the family's problems than they can handle. They should know when times are tough, but they shouldn't be given the anxieties or responsibilities of a parent. You can be honest and open without leaning on them.

As I have urged before, try to stay in the same location for as long as possible after the change in your status. Your child has had enough upheaval in his life, and needs the stability of the same neighborhood, school, and friends. Unless he is terribly unhappy where you are, delay any change at least until the end of his current school year, and when you do decide to move, involve him in your plans. Let him go with you to look for houses or apartments; go with him to visit schools in the neighborhood you're considering; check out the recreational facilities of the new locale. Don't move your child into an environment inhabited solely by adults and expect him to be happy; seek out an area that has other children his age.

There is nothing so important as doing everything you can to establish a sound base upon which your child's future will be built. There are too many dangerous avenues open to the unhappy child. As a parent alone you are at a disadvantage, but there are precautions you can take to avoid trouble. And if it does occur, there are steps you can take to help your child.

RUNAWAYS

Nearly a million children run away from home each year, and many are from single-parent homes. FBI statistics show that the median age of the runaway has dropped to 13 and that more girls leave home now than do boys. The problem has become so acute that Congress has passed a Runaway Youth Act that will increase and improve services for children who have left home, so that they will have havens available for counseling and aid.

William Treanor, director of Washington, D.C.'s Runaway House, described to a Senate committee the kind of child *least* likely to leave home. The child is likely to be "a young person who has at least one other sibling, who is living with both of his natural parents, who has not moved during the period that he has been in school—his family has not changed houses, or at least neighborhoods—and whose family has some kind of value system that they are trying to transmit to the child and are consistent about it. I do not recall ever seeing a runaway that was raised that way."

Obviously, those of us who are raising our children alone are at a certain disadvantage. We cannot be both mother and father; and we often must change locale. But, with open communication and a lot of love, understanding, and patience, many of us are succeeding in bringing up children who are happy in their homes.

If, in spite of your best efforts, your child does run away, report it to the police and apply immediately to your State Family and Children service department for advice. You will have to be particularly persevering in your search if you think your child has joined one of the questionable cult-type groups flourishing in America today. Basking under the mantle of respectability, many of a pseudo-religious orientation, such groups often beguile the immature mind—in effect, brainwash the child—to the extent that he will renounce his worldly family in order to become part of what he sees as a fulfilling substitute. Check with your local police department or the county or state attorney general's office for aid and information if your child has gone with such a group, or has shown interest in their meetings.

Experts believe that today's children are running *away* from an unhappy home rather than *to* the excitement of a new life. If we remember this, we may be able to concentrate on seeing that our children's lives are as balanced and secure as possible, even without the male parent. Frequently, children's adaptability and strength amazes us. It is not rare to see them become even happier and more fulfilled individuals after the loss of a parent, provided the remaining parent is loving and supportive.

HELP FOR BOYS

One of the problems involved in raising boys is the absence of an adult male with whom they can identify. If you do not have a responsible male relative or close friend who will act as a part-time father, don't hesitate to contact the Big Brothers Association. The organization is comprised of men from all walks of life, from teachers to lawyers, from athletes to policemen, from druggists to businessmen, who have in common an interest in and a desire to help fatherless boys. Check with your local "Y" for information about programs they may have for boys alone—they will be well-supervised and will give your son a chance to be with other boys and young men in an informal atmosphere. Look in the yellow pages of your telephone directory for other organizations that are available to you and your son; you'll be surprised at the diversity of services offered. Don't overlook the Boy Scouts as an ideal way for your son to share wholesome experiences with other boys and an adult male.

Help for Girls

The mother of a girl has a different problem. A daughter has an adult with whom to identify—you—but she may also feel a subtle rivalry. This is not unusual, and you will have to be diligent in your efforts to let her know that there is more than enough room in your home for two females in a close, loving relationship.

There are organizations to meet her special needs, too. The Campfire Girls and Girl Scouts offer programs of learning and service, and are under the dedicated leadership of other mothers. If your time allows, become involved and work with your daughter. If you are unable to give time during the week, suggest that field trips be planned for the weekends so that you can participate.

If neither of these groups appeals to your daughter, you could organize a club for her and her friends centered around their particular interests. Do they like to hike, or sew, or paint? If you don't feel qualified to lead them, ask the school principal for the names of mothers who are. The object is to let your daughter know that you are interested in her welfare and happiness and want to be involved in her life. Above all, make it possible for her to talk to you. Try not to overreact or be shocked by some of her questions and ideas. It's better for her to try them out on you than on someone less understanding.

One thing you must guard against is the temptation to relive your own youth through your daughter. Except for the normal interest and observation such relationships deserve, try not to become involved with your adolescent daughter's romances to the possible detriment of the boy-girl relationship or, more importantly, the mother-daughter relationship. This is the point for a little benign neglect; if you have given your children a firm set of standards of behavior you will be able to trust them in any situation. If you have long since established the fact that you look upon your daughter as a person with good judgment in whom you have complete faith, she will not hesitate to come to you for advice if she needs it. But you can't live her life for her, and you can't relive your own through her. She must be free to make her own mistakes, and suffer her own heartaches, for only in that way will she become a mature woman. Don't worry that she will turn to promiscuity in a search for masculine approval; if she has a good, two-way relationship with you, she will have a strong sense of her own worth and will not have to establish shallow sexual relations to prove that she is lovable. As much as you would like to, you can't protect her from everything unpleasant she will face; you can only equip her with the strength and determination to face them herself, and the knowledge that you are there if she needs you.

This same benign neglect must be allowed in other areas of your relationship with your children. You must be careful not to overcompensate for the lack of a father. You will, of course, give them your constant, unwavering care and devotion, but you must establish the fact that you are an adult and have a life of your own to live. It does not *exclude* them, but it does not involve them to the extent that you have no life except the one centered around them. As you are training them to accept adulthood and an eventual life away from you, they will realize that you are already an adult, and you, too, must have a part of your life that is exclusively yours.

There are splendid organizations formed to help parents alone meet with others in similar circumstances. They are *not* dating clubs—although through them you may meet men tackling the job of raising *their* children alone. These clubs constitute a form of group therapy; in them you will find that your problems are not unique, and some of the solutions and insights offered by the members may be of help to you.

DRUGS AND DRINK

The nightmare of every parent, no matter what the marital status, is that the child will turn to drugs or alcohol in an effort to tune out the world, become part of a selected group, or try to prove something. The thought that your child is a potential user or addict is frightening, and in this case, at least, you are not better off if you live in a small town. Drugs and alcohol represent an "out," an escape. Wherever you live, education about the dangers of drug and alcohol abuse is the best preventive, coupled with vigilance and concern on the part of school personnel, law enforcement officers, and parents of the community. If there is no counseling service in your area, organize one, and include a teacher who is respected by the students, a doctor, and a youth-oriented religious leader. Ask your police department to send officers to the school to give informal talks covering the identification of the various drugs, their effects, and the penalties attached to their illegal use. Have them stress the long-term penalties—

the criminal record, the lifetime loss of rights by the felon. Get a former alcoholic to tell them of the dependency and harm caused by excessive use of intoxicants. Have a doctor tell the students of the physical effects of drugs and alcohol use—early death, or neglect of health. The words of addicts will be worth much more than those of laymen. They will stress the expense involved in perpetuating the habit, and the depths to which the user can sink.

The National Safety Council (450 N. Michigan Ave., Chicago, Ill. 60611) has available a frighteningly graphic motion picture of car accidents caused by drinking. Most large cities have several federally funded drug-related programs, from halfway houses to counseling and treatment centers. Ask your local health department for information about any in your area. But if your child *does* try drugs or alcohol, don't turn away from him; he will need you more now than ever. Don't feel that you have failed your child. And don't let self-pity cloud your actions; your son or daughter doesn't need guilt added to the already overwhelming distress. Just seek the best help available and let your child know that your love is unwavering.

The Cost of Being a Parent

Even though your children may never cause you more than the normal concern connected with raising them, they will create financial burdens that will increase with the years. According to one conservative estimate, it requires $125,000 to raise a child to maturity, and any parent faced with clothing, food, medical, dental, and educational bills probably feels that the estimate is conservative.

No matter what your source of income—insurance money, Social Security benefits, alimony and/or child support, your salary—there will never be quite enough to do all the things that you would really like to do for your child. Be comforted. It is the quality of your care of him, not the amount of "things" he has that is important. Nevertheless, he *will* have to have shoes and shots and soup, and you'll have to pay for them.

You may encounter problems, if you are a widow, with the terminology and provisions of your husband's will. Unless he left a good will, you may have suffered the indignity of having been appointed your children's guardian, thus having to post bond and account to the court about the monies spent. You probably will not be able to alter the payments as stated in the insurance policy because minor children are involved. And when you undertake to administer government funds such as those from Social Security, you will be under the strictest regulations concerning your record-keeping. If you are a divorcee, your accounting must be no less accurate.

It can all be intimidating and a little overwhelming, and you wouldn't be normal if, occasionally, the thought didn't come, unbidden, into your mind, "What if I didn't have these responsibilities and expenses? Couldn't I manage better alone?" Don't feel guilty about it; we've all wondered the same thing at one time or another. It's a natural reaction to the enormous responsibility of raising our children by ourselves. It's frightening to know that the actions and reactions of another human being, for the rest of his life, will be the direct result of your guidance and example. But the blessings far outweigh the burdens, and whatever phase of child-rearing you're in right now, it will pass and will be followed by another—not necessarily an easier one, but a different one. At least you'll never be bored!

CHILD CARE

If you find that it is necessary for you to work while your children are small, paying for their care will be an extra expense.

You will indeed be fortunate if you work at a factory or business that operates a day-care center for the children of its employees. The cost will be minimal, and the additional transportation expense will be eliminated.

Before you entrust your child to a commercial day nursery, inspect the premises carefully. Ask for the names of patrons, and call for references. Look at the help employed: Are they clean? Do they seem interested in the children? Are there any young women who might play with the children? Do the children seem happy and comfortable with the employees? All these things must be considered carefully. Your child may be spending more time with these women than with you. Find out what local ordinances regulate the cleanliness and safety of child-care centers and nurseries. Are health examinations required of the employees? Is a doctor available if needed? Are there strict quarantine rules so that an infection doesn't spread unchecked among the children? What fire safety precautions are in effect?

If you are unable to find a care center with which you are satisfied, you will have to consider having your child cared for at home. Advertise, ask your neighbors, turn to your friends and family. (Using a family member can pose a financial problem; I'll explain later.) If you select someone previously unknown to you, demand the best references possible— no less than three, and none older than two years—and check them meticulously. You would be derelict in your responsibilities if you did any less, for you are inviting a strange woman into your home to care for your children.

You may find that it will be best for you and your child if your mother comes to live with you to care for the child. Enter into this arrangement cautiously; the benefits must be weighed carefully against any possible disadvantages. I would condone it only if your children like their grandmother, if she is patient and capable, if you and your mother are on the best possible terms, and if you have a clear understanding and agreement about the way the children should be raised and disciplined. If you anticipate no problems, attempt the arrangement on a trial basis, for a predetermined period of time; make clear the option to terminate the plan, with no hurt feelings, if it is best for all concerned.

The advantages of having your mother care for the children are many, not the least of them being the fact that she can give to your children, at a time when it is important to them, a feeling of the continuity of their family and its heritage.

The financial problem I mentioned earlier involves your using any family member (except a cousin) to care for your children, if wages are paid for the services. The Internal Revenue Service will allow you to deduct a portion of your child-care expenses, whether incurred within or outside the home, if you itemize expenses on your tax return, and if certain criteria are met, but not if paid to any relative but a cousin.

To qualify for the deduction you must have been gainfully employed (includes self-employment) during the period covered by the expenses, you must have maintained a household for the dependent, and the care must have been necessary to enable you to work. If the child was under age 15, and can be claimed as your dependent, you can deduct up to $400 per month for care within the home, or a maximum of $400 per month for care outside the home, in amounts as follows: $200 for one child, $300 for two children, and $400 for three or more children. Total care deduction, inside and outside the home, cannot exceed $400 per month. If you have a disabled dependent who is mentally or physically incapable of caring for himself, his care may be deductible only if it takes place in the home, and only if the expenses are reduced by his adjusted gross income and disability benefits that exceed $750 per year. (An institutionalized dependent's expenses would come under medical deductions, if he were there because the institution's resources are being used to alleviate his handicap.)

In order to claim the child and dependent care deduction, in addition to the above qualifications, you must have furnished over half the cost of maintaining the household in which the dependent lived. These expenses include property repairs, taxes, mortgage interest, rent, utilities, upkeep and minor repairs, property insurance, domestic help, and food consumed in the home. Interestingly, you cannot include the cost of clothing, education, medical treatment, and transportation.

The necessity for accuracy in your record-keeping cannot be emphasized too often; you will have to complete a form showing your child-care expenses and attach it to your tax return. Keep all receipts showing your payments and tally all your household bills. One other tax matter that will concern you: If you pay an employee more than $50 during a calendar quarter you will have to pay FICA (Social Security) taxes for that quarter. You may pay the entire amount or you may withhold one-half, while the employee pays the rest. For complete information about your specific liability, contact your IRS office.

No matter by whom your child is kept, don't feel alarmed if he looks to her for information or understanding. He is with her all day, and you want him to be with someone with whom he feels comfortable. She isn't going to take your place in his affections; be grateful that she is on hand to take care of problems when they arise, so that when you come home your time with him can be special.

Teach your children to understand money. No matter how young they are, they can be taught to save part of their allowance (or salary, when they're older), put part aside for church or charity (if you're so inclined), and have the luxury of being able to spend the remainder as they see fit.

When your children are older, they may want to work, and you will be wise to welcome their help. The money they earn can eliminate the need for an allowance, and may help with the clothing budget. If they are driving, the extra money can be used for gas and automobile expense, or for helping to pay for the increased automobile insurance coverage necessitated by their youth. Urge them to save as much as possible, and have the savings account list you as co-owner, with your children's approval. But do let them have some of the money they earn for their own use; that's half the fun of working, and they *did* earn it.

CHILDREN WORKING

The variety of jobs open to teenagers is limitless, and can be part-time during the school term, full-time during the summer, or whenever convenient if he or she is self-employed. The student can find jobs clerking in stores; packaging groceries; baby-sitting; working in a car wash or a fast-food chain; delivering newspapers or typing other students' school papers; working in church nurseries or the library; taking photographs at children's parties; teaching something at which he or she is adept, such as music, dancing, or painting; taking a summer job with the government, or working at a children's summer camp. There is always a need for co-operative, reliable, responsible young people in various fields. Their pay may not be fantastic, but it will probably be welcome.

If your children are receiving Social Security survivors' benefits (which will be available until age 22 if they are full-time students), they are entitled to earn up to $2520 per year without losing any of their benefits. If they happen to find a job paying over that amount during the summer (highly unlikely), they would still be eligible for the full benefits during the other nine months.

When your child is hired, instruct him to fill out a W-4E form and have it on file with his employer. This is different from a W-4 and will enable him to have the use of more of his money when he earns it. If he is eligible to file the W-4E, no United States withholding tax will be taken from his salary. The FICA tax will still be withheld, but the federal tax will not. He is eligible to claim this exemption from the tax if he did not have a tax liability the preceding year and anticipates none for the current year. (He will have no liability if he earns less than $2050 for the year and had less than $750 in unearned income—such as interest.)

You will still be able to claim him as an exemption, no matter how much he earns, if you can claim him as a dependent and he is a student for five months of the year or is under age 19.

Nothing will help a child achieve a sense of independence like earning money of his own, and nothing can be so helpful to his mother. But just as many marriages founder on money problems and conflicts, so can a mother-child relationship. As both sons and daughters approach adulthood, they typically begin to resent and resist parental authority. They know that the time for them to be on their own is near, and the more mature they become, the less they want to be indebted to anyone for their food, clothing, and education. Often the situation is trickier in the case of an almost-grown son dependent on his mother. Approaching manhood, he resents the fact that the figure of authority in his life is a woman.

Nor is the mother free from resentment toward a near-adult she is still supporting at greater and greater expense. The potential for friction increases daily. The wise mother realizes this, and gently pushes the child from the nest, all the while guiding him or her toward financial solvency. But the money problems, particularly if the child goes to college, will continue to be abrasive. As single mothers wanting the best for our children, we may find ourselves trapped by the typically American desire to see each generation advance one notch higher on the success scale than the last. Before World War II only an elite 2 percent of high school graduates—male and female—went on to college. Since the war, and especially since the Vietnam draft exemption for college attendance, the number has increased to about 50 percent.

COLLEGE

Although I am not opposed to college for those students who will need a degree in their professions, or those who really want to learn, I do not think that college is for everyone. (Some educators estimate that only 15 percent of the members of the work force need degrees.) The prolonged adolescence and financial dependence that we are imposing on our young can be harmful to their potential to become productive, self-sufficient adults. This additional strain on the family relationship should be carefully assessed and avoided, if possible. In other words, train your children from childhood to anticipate the time when they will have to help you with expenses and can aim toward the day when they will be financially responsible for themselves, whether or not they continue their education.

If the decision *is* for college, there are numerous avenues open for the prospective student from a family of moderate means.

The most important source of information and help will be your child's high school counselor or, if the school doesn't have one, the principal or senior class teacher. These professionals have available to them the lists of grants-in-aid, scholarships, and loans for which your child may be eligible. You will have to complete a financial statement that is absolutely confidential and mail it to a national clearing house; no one at the school will ever see it. In some cases, colleges will require that the student himself complete a financial statement. Either way, there are many types of aid for students who need it.

Families who have an adjusted gross income of less than $15,000 can probably qualify for a government-backed low-interest (7%) student loan of up to $2000. Such a loan does not have to be repaid until the student has completed college and can pay it himself. For complete information, and to see if you are eligible, write to the Office of Education, Student Financial Aid Section (Washington, D.C. 20202) and ask about available aid. Many states offer similar loans, and some in certain fields need never be repaid, nor do some specifying that the student remain within the state for a period of time after graduation. Check with your state department of education for full details.

A federal grant-in-aid may be given to a student whose family and personal income qualify him for the benefits. My son is receiving the Educational Opportunity Grant, which is paying the entire cost of his tuition and books. He is not receiving the maximum annual amount of $900 because he also receives Social Security benefits, but this is a no-strings-attached grant that never needs to be repaid. He would be unable to attend college without it. The school counselor will give you application forms and full particulars.

There are numerous "college finders" that will match the student with the proper college and with the financial aid available, but they cost money. However, these are diligent in ferreting out otherwise untouched scholarship and aid funds. (They have uncovered cobwebby scholarships for people with certain last names or particular family backgrounds, for example.) You can write for information to The National Association of

College Admissions Counselors (9933 Lawler Street, Skokie, Ill. 60076).
The fee is $10 and the Association will send a summary of the student's
qualifications and needs to 200 participating colleges. The College Admissions Assistance Center (888 7th Avenue, New York, N.Y. 10019)
has the same service, but its fee is $25. College Search Corporation (7
W. 51st Street, New York, N.Y. 10019) asks a fee of $15, and it has
2300 participating colleges, from which list a computer will select the
eight most suited to the student's needs. This agency also charges $1 for
an application form and brochure.

Or you can simply write to the college in which your child is interested
and ask for full information about financial aid available to its students.
The public library will have a complete list of the addresses of all colleges.

Although it is sometimes impossible for an entering college freshman
to select a major subject, it would be best to have some sort of idea before
the college is chosen. It would be foolish to go to a technological institute
if the student's inclinations are toward liberal arts, for instance, or to a
liberal arts college if the student wants to study veterinary medicine. But
the student should not feel locked into his first choice if his interests develop in another area. In selecting the college or university, however,
keep in mind that costs for in-state students are lower than for out-of-
state, and that transportation costs should be figured into the total projected
expenses.

What are the best-paying fields for college graduates? In 1974, according to a survey made by Frank S. Endicott of Northwestern University,
and based on the hiring practices of nearly two hundred large corporations,
the graduates commanding the top salaries went into engineering, accounting, chemistry, production management, math/statistics, sales/marketing,
economics/finance, liberal arts, and business administration.

Field	1974 Starting Monthly Salary	% of Rise From 1973
Engineering	$963	2.99
Accounting	920	3.84
Chemistry	890	3.61
Other	862	6.68
Production Management	850	1.43
Math/Statistics	848	1.56
Sales/Marketing	822	2.11
Economics/Finance	806	.50
Business Administration	756	3.14
Liberal Arts	741	.95

But as important as money undeniably is, the most important consideration in the choice of a career is one's happiness. Nothing is more miserable
than the prospect of spending the rest of one's life at a job that is not

enjoyable, and to which one's best efforts can't be brought. Urge your child to think carefully of all of the aspects of his career choice, and to talk with people already in that field about the possible drawbacks and rewards. Then, whatever he chooses, encourage him and offer him whatever moral or monetary assistance you can.

When he is in college, investigate the possibility that he may be eligible for food stamp assistance. No longer are food stamps offered only to those on welfare; they are now available to anyone whose income is below a certain level. Nor is your child's eligibility dependent on *your* income; his own is the only criterion for qualification. Although the program is under the authority of the U.S. Department of Agriculture, it is administered county by county so check with the department in the county in which the college is located. The stamps can be a tremendous help for your child who lives on campus, and for you, too, if you are eligible. The determining factors are income and size of family, and means that your food costs can be reduced by a substantial amount, generally almost one-third of the total.

CHILDREN'S SCHOOL RIGHTS

While your child is still in primary or secondary schools, he will probably be affected by recent laws and rulings from the federal government.

Late in 1974 President Ford signed into law a new Elementary and Secondary Education Act ("new" in reference to Lyndon Johnson's 1965 legislation passed by Congress) that has been termed "The Education Amendments." They include such disparate items as busing and experimental projects; there is one section of vital concern to every parent, and that is the part dealing with your child's school records. Don't think that these files contain only data pertaining to your child's grades, attendance, and conduct; they can include comments about your family's politics or the fact that a teacher attributes your son's friendships with other boys to "indications" of latent homosexuality. These records now can be inspected by the parent or by the student himself if he is 18 or over, or if he is attending a post-secondary school or college. If school officials refuse to allow you to see the records, federal funds will be withheld from the school. If you have any questions about the law and your rights, you can call the National Committee for Citizens in Education at 800-NET-WORK (800-638-9675). This group has been partly instrumental in having the confidentiality of school records lifted, and will give you complete information about the subject.

Another recent landmark ruling that could affect you and your child was a decision early in 1975 in which the Supreme Court stated that pupils suspended from public schools have a constitutional right to know and answer the charges against them. The ruling applies to students suspended for ten days or less, and could simply be an informal hearing or discussion involving the student and the school official. Students suspended for longer periods or for behavior that is considered dangerous or disruptive may require formal procedures. In any case, investigate and get all the facts so that your child's rights will not be abridged and so that you and the school will agree on his punishment, if necessary.

It's always a good idea to schedule regular conferences with your child's teachers so that you will know of any problems before they can cause real trouble, and so that you can intelligently evaluate your child's complaints of a teacher's unfairness. Keep in close touch with your principal and work with him or her so that your child will receive the greatest possible benefits from his education.

TIME WITH YOUR CHILD

As single parents, we are faced with the alarming statistics that indicate that our children are more likely to be arrested for a crime than are the children of two-parent homes. As one judge said, "You've got to have parents who have time. Where there's only one parent, it's hard for the parent to find the time and energy. You've got to feed them before you play with them." I thoroughly agree that children deserve as much time as can be devoted to them and I am aware of the statistics, but I disagree that the mere presence of two parents makes a better child. It is the *quality* of parenthood that is important; no matter how much time is spent with the child, it is the *way* the time is spent that is significant. I have seen too many nuclear families in which the children were unhappy or were delinquents, and I have seen an equal number of homes in which one parent alone was raising happy, well-adjusted individuals. If the mother is interested in everything that interests the child; if she shares much of her own life with him; if they share time and fun together (and some problems, too); if she sets certain standards of behavior as a guide for living; if she dispels any doubts about her love for him, and lets him know that he can always depend on her for understanding, friendship, and love, then the child will not be deprived of any benefits he might have had in a home complete with both parents.

But there is always the possibility that your child will be involved in some way with the police, and it is best to prepare for the eventuality before it happens.

YOUR CHILD AND THE LAW

Probably the one attribute that will ease any encounter with the police most will be courtesy. Whether or not your child has been arrested or detained rightly or wrongly, the first goal should be to obtain his release, and the best way to achieve that is for you both to be polite and cooperative. Law enforcement officers are human, and are more likely to try to ease the experience for a friendly person than for one who is belligerent. Advise your child to watch his language and to avoid challenges to the policemen's authority. Instruct him to ask permission to call you immediately so that you won't be worried by his absence. When he has called you, ask to speak with the officer making the charge, get all the details, find out if your child will be released or held for trial or hearing, and whether or not bail will be set. Contact your lawyer and have him go with you to the station, post bond, if possible, and have your child released to your care. If you don't have a lawyer, contact the Legal Aid Society and ask for help. If necessary the court will appoint an attorney to defend your child if he goes to trial.

As distasteful as the prospect of arrest is, it is best to know what to do, so instruct your child that his manner can have an influence on the way he is treated if he *should* be arrested.

YOUR CHILD AND SEX

Another vital area of discussion with your child should be the subject of sex, and in no other will you need such wisdom and skill. Your child's attitude toward what will be one of the most important parts of his life may be determined by your own attitude and instruction, so tread carefully.

Don't wait for the school to teach the necessary facts of life; too often the sex education course is no more than the old hygiene course you remember from your own school days. For suggestions about how much to tell and when, consult the books available at your library, or ask your doctor for pamphlets he recommends. There are excellent booklets prepared by manufacturers of sanitary products; your druggist can give you the correct addresses. If you feel uncomfortable talking about sex, ask your doctor to help you, and ask him to be explicit. It is likely that he can guide you in your discussions with your children, helping you with what to talk about, how and how much. You may want to help plan a better sex education program at school if you don't think the existing one is adequate. You should know what the school's educational philosophy is, at any rate.

One thing is important: Answer your child's questions, to the best of your ability, when they are asked. If you are caught off guard and you'd like time to be able to answer in the best way, be candid—say so! And don't fail to take up the subject later. Whatever you do, don't ever give the children the impression that sex is dirty or unpleasant. Teach them that used correctly, it is the most beautiful experience they will ever share with another human being, and stress, if you feel so inclined, the various views on chastity and faithfulness. If you have a church affiliation, ask your clergyman to discuss the attitude of the church toward pre- and extra-marital sex.

No matter what are your own or your church's stands on sex outside marriage, realize that sex is the most vital life force on earth; your child may not know how to handle these brand-new desires and needs. Recognize the fact that the current generation's attitudes toward sex are not the same as yours, and take practical steps to protect your children both physically and emotionally. Certainly both sexes should know all the facts about conception and pregnancy, about contraceptives and abortions, about venereal disease of every type, and about the emotional implications of physical intimacy for both boys and girls.

I instructed my doctor, after George's death, that he had my permission to treat any of my children without my knowledge or consent, and that he could prescribe contraceptives if requested. This simply means that I am a pragmatist. I know that the boys, particularly, would normally have gone to George for advice and help, if needed. I didn't know if they would come to me as openly, and I didn't feel that I could cope with it at that time if they did. I have no idea whether or not my children have availed themselves of the services that they knew were available to them; I do know that I would much prefer *that* than that one of them had contracted VD and been untreated, or had been a partner in an unwanted pregnancy. The Department of Health, Education and Welfare has conducted studies showing that of every ten teenagers who have had sexual intercourse there is at least one pregnancy, that three-quarters of all teenage pregnancies occur outside marriage, and that the cases of adolescent venereal disease are at an all-time high.

Fortunately, since the age of majority was lowered to 18 in 1971, more and more states are making contraceptives, pregnancy care, and abortions legal for young people without parental consent. Although I do not necessarily condone teenage sex, I do feel that if young unmarried people are going to have intercourse, they should know *all* they need to know before intimacy begins.

The age of consent varies from state to state and for the different services, but they all mean that your teenager can obtain, without your permission, the entire range of public health care relating to sexual activity. Six states—Kansas, New York, New Hampshire, Illinois, Mississippi, and Michigan, plus the District of Columbia—have no age barrier for the distribution of contraceptives, for pregnancy care, or for abortions; others, such as Washington and North Carolina (and ten others) require that the teenager be 18 or over. Some states have different ages for different services. Georgia, for example, has no age barrier for the users of contraceptive devices, but the recipient of pregnancy care or an abortion must be 18 or over. Delaware requires that contraceptive devices may not be dispensed unless the recipient is 18 or over, but offers pregnancy care and abortions at the age of 12. What a contradiction!

For specific information on the laws in your state, contact your county or state public health service. And if you don't feel that there has been adequate attention paid to the dangers of VD, or if the information has not been complete, you can contact the nearest Travelers Insurance agent and ask that this company's film, *How to Talk with Your Teen-Ager about VD,* be sent (free) to your social or civic group.

SINGLE MOTHERS

I have not yet mentioned a special group of mothers: those who have never married, and are natural or adoptive parents. Like Joshua's wheel within a wheel, they are a new phenomenon within the new phenomenon of women alone. Not only are there more unmarried mothers who choose to keep their babies to raise rather than putting them up for adoption, but with relaxed adoption laws, there are single women who are creating their own families outside of the structure of marriage.

This choice, to raise a family without a father, is one that I personally admire, but I don't know if I would ever have tried it myself. Raising a child alone is difficult at best, as those of us who are widowed or divorced are learning, so it must take a very special type of woman to face the problems voluntarily. I can readily understand the natural mother who chooses to keep her child; but a woman who undertakes, deliberately, the responsibility of raising an adoptive child fills me with the utmost admiration.

Even though most agencies are no longer hesitant about the single parent as a good adoptive risk, in thirty-three states they still require that the child and parent have the same religion. This can present a problem to the mother who wants to adopt a baby of another race or from another country, but these hard-to-place children can offer untold rewards to their new mothers, and should not be forgotten if you are interested in adoption. Contact your state Family and Children Service and find out if your state will help you to locate the child you want.

But no matter how you became a mother—with marriage or without, by birth or by adoption—you are, in raising your children, handling the hardest, most demanding, most rewarding task you will ever undertake. You are the primary influence in their lives: their social arbiter, their guide in belief and behavior, their figure of authority, and—if you're very fortunate —their friend. It's an awesome task, but it's a lot of fun, too.

THE BLESSING OF CHILDREN

You're especially blessed if you really enjoy your children, and are interested in whatever they do. There are so many things you can share together, and while they are learning from you, you can see the world anew through their eyes. They will introduce you to wonderful things you had forgotten existed; they will keep you in touch with the world in which they are growing and forming opinions and in which they will someday be the adults.

No matter how exhausted you may be, take some special time for them. Provide a time that is for them alone, and talk. *Listen* to them—this is one of the greatest gifts you can give your children.

Once my daughter told me I never listened to her any more. I was shocked, but when I thought about it, I realized that I had become so wrapped up in my new job that I was listening to my children with half an ear, and that wasn't good enough. I sat down with them, and told them everything I could about the job, and asked their indulgence until I was a little surer of myself. They agreed on condition that I tell them about the various happenings of each day. From then on, I delighted in telling them about my activities, and in so doing I was able to relax from the tensions of a demanding job, and to make them feel that they shared in that part of my life.

Of course, you can't be with your children all the time; it wouldn't be fair to any of you. You need time alone just as they do. Don't feel guilty about it, but arrange it so that they will be well-cared-for while you are gone. If there is not a baby-sitting group in your area, organize one. The idea is simple; about twenty-five people form a cooperative and swap child-care times among themselves. A schedule is drawn up listing ages of the children and convenient times for various sitters to have a certain number of children. No one will be paid, and you can keep track of how many times each of you sat for the others. You can use the same group for helping with medical and dental appointments and for special outings.

There are so many dos and don'ts about child-raising that assume added significance for those of us raising our children alone. We must be ever alert against taking out our fears and frustrations on them. We must take particular care to share their joys and sorrows and triumphs. And let them share in any of our own that are within the scope of their understanding. We can aim at being the best kind of parents, not demanding the constant attention and assurance of their love. We can avoid at all costs making our children feel indebted to us, at the same time hoping that they will some-day be mature enough to realize that gratitude is a gracious quality.

We can hope and pray for the strength and wisdom to cope with their love affairs, their school problems, their driving. If we are widowed or divorced we must remember that their father's parents are their grand-parents and should not be denied the pleasure of their grandchildren's love and company. We can take pride in the accomplishments of our children, and comfort them when they fail. We can welcome their friends, and never embarrass them by criticizing or punishing them in front of others. We can remember that childhood is short, and should be enjoyed. A happy childhood, like a happy marriage, is to be treasured; its memory will sustain the child in years ahead. We must prepare our children for the day they will be adults, and we must be willing to let go when that day comes. If we are fortunate, they will always remain close to us and will be eager to be with us as much as possible.

We must take care never to be patronizing to them; they hate it as much as we do. If there is some action or behavior that you feel should be changed, discuss it with them and let them see that another course would be more suitable or satisfactory. Try never to use sarcasm on children—it is not constructive and they despise it. Let them be themselves, not carbon copies of someone else. Each one of them has something special to offer the world; nurture and cherish that difference.

Respect their privacy. If you can't give each child a room of his own, at least give him an area that is his alone, with his own bed. Under no circumstances should a child of either sex share an adult's bed. It can lead to emotional traumas for years to come.

If you belong to a church, worship *with* your children—don't drop them off at the door and plead that you're too busy to spend one hour a week in an uplifting, soothing experience with them.

Treat your children as human beings, not as adjuncts. They are not possessions or extensions of yourself; they are people. Never violate their faith in you; don't read their mail or diaries, or listen in on their telephone conversations. It's easy to excuse such actions by saying you "need to know," but if you have kept the lines of communication open, they'll tell you what you need to know.

Children are fragile yet strong; they can accept a terribly destructive situation—the shattering of their lives as they have known it—and, with love and guidance, can turn the challenge into a victory. The experiences of my children have not been unique, and I think that they typify the way most young people can respond to grief and a new life. It hasn't been easy for them, and the problems have been many, but they have matured and developed into self-sufficient, poised young people who are at ease with me, themselves, and the world. They have coped with their grief and loss and have grown in wisdom, in maturity, and in stature as productive human beings.

10

Welcome to the World

Whether you already work, are looking for a job for the first time, or are re-entering the job market after a number of years' absence, you will find no other area of your life so challenging, frustrating, and rewarding. You will encounter discrimination (no matter that it is illegal and more difficult to pinpoint because it is subtle), and you will have to be a superworker— both because you happen to be a woman. You will be introduced to an entirely new world of experiences, people, and ideas, and you will witness changes in yourself—your attitudes and reactions and outlook on life in general and on work in particular.

If you've never worked for a living before, take comfort in the fact that you are not alone. Every year tens of thousands of women search for their first jobs, swelling the ranks of working women to an all-time high of more than 33 million. According to the U.S. Department of Labor, nearly one in four of that number is single, and one in five is either widowed, divorced, or separated. In other words, we are our sole source of support, and we are working because we *have* to earn a living.

SHOULD YOU WORK?

Before you try to enter an already glutted job market, sit down and assess your capabilities and liabilities, your financial needs, your home responsibilities, and your access to a job.

If you are just out of high school or college, you have, hopefully, aimed your studies toward a specific employment area. If not, consider any skills you might have attained during your school years. Are you good in math? There are courses available in computer training or accounting. Do you have an artistic flair? Think about a career in fashion or advertising. Were you on the school paper, or did you study journalism? You might want to try newspaper, radio, or television reporting. Of course, if you type, everyone from the government to private business wants you, and, if necessary, you can always take additional courses to learn shorthand.

The point is that you should try to utilize your particular interests when you consider your assets. The same is true for the widow or divorcee who has never worked or has been out of the market for some time. If you worked before, you may have to take a refresher course. There have been astonishingly rapid changes in everything from medical techniques and resources to equipment used in stores and offices.

But don't overlook your home-related skills attained during the years you were a housewife. Don't think for one minute that because you've never worked, or haven't worked in years, you can't do anything. You can do anything you like with determination and self-confidence and the necessary amount of training.

You will have to decide on the minimum amount for which you can work. If you are receiving Social Security benefits, you will have to find out exactly what your take-home pay must be in order to offset the loss of this tax-exempt money. Keep in mind that you can earn up to $2520 per year before your benefits are reduced, and that after that amount you will still receive one dollar for every two that you earn. So if the job pays a small salary, out of which will be taken taxes and Social Security contributions, it may pay you *not* to work. However, if you want to take a low-paying job that will enable you to retain your benefits while you are gaining experience and confidence, it would certainly be worth trying for a while. Balance against your take-home pay, however, any costs of child care and of clothes, lunches, and transportation. In considering going to work, you must consider all aspects of the situation, not the least important of which will be your home responsibilities. If you have children at home, their care must be a prime factor in your decision; but with the options discussed in the last chapter, this is not necessarily a deterrent.

The last thing to be weighed is your access to transportation. If the only jobs you feel suited to take and that are available to you are located a great distance away, you must add up the total cost of time and money involved. Public transportation, of course, is the cheapest and the most practical; you won't have to worry about driving in bad weather, about the cost of running the car, or about the high cost of parking. In most cities, the travel time is about the same for surface transportation and private cars—they're both tied up in the same traffic jams—but subsurface and rapid transit travel are to be chosen over automobiles for speed. If your area doesn't have good public transportation and you'll have no choice but to drive or join a car pool, add these costs into your expenses and subtract them from your projected salary, so you can come up with a figure that will tell you the lowest possible salary you can accept.

PREPARING TO WORK

If you feel that you will need to take a refresher course before you begin applying for work, there are numerous programs available to you at minimal costs. Check with your community college or your high school or college adult education branch to see what they offer. The cost is generally $25 to $30 per course, and they range from learning to operate computers, automatic typewriters, and calculators to bookkeeping techniques and speed writing. Some courses are available in more esoteric fields such as pottery or art. Select the best course available to you; the employment competition is going to be keen and the few jobs open will be given to those women with the best training. If you have any question about the legitimacy or adequacy of a vocational school in which you are interested, write the Department of Consumer Information (Pueblo, Colorado 81009) and ask for the free government booklet, *Pocket Guide to Choosing a Vocational School.* If the school in which you're interested isn't listed, contact the Better Business Bureau in your area for specific information.

For all women who are in the work force now or are preparing to enter it, there are many excellent college programs. You can take evening courses while you work, or you can attend full-time before you're employed. There is no question that the greater the amount of education the worker—male or female—has, the greater chance he or she has of obtaining and keeping better jobs, and of advancing to higher levels of responsibility and salary. But, of course, it is even more important for a woman; like it or not, there is still discrimination. But more of that later.

Among the most interesting programs is one sponsored by the Clairol Company for women over 35. It's a scholarship offered for those who want to return to college but are unable to do so because of their age, their financial status, or the fact that they want to attend part-time. Contact the college of your choice to see if it is a participant in the program, and ask for complete information.

Many colleges offer courses in the new area of women's studies. They are in most states, from South Carolina to Hawaii, from New York to Washington, and they offer both bachelor's and master's degrees, as well as credit toward your minor. For a complete listing and further information, write to Clearinghouse, The Feminist Press (Box 334, Old Westbury, N.Y. 11568).

If you feel that you can't devote the time or money required to attend college, the answer might be for you to select a good home-study course that will help you earn your degree. (Most colleges insist that at least some of the course be in-class.)

Contact the nearest college or university and ask if it offers any of these home-study courses, or write to the National University Extension Association (1 Dupont Circle, Suite 360, Washington, D.C. 20036) for its *Guide to Independent Study*. It costs $1, prepaid, and lists 73 colleges that offer courses for accreditation toward a college degree. For $1.95, prepaid, you can order their *Directory of U.S. Colleges and Universities for Part-Time Students,* which gives by geographical location a listing of all degrees available through part-time study.

This is the perfect answer if you want to work *and* get your degree, and even if you already have a degree or don't feel that you will need one, there are similar courses that will help you improve your job qualifications or learn a new skill. For a list of accredited schools offering such home-study courses, write to the National Home Study Council (1601 18th Street, N.W., Washington, D.C. 20009) for its free directory naming more than 135 accredited private schools, and listing the hundreds of courses offered. These home-study courses can be expensive (up to $500 plus books and equipment), so study their brochures carefully, and understand exactly what they offer and what the cost covers. Don't sign a contract until you are sure that you know what you'll be getting for your money; check with the Better Business Bureau to see if there have ever been any complaints made against the school in which you're interested.

Today the career opportunities that are opening to women are limited only by the scope of our ambition, talents, and self-confidence. Twenty years ago, there were almost no female faces on television news or in the police force or behind the counter at the pharmacy. We were under the stereotype of the keeper of the hearth, and our great numbers in the labor force were limited to the "traditional" jobs of teachers, nurses, saleswomen, and office workers. But now sexual qualifications have blurred, the advertising for workers by sex has been outlawed, and in theory at least, we can work at any job for which we are qualified.

JOB DISCRIMINATION

Equal opportunity is great in theory; it's a pity it doesn't work in practice. On the United States Civil Service "Inquiry as to Availability," for example, the requirements for the employee (in stating a limitation on the number of members of the same family who may work simultaneously for the government), says:

> The term "family" as used in section 9 of the Civil Service Act, refers to those who live under the same roof with the head of the family and form *his*

fireside. When members of the family become heads of new establishments they cease to be part of the *father's* family. [italics mine] (260p. Atty.Gen. 303, 7/12/07).

Now, really, Uncle Sam! Granted that in 1907 the head of the family, in 99 percent of the cases, *was* the father, and granted that the cost of printing is high, next time a new batch of these inquiries is run off, let's update that wording a little!

Not only is it no longer viable to assume that a male is the head of a family, it is just plain stupid to say that there are "boy jobs" and "girl jobs," as if the jobs themselves had a gender. Why *shouldn't* a woman be able to sell cars or be a construction worker? And why *shouldn't* a man be a secretary or a nurse?

Women are not trying to take jobs away from men; we're out there for exactly the same reason—to support ourselves and our families—and no door should be closed to us because of our sex. Or our age. Too often jobs are open only to "recent college graduates" or are described as ideal for a "junior executive." (The Civil Service itself is guilty of this, and the United States government should be in the forefront of eliminating any hint of discrimination; after all, it *is* the law.) If asked about the ad specifying a young person, the interviewer may admit that the company (or government agency) cannot discriminate, but prefers to hire a young person so that the money spent on his training will not be wasted.

If you feel that discrimination has caused you to miss out on getting a job or a promotion, don't waste a minute in making a formal complaint to the employer and to the Equal Employment Opportunity Commission (1800 G Street, Washington, D.C. 20506) and the Women's Bureau (U.S. Department of Labor, Washington, D.C. 20210). Tell them all the particulars, and ask their help. Don't hesitate to go to the top, and don't worry about being a troublemaker; it is the *employer* who is making trouble by disobeying the law. And if you're threatened by dismissal because of your complaints, report that to the Department of Labor, too. Ask for the free booklet, *Equal Pay,* when you contact the Department; it has a complete rundown of your rights as a worker.

But all discrimination isn't blatant. It can appear in the interview, disguised as concern. The employer (frequently male) will ask, upon learning that a woman has children at home, "Who will be caring for them while you work?" Would that question be asked of a widower with children? A single father? Or a divorced father who has custody of his family? Never. It would be assumed that the man had the intelligence to make suitable arrangements for the care of his children so that he could work. Why, then, is not a woman in the same circumstances granted the same degree of common sense? I will concede that an employer is concerned that a mother may have to take time off if her child is sick, and I will also concede that a woman in a low-paying job ($6000 and under) will not be able to afford the amount of care that a person receiving a higher salary could. When an emergency arises, she *will* probably have to take time off. But according to statistics from the Bureau of Labor, in jobs that pay enough to enable the custodial parent—mother or father—to hire proper care for the child, women are absent less often and usually stay with the same job longer. So any hesitancy that might be felt in hiring a woman who has children is invalid, and the question about the care of the children is nothing short of insulting to her intelligence.

Another insulting question (and one that has absolutely nothing to do with the job or your qualifications) is this one: "Why do you want to work? For the money or for fulfillment?" Would anyone ask this of a man? Does this question mean that a nonworking woman can't be fulfilled? Or that a woman who works needn't expect fulfillment *and* money? Or that you must choose between the two? Let's face it; there are very few of us working solely to "fulfill" ourselves. We're working for the money. If we're fortunate enough to obtain a position that pays well and is at the same time "fulfilling," that's icing on the cake, but it is totally irrelevant as far as the employer is concerned. Of course a happy worker is a better worker, but that isn't what the question is after. Just remember that you don't *have* to answer either of the above questions. Or any other question that has nothing to do with the specific employment or your qualifications for same. Ask yourself, before answering any question, if the same question would be asked a man applying for the same job, and react accordingly. You can do it politely but adroitly, so that the interviewer will not be offended, but so that there is no doubt that you are there to discuss the job—period.

Another subtle type of discrimination is to be told that you are "over-qualified," which may only mean that your education is impressive but how many words a minute can you type? Again, you can intelligently turn the conversation to the qualifications demanded by the job and *your* qualifications. Remember that many employers are considerate and honestly try to find the best person for the job, no matter what is the sex of the potential employee.

JOB-SHARING

Among the job ideas you might want to explore is that of job-sharing, a new concept for employees and employers. In effect, the employer is getting all the work done, but by two employees who split the time and pay. An advantage this has over ordinary part-time work is that the job, because it is a full-time one, would pay more and the employees would be eligible for fringe benefits offered by the company.

When you find a job for which you think you are qualified, find someone

else who has similar qualifications and would be interested in entering into
the arrangement with you. See if the employer will accept the idea of having
two of you for the price of one. If he likes the plan, arrange your work
schedule and division of the other benefits with your friend. (Perhaps, if
you both have children, you can baby-sit for each other on the nonemployed
days.) You'll have to get an approval from the Social Security Administration so that both of you will receive the credit due you. I have seen the
system work satisfactorily, and it has many advantages for the woman who
doesn't want to work full-time and is willing to forego possible advances in
her career. For a detailed guide on the best possibilities for employment on
a job-sharing basis, send $1.25 for *The Job Campaign,* distributed by the
Catalyst (6 East 82 Street, New York, N.Y. 10028).

JOB-HUNTING

Once you have selected the type of job you want, the next step will be to
find it. You have three avenues open to you: You can answer advertisements, knock on doors, or register with employment agencies. Go armed
with a resume. This should include your name, address, marital status,
names and ages of children, your educational background, and professional
experience. Do not include your age; you will have to put it on various
forms when you're hired, but it has no place on a resume. List all your
professional experience, beginning with the most recent, giving dates of
employment. If you've never been salaried, don't hesitate to list work you've
done in civic clubs and organizations, and stress any domestic talents that
can be translated into the business world, such as budgeting, planning trips,
so on. Add your school interests, clubs, and honors.

Newspaper Ads

During an economically depressed period, of course, there will be fewer
openings and fewer ads in the papers, but they are still a good starting point
when you're job-hunting. They will give you an idea about the salaries
being offered in your field, and an estimate of the jobs needing more workers. (You may have to go outside your field for a time in order to work at
all; don't consider the time wasted. It will be good experience in adapting
to a different work situation, and you may find some way in which it can be
useful when a job opens in your area of expertise.) When you're looking at
the ads, notice that some say "fee paid"; this will not concern you unless
you are registered with an employment agency, and then it can make a
tremendous difference in your pay.

Employment Agencies

Let's face it—agencies are in business to make a profit, so someone, the prospective employer or employee, is going to have to pay for their services. The function of an agency is simple: An employer needs a worker; the worker needs a job; they register with an agency that tries to match the right employer and employee, and for that assistance a fee must be paid. The fees are stiff, so before you sign a contract with an agency, read it very carefully.

The contract usually runs for a period of two years, and by signing it you have authorized the agency to act for you in seeking employment. Make sure that the contract stipulates that you can cancel at will, at no cost to you. For its own protection, the agency will probably add to this that the contract will remain effective for a time (generally a year) after each past referral. This is only fair; it protects against the person who registers, is sent to an interview for a job, cancels the contract, then takes the job, thereby doing the agency out of the fee entirely.

The contract should also state plainly that if you do not accept a job for which you have been interviewed, no fee will be due. But watch out for the paragraph covering your leaving a job the agency has found for you. If you leave before the full fee is paid, the contract can commit you to paying the remainder within a week or ten days of termination of employment. And beware of a sentence saying that if you do leave the job for which the employer paid the fee, you will have to pay the agency the amount that has been reimbursed to him if you quit. Check the job carefully before you accept, to avoid over-hasty action that can cost you money.

And the fees are high. Tax-deductible, but high. For example, on annual earnings of $5,701 to $7,000, they generally run at 7 percent; on $7,001 to $8,000, 8 percent; on $8,001 to $9,000, 9 percent. The fee is usually the same percent as the number in the highest salary, so that by the time you are in the $12,001 to $13,000 range, the fee is 13 percent. But above $15,000 it stabilizes at 15 percent, although the fee for temporary employment is a great big 20 percent. If you accepted a job paying an annual salary of $10,500, say, your fee would be 11 percent, or $1,155. Not too bad, if you could spread the fee payments over the year in which you will earn that money, but the agency doesn't work that way. Its payment is usually set up so that you will pay no less than one-third of the total fee (in the above case, that would be $385) within fifteen days of starting work—when you draw your first paycheck. Another one-third will have to be paid within forty-five days, and the balance within seventy-five days. There is usually a sentence in the contract stating that a penalty of 10 percent will be assessed against the employee for any balance still due ninety days after date of employment. These fees are pretty well standardized among the various types of agencies throughout the country.

Most agencies accept the fact that you will probably register with others, so make sure that there is no restrictive clause in the contract. The final thing you should verify before you consider signing a contract is a statement that you will be in no way hindered from seeking employment through any other source.

Knowing all these conditions, should you consider using an agency? Yes, if you have been unsuccessful finding a job any other way, and if yours is a specialized field that requires that you be put in touch with a certain type of employer. Just be sure that you understand the contract, and that you have on hand enough money to cover the fee. You can, as a means of self-protection, tell the agency that you will accept interviews only for fee-paid positions, so that the burden will be on the employer. Don't be beguiled with talk of the fantastic jobs that are available, but on which, alas, you'll have to pay the fee. Naturally, they want to unload those because they outnumber the others, but stand firm; they'll find something else for you.

An alternative to using a private agency is to use a state agency. There will be no fee, but there may not be the variety of jobs available, either. Check to see if its waiting lists are long for the type of job you want.

Although they cannot be truly classified as agencies, you should not overlook your city, county, state, and federal employment registers. The municipal and state organizations will vary in each locale as to their methods of accepting prospective employees—some require written tests—but there are so many varieties of jobs with all branches of government that nothing should be ignored. Most states, following the lead of the federal government, give job preference to former service people and to widows of servicemen, and add five or ten points to the scores of the competitive exams. If you're dissatisfied with your test score, you are entitled to take the exam over for a better grade. State and local jobs are usually well-paid, have good hours, and offer attractive fringe benefits. They are generally void of discrimination of any kind and offer opportunities for advancement.

The federal government—Civil Service questionnaires notwithstanding—offers an ideal job situation for everyone, but particularly for women. Civil Service jobs cover almost every type of employment conceivable—as maids, secretaries, statisticians, nurses, interviewers, writers, telephone operators, lawyers, doctors, psychologists, and on and on. It really *is* virtually without discrimination, the pay is good, the raises are regular, the benefits are numerous, the working days and hours are excellent (generally weekdays only), and the job security is comparable to that in the private sector, if not better. For these jobs a good score on the written examination is necessary, but there are books available that can help you study for the kinds of questions that will be asked.

Your test score will be placed on the Civil Service register according to grade, and when jobs are open applicants will be called for interviews, beginning with the highest grades and working down. (Remember that veterans and widows of veterans receive additional points added to their scores.) If your score is only average, don't despair; some of the people above you on the list may not be nearly as well suited to the job as you are, or may not want it at all.

You can state, on your personnel sheet, that you would like to be located in another city or state—or overseas—or that you would like to travel. If you do leave the service, you can always come back into it at another time, and receive credit toward grade and retirement from your previous employment. And even after retirement you can probably come back to work seasonally, or part-time. I can find few drawbacks in federal employment. True, you may be able to command a larger income in some very rarefied strata of private business, but balancing that is the fact that you are not at the whim of a temperamental employer who can fire you with little or no warning or cause. If a federal employee has a grievance, there are prescribed channels through which he may go to obtain aid and consideration, and he may call upon the union for more stringent assistance.

Personal Contacts

If for any reason you don't find the work you want any other way, there is always the possibility that you may knock on a door that will open to the exact job you desire. That's the way I found the first of the three jobs I've had since George died.

I had been a regular listener to a particular radio station in Atlanta, but was annoyed at the many inaccuracies I heard. When the time came for me to start looking for work (after I had closed George's office), I applied to the station for a job as researcher. When I finally had built up my courage to try to sell myself, I went in, filled out an application, was interviewed, and got the job! And I began two of the most exciting years of my life.

So don't hesitate to go after any job that interests you. Ask your friends for suggestions; you never know who has just heard of an opening that would be ideal for you. Apply, apply, apply; one of those application blanks you complete may be for the position that will be exactly what you were hoping for.

THE JOB INTERVIEW

Probably the hardest thing the job-hunter faces is the interview. Here you are, trying to convince another person that he should gamble on your ability, your conscientiousness, and your reliability, and he should pay you a good salary while he's doing it! You'll have to sell yourself as the one person who is ideal for the job, and assure him that no one else could do the work better or faster or more accurately or with better cheer. All this time, of course, you are trying to maintain an air of aloofness, conveying subtly that he'd better hire you fast, because dozens of other employers want to add you to their payroll. It takes guts to go to a job interview, and skill to maintain that delicate balance.

I developed a philosophy and a technique for interviews. Before I began seriously looking for work, I answered as many ads as I could find that offered jobs that I felt qualified to handle. I wasn't seriously interested in any of them, so if I didn't get them, I wouldn't be disappointed. But I went, I answered questions, I asked a few myself, and I learned what to expect from an interview and what to avoid. Because I didn't care about the jobs, I could be casual and relaxed—*not* indifferent—and could eventually turn the conversation so that *I* was interviewing, to learn exactly what type of employee the employer seeks. The information was invaluable.

The prospective employers all agreed that appearance is almost as important as ability. Not ravishing beauty, but suitability of appearance for the job is important. (Obviously, there are special jobs dependent on looks alone, but I'm speaking now of the average woman applying for the average job.)

The employers I interviewed agreed that a woman's clothes, hair, and makeup should blend into a pleasing overall look of taste and appropriateness to her age. They didn't care for faddish clothes that looked uncomfortable. They didn't like the applicant to chew gum, and most were divided about smoking, depending on their own preferences. They all agreed that the prospective employee shouldn't light a cigarette unless the interviewer suggests smoking.

They liked open responses to questions, and when the woman had no previous work experience, they liked her to give an honest appraisal of why she thought she could do the job well. They were all impressed with college degrees, although most said that the lack of one wouldn't influence them against a qualified applicant. They all rated poise as being one determining factor in their selections; they felt that a woman who can maintain her aplomb under the trying conditions of an interview probably would do the same at work.

They all liked ambition, and didn't mind if the applicant stated frankly that she hoped to advance in her career. But they were unanimous in their dislike of a woman who let it be known that she would look on the job as a mere stepping-stone to another. They liked women with good health backgrounds, although physical handicaps were not a deterrent to certain types of employment. And they were overwhelmingly in favor of enthusiasm—an objective and lively interest in the job. They appreciated questions about details such as working conditions, hours, days off, benefits, salary (of course), and opportunities for advancement. They particularly appreciated being told of any family situation that could involve absences from work, and assurances that these would be kept to a minimum.

Armed with the above insights, you should be ready for your interview. Get a good night's sleep the night before, try to stay calm, and maintain your self-confidence. Promise yourself a small treat at the end of the interview so that whether or not you are hired, you'll have something to look forward to, and with which you can unwind.

ON THE JOB

When you do get your job, you'll have more hurdles before you. Starting any new job is just like starting the first, so those of you who have worked are in exactly the same mental state as the beginner. No matter how much training or experience you've had, each place of employment is different, and you'll be working with different people to whom you must become accustomed. Take your time, don't hesitate to ask questions, and learn as much as you can absorb during the first day or so. The specifics of your work may take much longer to learn, but you can get the basic routine down very quickly.

Your Paycheck

Remember to complete your W-4 form to your best advantage, as we've discussed. Don't be rushed; ask if you may take it home to complete. Decide, if you have the option, which company benefits you'll want, and select only those that offer better services for lower costs than you can obtain by yourself. For instance, if you already have adequate health insurance, you may elect to bypass the company plan; but you may find that its life insurance program offers greater coverage at lower premiums than you could find privately.

Before you sign for too many of the company-sponsored programs, however, do a little addition and subtraction to see how much is going to be taken from your salary before you even see it. By the time taxes, insurance, and retirement contributions have been withheld, you will be taking home a diminished paycheck. Remember that not all pension plans may be good for you; investigate the one offered before you agree to participate.

Unions

You may not have a choice about joining a labor union; it may be a requirement of employment. Dues vary according to union, job, and location, but there is generally an initial fee for joining and a subsequent assessment from each paycheck. If you're working in a closed shop, everyone will be paying dues and will be entitled to vote on union matters, including strikes. If you are working where there are both union and nonunion members, the union may vote a strike and if you're not a member, you'll be faced with the prospect of staying out of work to honor the demands, or of crossing the picket lines and antagonizing the strikers. The decision in a case like this will have to be your own; whatever gains the union achieves will be enjoyed by all the workers. However, during the strike you will not be able to draw on the union's emergency funds for food and other necessities if you stay off the job. On the other hand, strikes sometimes flare into violence, so you may run the risk of injury if you cross the lines. The imponderables are too numerous; the decision must be yours. (If you *do* join a union, be an active member, so that you'll have a say in future strike decisions and so on.)

Office Friends

If you are a woman over 35 and are re-entering the job market, or are entering for the first time, prepare yourself for a shock. You're going to find yourself competing with women decades younger than you, and the strain will be terrific. Just keep in mind that you have maturity to counteract their youth, and that although you may not have professional experience, you can surpass them in life experience, and can hold your own on an equal basis. Make friends with these younger women; you'll both benefit from the association.

Your office friends should be chosen with care. Avoid the toadies who seem to inhabit every office. They're the kind who hope to make points with the employer by reporting every word or sign of criticism or disapproval of the status quo. Similarly, avoid cliques; the one that is "in" today may be "out" tomorrow. Avoid office politics; don't be forced to choose sides in a pointless power play. If there *are* office problems, take time to assess the situation and to decide on your best course of action— which may well be *inaction*. Shun the dissident little group whispering around the water fountain; this spells trouble.

And don't let yourself be used, by employees or employer. There is a fine line of distinction between being an efficient, cooperative employee and being a patsy. Being asked occasionally, in a real emergency, to stay late to help, or to run an errand, or to fix the coffee, or to skip your break may be acceptable, but don't let it become a habit. Be polite but firm, and let it be understood by employers and fellow employees alike that you will not be taken advantage of in any way. They'll respect you for it. But be meticulous in adhering to the company's policies about the time allowed for your breaks and lunch, and try to avoid being late in the morning.

Avoid employment in a concern that has had a large turnover or frequent changes in office management and employees—something may be terribly wrong in the organization. Look for stability in the establishment in which you are interested.

Sex at Work

You may as well accept the fact that in work situations, there will be three categories of men: those who treat you fairly and as an equal, those who are aggressive in their advances, and those who are antagonistic. The office lecher still regards a working woman as fair game, and some men feel threatened by any female near or on a level with them at work. In both of these cases, the less done by you the better. I don't have to tell you how to fend off passes; do it as you've always done, and try to make the man a friend. Office affairs have so many hazards that they are hardly worth the time and effort involved, but if one of your fellow workers or your boss is someone you'd really like to know, become better acquainted after hours. Keep romance out of the office; it has no place there. It can be detrimental to the business at hand. And you'll find that the fewer people in the place who know about it, the better. It will probably end at some future time, and if you both remain in the same office, you'll want to be spared the innuendos and sly glances that may come your way.

It's best not to talk over your personal problems at the office, anyway. Everyone else has their own problems, so try to be cheerful and stress the positive. If there is a real calamity, never fear, your friends will rally— but not if you've cried "wolf" too often.

Raises

When your employer speaks to you of future advancement, find out exactly when it will occur and what the contingencies are; don't go out and buy a new wardrobe on promises. Know exactly what is involved, and wait until you get your raise before you spend it. And *never* allow yourself to be satisfied with a title in lieu of a raise. Some employers are good at this trick; they'll tell you that you have shown such a grasp of the job that you should be made So-and-So in charge of Such-and-Such. In plain English, that means that you are going to be given more work and responsibility, but at the same old salary. Decline with thanks, insisting that you can't accept the position without an increase in pay. Don't worry that you will be fired for being uncooperative; you'll be respected for your stand. Be firm; if you're worth what you are being paid, you're probably worth more to someone else. (It never hurts to keep an ear open for better-paying jobs, anyway; you might want to change at any time.)

The standard procedure in almost every office is to give all employees a raise every year, but the ideal would be for each employee's work to be reviewed at least twice a year, with extra raises given to those who have earned them. Don't be afraid to ask for a raise if you feel you deserve it; you won't be fired for asking. But don't allow yourself to be put off with excuses and promises too often. By the time you're entitled to a raise you will be familiar enough with the firm's financial status to know if it can afford to give you one. You'll probably *have* to have one by then, anyway, to break even on your living expenses. A study published by the congressional Joint Economic Committee showed that a family of four whose income in 1973 had been $12,626 had to have a raise of $1,840 in 1974 just to maintain its living standards. (The Bureau of Labor Statistics calculates $14,466 as the amount necessary for such a family to maintain a modest standard of living in 1974—*that's* a laugh!) The study also showed that in 1973, half of American families earned under $12,000; women averaged less than $7,000!

If you are due reimbursable expenses in your job, keep careful records and check them with the bookkeeper; in fact, it's a good idea to go over every paycheck to verify that too much is not being withheld. Bookkeepers, human or mechanical, do make errors occasionally, so know exactly the amount to which you are entitled each pay period and see that you get it.

Lunchtime

Your lunchtime can be the most valuable period of your day. You can use it to rest, to walk or exercise, to shop, to catch up on your reading or needlework. You can conduct your personal business, visit friends, write letters, visit museums, make personal calls, and oh, yes—eat. Be careful about eating, though. The temptation to overeat because the food is available is constant, but if you have to watch your weight—and very few of us don't—breaks and lunches can be disastrous. Try to avoid those luscious fattening coffee rolls and cookies. Bring an apple or pear from home; it's much cheaper, generally, and more nutritious. In fact, you can save as much as $10 a week by bringing your lunch from home. Even if you're on a weight control program, you can prepare attractive, delicious meals that are low in calories and cost, and high in the nutrition you need to function at peak efficiency.

The "Blahs"

There are bound to be some mornings when the idea of facing another day doing the same work with the same people is more than you can bear. If you have any kind of annual or sick leave accrued and your work will not suffer, take the time off and treat yourself to a day that is out of the ordinary. If you're in the mood to polish silver or wash and wax floors, spend a day indulging those nesting urges that usually come in the spring and fall. Or if you'd like to spend the day in bed reading or watching television or sleeping, do it. Or give yourself a day on the town; have your hair done, or shop, or sit for hours watching movies. Spend the day outdoors, walking or gardening or just lying on your back watching the sky. Go for a short trip out of town and explore the countryside. Call up a friend you haven't seen lately, and get together for a relaxed visit. Whatever you do, don't watch the clock; let your day flow, unlimited by time and schedules. You'll return to work the next day refreshed in body and spirit.

If you can't take a day off, do as show business and sports personalities do before an appearance or game: "Psych yourself" for the day ahead. This simply means to get yourself in the correct psychological mood for the job at hand, to use positive persuasion to convince yourself that you're preparing to do the thing you'd rather be doing than anything else in the world. Tell yourself how lucky you are to be able to work and to have a job. Set yourself a goal for the day, decide the amount of work you intend to have finished by the end of the day, and give yourself something to look forward to when you get off from work. (It can be as simple as having a new book or magazine to read, a favorite TV program, some new hobby to try, a different bath oil.) When you're dressing for work, select your most attractive outfit to give your spirits an added lift, play soothing music, and take a different route, if possible, to work. If you ride public transportation, take a new paperback book to read, or just sit and enjoy the early-morning scenery and the people around you. Make the whole day different so that you won't have a chance to be bored.

If a time comes when you're facing that boredom every day and can do nothing to change the cause of your trouble, it would be best for you to look for a new job. Nothing is more debilitating than tedium or frustration caused by a dead-end job. No one denies that promotions are painfully slow for most women, and we often find ourselves on a treadmill. That's the time to investigate new employment—but don't burn your bridges behind you until you know what is ahead. You don't want to join the large number of the unemployed needlessly. When you are sure of another job, you will have to give notice to your current employer; two weeks is customary, but a week may be sufficient. It may be necessary to give your notice in writing; make it brief and noncommittal. State the reason for leaving (better pay, opportunity for advancement, different field of interest), and add a ritual word about having enjoyed working there; after all, you'll be wanting a letter of reference. Check with the bookkeeper to see if you can continue your group life and health insurance; there should be no problem, although the premiums will be higher. Find out about any funds you have paid into a retirement or profit-sharing plan. Check on any accrued leave to which you may be entitled, and for which you might be paid.

Unemployment

The average unemployment period for women, if they leave their jobs voluntarily, is ten weeks; twenty-seven if they're fired or laid off. One reason for the difference is that the latter can probably draw unemployment compensation if they've been dismissed involuntarily, and the weekly checks can offer a chance for a breathing spell while they're looking for the next job.

If you are unemployed, apply for compensation at your state Department of Labor claims center. The unemployment payments will vary in amount according to the salary earned and the state in which you live, but the average throughout the country is $70, and the length of time to which you may be entitled to draw them is determined by each state. The usual span is twenty-six weeks, but during periods of increased unemployment, the time is generally extended for an additional thirteen. The money is tax-free and can help tide you over while you're job-hunting, but it is not enough to maintain a household. The weekly checks will not come in for too long, remember, and to receive the funds you must obey certain rules. You'll have to report, either by mail (after the first few weekly visits) or in person, to the State Unemployment Insurance Service in your area, and will be asked, each week, if you are actively seeking employment. There are generally a few strings: You must not have been fired for failure to obey reasonable orders or to perform the duties for which you were hired; and you may be unable to receive compensation for any week during which you are unemployed due to a labor dispute or are too ill to look for work. I think that last condition is totally unfair.

This money can be a godsend when you're unemployed, so make sure that any future employer is required to pay the unemployment insurance tax. For example, in most states, you cannot establish an unemployment claim if you were working in agricultural, domestic, religious, insurance (only if on commission), and real estate sales. If you find that you are not eligible for state unemployment compensation, you may be covered under the Special Unemployment Assistance program. The benefits offered by SUA may also be available to some persons who have exhausted their state benefits. This is a temporary program paid for with emergency federal funds, but Congress will probably extend it as long as the economy is depressed.

Several other unemployment-related areas you should check out at your prospective place of employment are the job security, if any (is it under a merit system, or at the capricious discretion of your supervisor?); the amount of severance pay given to fired employees; appeals procedures to be used to protest dismissal; and a layoff plan conducted on a basis of seniority.

Although you may experience a period of unemployment, your goal will be to find another job and to settle back into the working routine as soon as you can.

Part-Time Work

There are many part-time jobs that can provide you with a modest income and yet allow you free time at home. You could take a lunchtime job at a school or at one of the fast-food chains. Or you could register with an agency that supplies temporary office help. The work is diversified (one week you may work in an office, the next as receptionist at a convention), and the pay is usually about twice the required minimum wage. You may work whenever you like, and may remove yourself from the register as you wish. There is no fee to be paid by you; the temporary employer pays the agency, and it pays you.

If you like the idea of selling real estate, you will probably need to take an examination qualifying you as an agent, but you will receive good commissions, have pleasant working hours and conditions, and may be able to set the days you want to work.

Register with your local election officials and ask to be put on their list of poll-workers; the pay is ample and you'll meet interesting people. The hours are long, generally from seven to seven, but voting days don't come so frequently that you will be exhausted.

Keeping House While Working

Plan your menu for the week, and do all your grocery shopping at one time. Use as many convenience foods as possible. Make dinners ahead and freeze them. Do a load of laundry in the morning before leaving for work (but don't leave the dryer running while you're gone). Fix your lunch at night, and plan and lay out the clothes you'll wear the next day. Clean a little each evening, so that you won't face a big chore on the weekend. Polish silver or give yourself a manicure while you're watching television in the evening. Establish and maintain a checklist of chores for each member of the family, rotating the schedule as much as is reasonable. Set the breakfast table at night, and put everything you'll need the next morning on a tray in the refrigerator or cupboard. Plan to serve frozen dinners on the evening you do your grocery shopping; they can be cooking while you put the groceries away. If you *must* iron (I am an ardent advocate of having as many wash-and-wear items as possible), do it one evening while your hair is drying or you're listening to your favorite records. (This is an excellent time to learn a foreign language by record.) Do as much of your shopping as you can by phone.

Keep a running list of things you'll need the next time you shop for groceries and personal items. Develop the habit of writing down an item as soon as you begin using the last you have; then you'll never run out of anything—from mascara to tomato sauce. If you have a pressure cooker or electrically controlled stewpot, take full advantage of their possibilities. Make friends with the operator of the neighborhood coin-operated laundry so that you can leave your load of wash while you do your grocery shopping. Take advantage of the coin-operated dry cleaning section offered by most self-service laundries. If there are several of you in the house getting ready for work or school at the same time, arrange a staggered schedule for use of the bathroom. Pack school lunches when you pack your own; you can save about $3 a week. And when you cash or deposit your paycheck, get a supply of coins for fares, tolls, coin machines, or school milk money. If you drive to work, stop at a car-wash on the way home one evening to avoid the weekend rush. Set aside one Saturday or Sunday each month to clean and do minor repairs on your car. And plan ahead so that you will have one day every few weeks with as few chores as possible—you deserve it.

Domestic Help

If you find that you won't be able to cope with a job outside the home and do housework as well, you might want to consider hiring domestic help. Unless you have friends who can recommend someone, you will probably have to go to an employment agency, either state or private. (Remember that you'll have to pay a fee if you go to the private one; you can't expect a domestic worker to pay it.) Tell the agency exactly what type of worker you want, the days she'll be required, and the kind of work she'll be doing. If the prospective employee has worked before, request three references, and check them carefully. Find out the current rate of pay for domestic help; you must pay minimum wages at least, and will probably have to go higher. The 1975 minimum is $2 per hour, but that will be increased in 1976 to $2.20, and to $2.30 in 1977.

Be prepared to pay Social Security for your employee if her salary from you exceeds $50 a quarter. You are required by law to pay a portion of the tax, but may elect to pay it in its entirety, as a fringe benefit. Outline her duties, her working hours, the days she'll have off, and holidays. It's best to have all of this in writing with a copy for each of you, so that there will be no future misunderstanding. Various organizations of domestic workers recommend that a day-worker be given one day of paid vacation per year for each day per week that she works for you, and that a live-in worker should receive two weeks of paid vacation after a year's employment. These organizations suggest that you allow one paid day off for sick leave for the day-worker per year, and six for the live-in helper. They recommend that the day-worker be given one paid legal holiday annually, if the holiday falls on a normal work day, and that live-in employees should have the same days off given to federal workers. Understand that these are merely suggestions; you can make your own arrangements with your employee.

Be sure that she is covered in your homeowners' or tenant's insurance policy in case of injury while on your premises. And if she has small children, decide if she may bring them with her during school vacations or in other specific instances. Discuss with her whether or not she would like you to withhold taxes from her salary; FICA taxes are mandatory, withholding are not. If you do withhold the tax, you will have to include in the total to be taxed any non-cash items such as food or clothing that you have given her as part of her pay. (These are *not* included as FICA wages.) But don't offer either item as salary or as gifts if you think that she will be offended. Give her the same courtesy and consideration that you expect from your own employer.

Call the Internal Revenue Service and ask for the "Employer's Tax Guide" (Circular E); it will furnish you with charts showing exactly how much Social Security should be withheld from her wages, and will guide you if you do withhold income tax, as well.

SELF-EMPLOYMENT

You may decide that the workaday world is not for you, but that you *do* need an income. The obvious answer for you is to become self-employed. There are more than 1½ million women who are doing just that, and the opportunities are boundless. This option is particularly appealing if you have small children whom you prefer not to leave in someone else's care.

Once again, you can call upon your domestic talents, if you have had no previous work experience; if you are a recent high school or college graduate you can utilize your special interests and hobbies. Remember never to say that you can't do anything; you've been doing *something* all your life, and now you have the chance to make good use of it. For instance, one young woman has turned her hobby—watching television —into a profitable operation. She watches soap operas and publishes a daily resume of the happenings for those fans who have to miss an episode or two. She sells subscriptions to her monthly newsletter for $7.50, and receives approximately one hundred new ones a week.

You can use the same sort of imagination and ingenuity to earn money at home.

To use one obvious example, if your talents lie in the kitchen, you can cook for profit in a variety of ways. (Before you begin, though, check with you local health board about any regulations concerning preparing food for the public.) If you have the space and equipment, you might like to offer cooking classes for students or young married couples. (Don't be surprised if as many men show up as women.) You can offer a catering service for children's parties or for weddings. You can cook your specialty for sale on certain days from your kitchen, or you can plan to deliver to your customers. (Figure travel time in your cost.) If you're good at cakes, supply them for birthdays and weddings. If you live close to a business district or vacation area, prepare sandwiches or complete lunches in attractive bags or boxes. Specialize in party foods, appetizers, or desserts if you don't want to cater an entire meal. Keep in mind that you are in competition with professionals and fast-food chains, so your service and food must be exceptional. If you do cater, work closely with the hostess and plan the menu to coincide with her party theme or decorations. (You might want to offer a line of decorations yourself.)

Making a Profit

Determining your price will be difficult; you'll have to see what others are charging and use those prices as a guide. As for specifics, when you total your expenses, include everything—food, electricity or gas, advertising, travel, the telephone, and your time. Keep accurate records to determine your overhead and the business deductions you will be entitled to take on your income tax return. As an example, if you are baking a cake, add the cost of materials and utilities plus a pro rata share of the other costs for the one item (use of telephone, so on). If you figure your time to be worth $3 an hour, and the expenses totaled $4, you'll have $7 in the cake, and your charge should reflect a reasonable profit, so you might want to charge anywhere from about $8.50 to $10. If you cater, your charge will be for each person served, so figure your costs the same way. A seated dinner may run as high as $12 per person (consider one-third of that to be profit); a buffet should run about half that amount; and you can cater a children's party for about $3 per guest. The amount you charge will depend on the costs in your area, the prices charged by your competition, and the quality and originality of your service.

Other Ways to Make Money at Home

If sewing is your thing, teach classes in dressmaking or needlework, and make items for sale. Turn a room of your home into a boutique, and invite other talented women to offer their goods for sale, giving you a share of their profits. Do some dressmaking or specialize in making items such as shawls, handbags, or skirts.

If you type well, you can do stenographic work and you can teach classes of beginners. (One at a time until you can buy additional typewriters.) The standard rate for stenography is generally $.75 to $1 a page, or a flat rate for a sizable job.

"Taking in laundry" has a Mrs. Wiggs of the Cabbage Patch sound to it, but why not give it a try? You could specialize in hard-to-launder items and those that require hand laundering and blocking. A fair charge for, say, an expensive cashmere sweater trimmed with jewels or fur would be about five dollars. You can consider renting your laundry appliances, if they are in good condition, to students and newlyweds, setting specific days and times and rules for care and use of the equipment.

Don't overlook the fact that many girls today have never learned the basic housecleaning skills; you could conduct classes in the art of housework. There's even a market for housecleaning services that offer doing weekly or monthly chores such as vacuuming, cleaning bathrooms, or waxing floors. The price would have to be set by the size and scope of the job. You would have to supply all the necessary tools and equipment. Advertise in a wealthy neighborhood, and ask your customers to recommend you to their friends.

If you are good with plants and flowers, turn this aptitude into profit. Teach flower arranging or horticulture, or open a small plant nursery. You can raise and sell vegetables and flowers, and do arrangements for churches, weddings, and parties. Again, add the total costs of materials and transportation, plus your time, then add a margin of profit.

There are more obvious methods of making money at home—telephone surveys and sales, housewares and cosmetics parties; but you might want to try some ways that are not so obvious, such as being a house-sitter for vacationers, watering plants and feeding pets. Or you might like to do personalized shopping for businessmen.

If you have any talent for arts and crafts, there is undoubtedly a ready market for the product or for your ability to teach the skill required to make it. When you conduct classes in anything, either have the students bring their own supplies or include the cost, if you supply them, in the price of the lesson.

There is no limit to the kinds of classes you can give, from music to painting to dancing to exercising. Just create a pleasant corner or room, and start teaching. In whatever you instruct, charge so much per session and offer a slightly lower rate if the student pays monthly or quarterly.

If you like to write, contact your neighborhood or church newspaper to see if they would like a how-to column on your speciality. Or check with a local publisher about free-lance proofreading or editing. Many businesses have employee magazines, for which feature articles are needed. And many people earn a living by writing articles and/or stories for national magazines.

The field is wide open for anyone interested in child care. You could begin by giving classes to expectant or new mothers, and go on into actual care of the children themselves. You could open a nursery or day-care center for other working mothers or contract to baby-sit at specified times.

You might want to investigate the feasibility of purchasing a franchise, and if you don't want the responsibility of the actual operation, you could hire a competent person to manage it for you. There are franchises for everything from fast-food chains to diet clubs to exercise and dance studios for sale, but be sure that the one in which you're interested is reputable and well-known. The more popular ones have waiting lists of prospective purchasers, and their costs may be prohibitive, but they generally make a good profit. Be careful to do some arithmetic before you decide; the overhead and purchase price may eat up all your profits. No matter what type of business you undertake there are three areas with which you must be concerned: advertising, local and federal laws, and your income taxes.

Advertising

Expect to set aside a certain amount of your income for advertising, but try to get as much free publicity as you can. Notify the feature editor of the newspaper about your occupation if it is unusual, and contact local clubs and service organizations about your services. If you make something, donate your wares to civic and religious bazaars, with your name prominently displayed. Enter every kind of exhibition that will feature your product. Put notices on school, supermarket, or church bulletin boards, and notify everyone you can think of who might be interested in your efforts. And if it isn't prohibited by local zoning laws, put a sign on your front lawn or on your house.

Laws

You will have to check out all local, state, and federal laws that may govern your particular business. For example, child care is strictly regulated by local health and welfare departments; food production is covered by rules of the state health department and by federal regulations of the Food and Drug Administration. Your state insurance commissioner will tell you the kinds of liability policies you may need. Ask government agencies to send all the information they have about operating a small business in your locale, and for federal information you can write to the

Superintendent of Documents (Washington, D.C., 20402) for *Starting and Managing a Small Business of Your Own* (35¢). This informative little book is published by the Small Business Administration; it also offers a free pamphlet, *Handicrafts and Home Businesses,* that is excellent. To get it and a list of other SBA publications, write to Small Business Administration, (Washington, D.C. 20416), ask for the booklet by name, and request SBA 115A and SBA 115B.

I've already stressed the importance of keeping accurate records, but if you operate your own business this is a legal necessity. As a self-employed person you will have certain tax liabilities, but you will also have substantial business deductions, too.

Taxes

Because your income will not be subject to withholding taxes, you will be required to estimate your taxes and pay them, with your Social Security contribution, quarterly. You will be required to file this estimate and pay the taxes if your total liability is going to be more than $100 *and* you can reasonably expect to receive more than $500 from your business or interest, dividends, and pensions, *or* if you expect your gross income to be more than $20,000. Your estimate can be based on the current year's income, using as a guide the total tax paid the previous year, or last year's income, or the actual tax for the current year. You must compute not only your income tax, but your self-employment (Social Security) tax, too. If you are just starting a business it will be difficult to anticipate its possible success, but you won't begin your operation unless you have some advance orders, probably, and if you don't make a profit, you can always amend the initial declaration and make no further payments. The first installment will have to be guesswork of a sort, but if you overpay your taxes, you will be entitled to a credit toward next year's taxes.

You may pay your estimated tax in full, if you wish, when you make your declaration, or in equal installments on or before the next April 15, June 15, September 15, and January 15 of the following year. If a payment is due you will have to send it with the first voucher. If you happen to have a salary during the same year in which you are self-employed, the amounts of tax withheld from your wages are considered payments of estimated tax made in equal amounts on the four installment dates, and you can request that your employer withhold larger amounts to cover any liability. If you want to file your Form 1040 with the final payment before January 31, you need not meet the January 15 deadline for that payment alone. Because estimated tax payments are merely a means of satisfying your tax obligation that would ordinarily be due for the year, you will still be required to file the return as usual. (Of course, you'll be eager to do that anyway, so that you will be able to deduct your business expenses.)

The self-employment tax provides Social Security coverage for those persons who earn more than $400 per year in self-employment income. This is a tax predetermined by the maximum amount of wages covered by the law in a certain year. For example, the maximum amount in 1974 was $13,200, in 1975, $14,100. The amount earned is multiplied by .079 to find the tax, so that if your income from self-employment is $8000 for the year, your tax will be $632. This is figured into the total estimated tax and will be paid quarterly with each voucher.

You will be allowed to deduct certain expenses incurred in the conduct of your business. In addition to the obvious ones for supplies and necessary equipment, you will be able to deduct what the IRS terms "office in the home expense." To deduct a pro rata portion of the usual maintenance and depreciation costs of a house or apartment, you will have to be able to establish that you regularly use a part of your residence to earn your business income, what portion is so used, and the extent of the use.

To determine the amount of space you use, you may try either the square feet method, or the number of rooms method. They are both simple: Figure the percentage used in your business and deduct that portion from your ordinary expenses of maintaining your home. For example, using the square feet method, if your home has 2,000 square feet of total floor space, and you use a room measuring ten by twelve feet, you're using 120 square feet in your business. Dividing 120 by 2000, you would find that the percentage would be six. Therefore, you would be entitled to deduct 6 percent of your total cost for business purposes. The number of rooms method is exactly the same; if there are eight rooms and you use two, the percentage would be two-eighths, or 25 percent.

If you are unable to allocate a room solely to your business and it must be available at other times for family or personal use, you will have to make a further computation based on time. For instance, if you use the square feet method, and have determined that your allowable percentage is six (using the above figures), but that you use the room only two hours a day for your business, then you will consider the two hours as two-twenty-fourths of the day (one-twelfth). That figure, multiplied by 6 percent, will be the deductible total. Assume that you had home expenses of $2,000; multiply that by 6 percent to get $120; and multiply that by one-twelfth, and the allowable amount will be $10. Not a large sum, but everything that is a legitimately deductible expense should be claimed on your return.

What are other qualifying expenses? They include depreciation, real estate taxes, mortgage interest, heat and electricity, water (if it is necessary in the operation of the business), and maintenance or repairs of the space you use for your business. These expenses and your business income will be entered on Schedule C, Profit or Loss from Business or Profession, and will be attached to your Form 1040, together with your computation of Social Security self-employment tax, on Form SE.

There is a lot of paperwork connected with any business, but don't be dismayed. You can receive help from the IRS in setting up your business and they will help you adhere to the law. Ask at any office for their Publication 334, *Tax Guide for Small Business,* and for all the forms and instructions you will need. If you go to any IRS office the tax representatives will show you exactly how and when the forms should be completed and filed, and will answer the numerous questions you are sure to have. And while you're there, investigate the Keogh Plan, which entitles you to set up a retirement fund that is tax-exempt up to $7,500 per year, or 15 percent of your yearly earnings, whichever is less. Your money will have to be on deposit with a qualifying financial institution or plan, but the plan affords you the opportunity to invest a respectable sum toward your retirement years.

If you need moral encouragement to spur you on your way to financial independence, don't lose sight of the fact that this is *still* the land of opportunity, and that there is always room on the market for the right product or service. Fortunes have been made by women and men acting on an idea whose time had come. Witness the success of home permanents, instantly developed film, and a philosophy and plan to aid overweight people. The satisfaction you will feel at even a minor achievement will be indescribable; you may even be one of the fortunate ones who will make a great deal of money.

When you work, there is an added benefit—you will be involved with people and ideas, and you won't have time to think only of yourself or your problems—work is a wonderful escape. Also, you will have to look well-groomed, and take an interest in your clothes and appearance—this never hurts a woman alone.

I am a firm adherent of the American work ethic; I'm a latecomer to the labor force, but a proud member of it. I enjoy work; I like the knowledge that I am capable of doing a job for which someone feels that I should be paid. I like the pride I feel in doing a job well, to the best of my ability and training. I like having a profession, and I like being an identifiable part of the business scene. I loved being Mrs. George Yates, and I loved being known as my children's mother, but in both cases, my identity was dependent on someone else, as if I had none of my own. Now I have—I enjoy a sense of being *me,* an individual, a person in my own right. That is fulfillment of the finest sort.

Before I worked for a living I often wondered how men could commit themselves to a lifetime of supporting and providing for a family. I found the answer the very first time I brought home to my family food and provisions that I had paid for with money I had earned. Not with money from insurance or Social Security or the architectural practice before I closed the office; all that money had been the direct result of George's labors. But my paycheck was *mine;* I had worked for it and I had earned it. Nothing can compare with that satisfaction, and nothing is more important to your sense of well-being than to do work that gives a feeling of accomplishment and pride and a full realization of yourself as a productive person.

11

COPING WITH CREDIT
AND WOMEN'S LIB

Not as Simple as You Think

You may wonder why credit and Women's Lib are given "equal billing" in this chapter. The reason is simple: establishing credit is a very important accomplishment for anyone in our credit-oriented society. It is almost impossible for a week to go by without our having to use some sort of charge card. The jokes about money becoming obsolete are too close to the truth to be funny; there is almost nothing that can't be bought on credit, from a pair of shoes to a tank of gasoline to a vacation trip. The woman alone must establish credit to run her household. And the woman alone, for reasons that are central to the very existence of the feminist movement, finds it particularly hard to do this. Many is the woman who, in applying for a charge card (even in a place where she is well known and trusted), suddenly finds that her identity as a separate, valid human individual is questioned. Time after time such applications are refused or returned as incomplete because a husband's name is not included. The women's movement is involved in the daily legislative, social, and economic battle for equal individual human rights; no matter where you stand in relation to Women's Lib, it is bringing about important changes in *your* life as a woman alone.

CREDIT

ESTABLISHING A CREDIT RATING

You should know the steps to follow in order to establish a good credit rating. First, go to the bank in which you have your checking account and ask for a signature loan. Such a loan is generally offered only to borrowers known to the officials of the bank, but as a depositor you may qualify. Nothing will be lost by asking, and if you are refused, find out the basis for giving such a loan so that you will know how to become eligible. If you are refused a signature loan, be prepared to offer collateral. It can be anything you own, but must be of a value at least equal to the amount you want to borrow. Ask for a comparatively small loan—$100 should be about right for the first time—and ask that it be repayable in thirty or sixty days. (Take the shortest term they will offer; you're only interested in getting the loan and paying it back as soon as possible.)

Do *not* permit the bank to require a co-signer; if the subject is even suggested, ask to see the president and lodge a formal complaint. It is highly unlikely that they would ask for a co-signer if a man were initiating the same loan; demand the same consideration.

When you've gotten your loan, put it into your savings account so that it will be earning the money to pay part of the interest you'll have to pay on the loan; after all, there's no sense of running the risk of being unable to repay it. That's *not* the way to establish a sound credit foundation. Repay the loan at the end of the period stated in the agreement. There is no particular advantage to repaying early except on some long-term loans; then the bank may give you a small rebate for prepayment. (Always check with the bank to find out whether or not they like early payments; some don't.)

Be prepared to pay interest on your loan, of course. It will probably run about 9 percent or more, but it will be worth that to establish a sound credit rating.

Continue taking out and repaying small loans, gradually increasing the amount. Each completed transaction will add to your standing in the credit world, and will make it easier for you to take out a loan when you really need one.

You'll have more trouble opening charge accounts, but your newly established rating should help. You will have to supply a fairly complete financial record, showing your income and debts, so that the company will know if you are going to be able to meet your charge commitments. Again, if you feel that your financial status warrants an account and it is denied, go right to the top. Generally, the pattern is the same whenever you apply for credit —the creditor is interested in your previous bill-paying performance, your residence (where you live, how long, whether you own or rent), your income and other assets. It will also want character references and employment records.

You can see the difficulty you are going to face until you have lived in one place for a while and have been employed at one job for an appreciable period of time. These standards may be set aside arbitrarily if your income and assets are large, but don't count on it. This cautious attitude taken by creditors is understandable, and would apply equally to male and female applicants, but when you have established yourself in the community, if you still encounter obstacles, go directly to the top of the organization and demand to know the reason for the discrimination.

Don't let me mislead you; establishing credit in your own name is not going to be easy, although each year we have gained new ground in our fight for financial equality. For instance, when George died in 1970 I canceled all charge accounts because I knew I wouldn't be able to maintain them. As card-carrying members of our "charge-now-pay later" society we had had many accounts, and used them lavishly. (I said "we" had accounts; of course you know that I mean they were in George's name.) I used to whip out those George Yates credit cards without a thought of what they represented, but when I was without them, I realized how convenient they were. Surprisingly, one oil company called to ask if I would like to have an account in my own name; I didn't realize it then, but when I accepted the offer I took my first step toward my new George-less identity. I was frightened and thrilled.

It wasn't that easy in other cases, however, and even today I can still open an account in his name more easily than I can in my own.

Congress is trying to help us. In 1973 the Senate passed an amendment to the Truth in Lending Act prohibiting discrimination in credit practices on the basis of sex or marital status. That's great on paper; but getting your potential creditor to honor it is another matter.

Martha W. Griffiths, Congresswoman from Michigan, has testified that "men and women today don't have equal access to credit. Banks, savings and loan associations, credit-card companies, finance companies, insurance companies, retail stores and even the federal government discriminate against women in all stages of life—whether single, married, divorced or widowed; with or without children, rich or poor, young or old." Virginia H. Knauer, the Administration's Director of Consumer Affairs, told the 1972 International Consumer Credit Conference that "the reasoning used to deny women credit is often a cobweb of myths and suppositions unsupported by research on the statistical risks involved or on the individual's credit-worthiness." Feminist groups are in the forefront of this battle for credit equality, often picketing stores that have a poor record in their credit relations with women. Spokeswomen for the groups say that we will continue to have problems until our access to credit equality is established as a right. They believe that every denial of credit must be challenged until credit is given as easily to a woman as to a man.

Hopefully, it will be easier for any woman who has met all the standards used by creditors (income, length of residence, so on) to obtain credit. In October 1975 the Equal Credit Opportunity Act went into effect, making it a violation of federal law to deny credit because of sex or marital status.

If credit is denied, you can sue in federal court for damages suffered, plus up to $10,000 in punitive damages. A class action suit on behalf of a group of applicants charging discrimination can cost the creditor up to $100,000. The drawbacks, of course, are that the denied applicant will have to take the initiative to bring suit (that will involve fees of various kinds), and will have to be able to prove discrimination because of sex.

There's no question that credit makes buying easier; you can have those things you want or need now, instead of waiting until you've saved the money for them. Credit buying provides a record of your expenses and of the deductible interest and finance charges. You can borrow for unexpected emergencies, and by planning your installment buying wisely, it offers a form of budgeting your major expenses. The advantages are numerous, but you must be realistic and recognize the disadvantages of credit, too.

THE COST OF CREDIT

You're going to have to pay, and pay well, for your credit. It is, after all, a service offered to you by the merchant or financial institution, which expects to be paid for allowing the use of its goods or money on an extended-payment basis. The finance charge is set by law at 1½% per month, for a total of 18% per year—a substantial rate under any circumstances—and you may have other interest and carrying charges as well.

But the biggest hazard of credit buying is the temptation to overspend. If you were paying cash you would be able to buy only those goods for which you could pay at the time; with credit, you can buy much more than with your actual cash on hand, and may saddle yourself with payments far beyond your ability to pay. You'll have to be cautious and know exactly what you're agreeing to spend.

Check over the credit contract carefully. Make sure it states the date of the transaction; the name and address of the buyer and seller (it will probably call you the debtor and the seller will be called the lender); the trade-in allowance or down payment, if any; the cash price; the credit price; the description of any property pledged as guarantee of payment; the total amount to be paid (unpaid balance); the amount charged for credit and an itemized list of any other charges; the number and amount of payments; any insurance coverage; and any penalties or other consequences if you pay late, miss a payment, or fail to pay. Don't sign until you understand all the terms of the contract, and be sure that you are given a copy. Put it with your other important papers and adhere to the payment terms religiously. You'll be building up your own favorable credit ledger each time you satisfactorily fulfill the terms of one of these credit contracts.

If anything happens and you are unable to make your payments, contact the lender immediately and come to terms with him about an extension of time, if possible. This is the very thing you'll want to avoid, however; a repetition of failure to pay will jeopardize your hard-won credit standing. If it does happen, however, and you learn that you have a bad rating, pay what you owe as soon as you can. You may want to take out one loan to consolidate all your debt payments into one. Then contact your local credit bureau to see what further steps will be necessary to re-establish a good rating.

With judicious buying, however, you're not going to let that happen, so use your credit wisely and enjoy it. Comparison shop among creditors exactly as you would among any other merchants, and make sure that the payments will fit your budget. You don't have to finance through a dealer— you can get a better rate from a bank, for example, with interest as much as 6% lower.

CREDIT PROBLEMS

So that you can guard against overextending yourself financially, the National Foundation for Consumer Credit has prepared a checklist of danger signals warning of impending disaster. If you answer "yes" to at least two of the following quesions, you are facing potential problems. If the answer is "yes" to three or more, you are already in trouble.

1. Do you charge small every-day expenditures—such as groceries and toiletries—because you don't have the money to pay for them?
2. Have you recently postponed paying a bill "until next month" due to lack of funds to cover it?
3. Do you have to borrow money to pay fixed expenses such as quarterly tax payments, insurance premiums, loan installments?
4. Are some of your telephone calls or letters from creditors demanding payment of overdue bills?
5. Do annual payments on long-term debts amount to more than twenty percent of your annual income?
6. Are you unable to say exactly how much money you owe on installment and other long-term debts?

If you answered "yes" to three or more, to whom do you turn for help?

The National Foundation for Consumer Credit, for instance, sponsors debt-counseling in more than one hundred communities throughout the country. Write for the location of the office nearest you to NFCC (1819 H Street, N.W., Washington, D.C. 20003). Send a stamped, self-addressed envelope for a prompt answer. Contact your bank about any counseling services offered (I mentioned this in Chapter 6) or ask your local family service association for suggested agencies. Most counseling agencies offer their services free or for only a small fee ($5 or $10). Avoid the debt "adjuster" or "consolidater"; he will charge an initial fee (usually $25 or more), plus 12 to 15 percent of the total debt.

BANKRUPTCY

If you ever find yourself head over heels in debt and have exhausted every other means available, you may have to consider filing for bankruptcy. (I think it is highly unlikely that this will ever happen to you if you continue to follow the rules for financial solvency we've already covered, but you should know all the facts, anyway.)

Forget the horror stories you've heard about bankruptcy; the U.S. Bankruptcy Act was designed to help the person unable to pay his or her debts, and in a period of depressed economy the courts are full of bankruptcy cases.

Find a lawyer who is familiar with bankruptcy laws. Consult your local bar association for recommendations, and select the attorney with whom you feel most comfortable. Ask him about the alternative to bankruptcy to which you may be entitled. Through the Wage-Earner Plan under Chapter XIII of the Federal Bankruptcy Act you may be allowed to pay your debts by installments—with the approval of your creditors—and on a schedule arranged by the court. If you can use Chapter XIII do so; if you declare bankruptcy you may be unable to obtain some types of future employment, and the record will be maintained with credit bureaus for at least seven years.

Filing for bankruptcy can be very expensive; the lawyer's fee (he'll agree to installment payments) will run from $150 to $400 or more, and it will cost you about $50 to file. Then, according to law, a statement of your assets and liabilities is given to the clerk in the U.S. District Court, it is referred to the nearest bankruptcy referee's office, and the referee takes over from there. He (a lawyer appointed by the court) will send a notice to all your creditors, call a meeting with them, and agree with them on a trustee who will collect and organize your assets and pay your debts. The trustee, under supervision of the referee, will liquidate all your assets and pay all your bills in a manner stipulated by law. Some creditors take precedence over others (any outstanding tax will be paid first), and some may receive nothing at all.

You will not be left destitute; federal law allows each state to determine what will be left to you, and all states insist that you be left a reasonable amount of money or assets. For example, California allows you to keep any house in which you have an equity no greater than $20,000, and all states allow you to keep clothes and "tools of trade," which in some cases could be a car. The entire process generally runs a year, and at the end of that time the referee will grant you a "discharge" from bankruptcy. If you haven't tried to hide any assets or perpetrated a fraud, the case will be closed, and you will no longer be held liable for any debts (except taxes) incurred before you filed for bankruptcy, so you may make a new financial start.

But you're not going to allow yourself to be put in the position of having to worry about bankruptcy; you're going to be very careful about over-extending your debt ceiling.

DEBT CEILINGS

Just how much can you safely owe? Credit payments (after housing) should be no more than 20 percent of your annual income after taxes; and short-term debts (loans or credit-buying for a one-year period) should be no more than one and one-half times your monthly income. Inflation can make the 20 percent too high as more of your income goes for necessities, so gauge your spending accordingly.

The U.S. Bureau of Economic Analysis has offered the following as the picture of the average nonmortgage credit debts of a family of four:

Debt		*Amount*
Installment credit		
Automobile		$ 895
Other consumer goods		775
Home repair and modernization		125
Personal loans		720
	Sub-total	2,515
Non-installment credit		
Single payment loans		235
Charge accounts		155
Service Credit		170
	Sub-total	560
Total consumer credit		$3,075

The chart is divided into installment and noninstallment credit because the payments, circumstances, and charges are entirely different. A car loan, for instance, usually runs for three years, although you may request a two-year note. The shorter the term, the smaller the interest. Even though the per-month interest payment will be greater, you will be paying it for a shorter amount of time. For example, if you have a $3,500 car loan, with a monthly payment of $115 (these are hypothetical figures) for a 36-month loan, the total cost would be $4,140, while the same loan, repaid in 30 months at $135 a month, would cost you $4,050.

The same rule holds true for any loan; the longer it runs, the more it will cost, so do some arithmetic before you buy—and don't be tempted by lower interest rates over a longer period of time.

If you'd like to find out exactly what the charge for any kind of credit should be, write to Consumer Information, (Public Documents Distribution Center, Pueblo, Col. 81009) and ask for the free booklet 075B, *What Truth in Lending Means to You.*

It is obvious that the sooner installment loans can be repaid the better, and the same holds true for charge accounts. There are several different kinds, and some can pose serious credit problems for the unwary consumer.

CHARGE ACCOUNTS

The basic department store charge account is generally called a "regular" account, although the name may vary from store to store. On this type, you are billed monthly for the purchases of the preceding month, and there is no finance charge if the balance due is paid in full. Revolving charge accounts allow you to make additional purchases, to be charged to your account, while you still owe money for previous purchases. If you pay in full within the next billing period there will be no added charges, but if you prefer delayed payment, you will pay interest or finance charges on the unpaid balance. The total amount that you can charge was limited when you opened your account; either you or the credit manager determined your credit line, and you will not be allowed to exceed it. The charges usually run from 12 to 18% annually, so you can expect to pay $12 to $18 a year for every $100 you owe. You'll have to be very careful about when you make your monthly payments; if they are received after the due date, the amount will still be carried on the books, and you will pay interest on it again next month.

There are two kinds of revolving charges, one requiring that you pay a percentage of the bill, and the other requiring a percentage of your credit limit. In other words, if you have the former, your bill for the month is $100, and the store requires that you pay 10 percent of each month's bill, you will pay $10, including interest charges. If the account requires a percentage of your credit line to be paid monthly, and your limit is set at $400, you will have to pay $40 a month, regardless of your balance. You might owe only $80, but you'd have to pay $40, anyway. I much prefer the percentage-of-the-balance type, but you'll have to accept the kind offered by your store.

Watch the statement's billing date; especially in the case of more expensive items, you can delay payment for two months if you shop at the right time. For example, if you buy a mattress just after the store's billing date, the item will not appear on your statement until the next month, and you will have until the *next* month's billing date to pay without penalty. You will be able to use this extended-payment method only if your account is carried on the adjusted balance system. If it is on the daily balance system, the sooner you pay your bills, the better. Check with the store's credit manager to see which method is used, and charge and pay accordingly. It's a tricky thing to try, though, so only use it if you really have to delay payment for a couple of months.

It goes without saying that you will check all your statements very carefully. Bookkeeping errors are common, and you may find yourself billed for something you haven't bought, for the same item twice, or you may find that you have not received credit for a bill already paid. If you notice a sudden change in your interest rate, call the bookkeeping department immediately for an explanation. You may have become the unwitting victim of a new twist on the credit game. Because it is no longer legal to send unsolicited credit cards through the mail (too many were being stolen and used by people for whom they were not intended, with the original recipient being billed for the amount due), some credit card companies are buying the credit departments of retail stores. As a result, you may find yourself being billed through a bank credit card system instead of through the store, and at a much higher rate of interest. If you are asked to pay a higher rate without prior notice, or if you want to lodge a protest, report the circumstances to the Federal Reserve Board (Truth in Lending Section, Washington, D.C. 20551).

CONSUMERISM

Everything concerned with credit is inextricably interwoven with the exciting new field of consumerism. At last the public is demanding—and getting—stricter controls on the quality of goods and services for which it is paying premium prices. Consumer groups lobby and disseminate information and influence legislation protecting every person in the country, and governments—nationally and locally—have established consumer action departments to investigate complaints and enforce compliance with the proliferating laws. Because of the influence of these organizations and the increasing public demands for protection against shoddiness and dangerous workmanship, the federal government is even regulating the safety of imported products. The U.S. Customs Bureau reports that the Consumer Products Safety Commission has begun new surveillance and inspection practices for customs clearance of goods from abroad.

But while the government and private agencies are protecting you, what can you do for yourself? You can become a better-informed consumer, and you can complain when a complaint is warranted.

You can read the various magazines dedicated to evaluating products and foods that are on the market, and become acquainted with the minimum safety and health standards required by the government. Consumerism is simply a new word for old-fashioned common sense and dollar-wisdom. No matter how much is done for you, it does you no good if you fail to take advantage of the strides taken to protect you and your money.

MAKING COMPLAINTS

We have been trained in courtesy from birth, and most of us shudder to think of causing a scene. But, sad to say, the old truism about the rusty wheel getting the grease is exactly on target. There's an art to being a successful complainer, and every consumer should learn it.

I repeat: Go to the top of any organization. Don't be stopped by an intermediary. If the secretary says that the person is out or is on another line or is in conference, keep calling back every fifteen minutes, politely giving your name and number each time, until you finally get through. (This will eventually happen, if only to clear the telephone line.) Make sure that you have a legitimate grievance, and be prepared to present the facts in a logical, unemotional way. When you talk with the person you wanted, make your point and see that he or she understands that you will not be satisfied until you have received justification or explanation or redress.

Don't worry that you will be halting the wheels of industry and business by taking up a few minutes of the executive's time. As a customer/consumer/client/constituent, you are entitled to be heard. Follow the conversation with a letter. Briefly review the reason for your call, the date and time it occurred, and express your thanks for the action taken or about to be taken on your behalf, or repeat that you will not be satisfied until corrective measures are in effect. Make copies of the letter (be sure the executive knows this) and mail them to the Better Business Bureau, a consumer action group, any professional association that might be concerned, and any state agency involved.

Never hesitate to contact your local legislator by phone or mail. Let him or her know your grievance; request action, if necessary. Suggest that appropriate legislation be introduced if none is on the books; make it clear that you expect results from your complaint. Don't worry about taking up the legislator's time, either. You (or some other constituents) put this person into office—and can take him out again—and his business is you and introducing laws to help and protect you. Become a one-woman lobby, and make yourself heard—if your complaint and cause are just, you will be. Develop consumer clout and learn to use it.

Be sure that when you have a complaint you send it to the right organization or agency. For any consumer problem, write to the Office of Consumer Affairs (U.S. Department of Health, Education and Welfare, Washington, D.C. 20201); referrals will be made to other federal agencies.

To report dangerous design or use of any product, write to the Consumer Product Safety Commission (Washington, D.C. 20207); any sales or business frauds can be reported to your state Attorney General or the Better Business Bureau (1150 17th Street, N.W., Washington, D.C. 20036). The Federal Trade Commission (Washington, D.C. 20580) will investigate complaints about deceptive advertising and fabric labeling, while questions about the safety or purity of foods, drugs, and cosmetics can be sent to the Food and Drug Administration (U.S. Department of HEW, at the address given for the Office of Consumer Affairs).

Complaints about mail service can be directed to the U.S. Postal Service (Chief Postal Inspector, Washington, D.C. 20260), and if you want to complain about the receipt of junk mail, write to Direct Mail Advertising Association (230 Park Ave., New York, N.Y. 10017). If you have problems with any major appliance and receive no satisfaction from the dealer or manufacturer, write to Major Appliance Consumer Action Panel (20 N. Wacker Drive, Chicago, Ill. 60606), and state your grievance. Be sure to include the make and model number of the item in question. And if you have had any trouble with the quality, utility, or delivery of any piece of furniture, contact Furniture Industry Consumer Action Panel (P.O. Box 951, High Point, N.C. 27261); for carpets, the address is Carpet and Rug Industry Consumer Action Panel (P.O. Box 1568, Dalton, Ga. 30720).

Take advantage of every legitimate means available to make your complaints; you will be doing yourself and other consumers a service.

WOMEN'S LIBERATION

When you apply for credit based on your own income and receive it; when you apply for a job formerly restricted to men and are hired because you are qualified; when you find job opportunities never before open to women; when you can go to any formerly all-male stronghold; when you see the awakened demand for women's rights to equality under the law; when you see the efforts being made to protect us from discrimination in housing, in the courts, in every area of our lives, you can be grateful to the handful of concerned women who have fought your battles for you. And you can be absolutely positive that you *still* wouldn't have those rights if they had not fought vigorously against discrimination, in spite of the most strenuous opposition.

You can thank the leaders of the Civil Rights Movement, too, because they unknowingly set the pattern of protest, and made America look long and hard at its inequitable treatment of some of its citizens. They altered the temper of the times, and set the stage for Act 2—the Women's Liberation Movement.

There have been a few hardy souls in the past who have tried to change our lot; they tried to get the vote for us for forty years before we were finally franchised in 1920. (Blacks—correction: black *men*—had been given the right to vote fifty years earlier, in 1870.) And the only reason women were *ever* granted that privilege was that a few hundred valiant women marched and chanted and chained themselves to iron railings to draw attention to the fact that females were entitled to suffrage. We can all be thankful for those women, and for the latter-day militants who have gained so much for us in such a short time.

From what do we want to be liberated? From the restrictions with which society (male) has bound us to make us fit a prescribed role. From being stereotyped because we are women, rarely considered as individuals. From being treated as if any intelligence we show is in spite of our sex. From being talked down to because we are women ("the little woman," "woman driver," "just like a woman").

Because we've never been hung up on anything as adolescent as machismo; because we aren't ashamed to cry, we're considered the weaker sex. Weaker than what? Or whom? Certainly most of us are not as physically strong as men, but what does that prove? We survive childbirth, menstrual cramps, and menopause, and they all demand physical and emotional strength unknown to men. We live longer, commit fewer suicides, kill fewer people, and don't start wars. We have strength of every kind. So why shouldn't we use those strengths now to achieve the equality that has been denied us?

The women's groups all have a few things in common: They all are concerned to some degree with abortion reform, establishment of day-care centers, the issue of equal pay, and the general status of women. They attempt to raise the level of women's consciousness about the conditions of women and to urge legislative reform.

ORGANIZATIONS

As with Civil Rights groups, there are factions within the feminist movement, and a group for almost any specific interest.

It all began with the National Organization for Women (NOW), founded by Betty Friedan; NOW is still the largest and most influential group, with approximately 50,000 members. Considered to be too conservative by some women, NOW works within each community to try to change the laws and discriminatory practices within that area. (It has chapters in every major city, and if you are interested in joining or in organizing your own chapter, write to P.O. Box 1455, Detroit, Mich. 48231.)

WEAL, Women's Equity Action League (7657 Dines Road, Novelty, Ohio 44072), is thought to be the second largest group and one of the most effective. It concentrates on economic oppression of women, limiting its actions to attacking tax inequities and discrimination in employment and education. OWL (Older Women's Liberation) is located only in New York, but is a good prototype for an organization concentrating on the problems of women over 30. This group has drawn up a "Housewives' Bill of Rights," demanding unionization, six-day work weeks, health insurance, and paid vacations. KNOW, Inc. (P.O. Box 10197, Pittsburgh, Pa. 15230) is primarily interested in disseminating information about the movement. FEW (Federally Employed Women) is especially interested in ending all discrimination within the federal government, and has chapters in various cities all over the country. (Contact the federal job information center in your area for particulars about the nearest chapter.)

I mentioned "consciousness-raising" in passing, and you will hear that phrase continually as you learn more about the movement. In simple terms, it means the gradual awareness of some of the slights and indignities we have accepted as our due, because we are women. We have always lived with these slights, but most women probably never really think about them until they encounter some of the knowledge vocalized by women's groups.

When you try to establish a credit rating you are thrust, ready or not, onto the battlefield of women's rights. Your consciousness may then be raised when you watch television ads depicting us as feather-brained ninnies who can't think beyond the evening's meal. Even men notice the way we're degraded. Norman Marks, writing for the *Chicago Daily News,* said of daytime television commercials that they "are overloaded with stereotypes of housewives as dutiful drudges—women whose real devotion is to their cats, dogs, their bodies, toilet bowls, sink drains or their husbands' stopped-up noses. Until those ads change their images of American womanhood, all the efforts of the woman's movement become meaningless in the face of the more important question: 'What are you hungry for when you don't know what you're hungry for?' The answer is Ritz crackers, not equality as human beings."

SEXISM

I haven't used the term "sexist" before, but we all hear it constantly these days. Basically, it is a catch-all word describing the attitude of most men—and sadly, some women—that it is in the divine order of things for men to dominate the world and everything in it, including women. (Of course there are women today guilty of sexist attitudes toward *men.* They are trying to obtain women's rights at the expense of men's rights, thus denying the principle of equal opportunity for all.) The most insulting thing a man can do is to pat us figuratively on the head with a "There, there, little woman, don't worry your little self about anything but woman's work. Let

me take care of the important things." Carole Fogel, head of the Human
Rights Commission in Saskatchewan, Canada, says that a good test of
whether or not a statement is sexist is to change the word "woman" to
"black." "Being a sexist is not considered necessarily a bad thing. Being a
racist is very bad. Nobody will publicly admit to being a racist."

I don't understand the oppostion of some women to equal rights. Men,
yes; they feel threatened, economically and sexually by the women's movement. And yet, in the 1974 Virginia Slims American Women's Opinion
Poll conducted by The Roper Organization, the answers of some of the
women were appallingly out of tune with contemporary conditions.

For example, three in four of the women polled refused to complain that
being a woman has prevented them from doing the things they have wanted
to in life. (My opinion is that either their goals were extremely limited or
they weren't being absolutely honest.) Two out of three preferred having a
loving husband to making it on their own. (Note the key word "loving," and
the term "making it on their own"; with choices like that, I'd vote the same
way. Why not ask if they would prefer marriage to a career? That doesn't
sound so negative. But why do we have to make a choice anyway?) And
over half deny that being born one sex or the other provides an advantage.
Girls! Where have you been? Surely not competing with men for jobs.
Surely not applying at a country club for membership. Certainly not fighting
off a rapist. And certainly not having the door closed in your face when
you apply for credit or loans or housing.

I suspect that the Roper questioners went to women who work for the
rest of the survey—I don't see how the women who answered the first
queries could possibly have been the same as those who answered the
following. More than two out of three thought they have to try harder and
be much better at their work than men to make it as business executives
and government officials, and almost half charged discrimination in getting
skilled jobs. More than half cited difficulty in obtaining charge accounts,
loans, and mortgages; and although 96 percent called marriage the most
satisfying and interesting way of life, nearly half were reported as preferring
a marriage in which the husband and wife share work, homemaking, and
child-rearing responsibilities. You've come a long way, baby, but you've
still got a long way to go.

Anti-Feminism

We who are ardent in our search for equality are frequently accused of
wanting to emasculate men, which isn't really surprising when you remember that many men equate money power with sexual power. But sex has
nothing to do with our struggle except to the extent that we will refuse to
be discriminated against because of our own. There are those who think all

feminists are anti-sex. And there are some who equate feminism with lack of femininity. Admittedly, there are some avowed lesbians in many of the activist groups; but they are probably in your office or PTA, too—they're just not as honest and open about it.

The anti-feminist who says that woman's place is in the home is pursuing a pointless argument; women have been in the classrooms and offices and restaurants and other people's kitchens and the hospitals, working and teaching and serving and helping others for fifty years. There are too many of us working (most because we have to) to make this objection valid. I wonder if these critics have really contemplated the disaster that would occur if we took their advice and *went* home? What if every woman in every office, every nurse in every hospital, every teacher in every school, every female worker in every factory, every clerk in every store, every telephone operator in every city, every waitress in every restaurant just walked out and went home? The nation would come to a shuddering, nerve-jolting stop. Sure, some of the jobs could be filled by men, but not all; the families the women were supporting would still have to be supported by someone, somehow.

The noted anthropologist Margaret Mead has said that "unless we change the status of women, giving them other jobs than having children, we will not know what we can do." She added, "In all of civilization it has been impossible to find out what women's gifts are because they have been so busy having babies. We have never yet tried out their brains on science or the arts. In every life we know anything about, the public life belongs to the men. Every time you liberate a woman, you liberate a man."

I'm convinced that the main issue separating the supporters of the feminists and their opponents has been a lack of clear understanding of the goals and objectives of the woman's movement. This lack of understanding is apparent in the tangle of half-truths and misconceptions surrounding the Equal Rights Amendment. Probably opinion has not been so sharply divided on any single issue since Prohibition or the Vietnam War.

Let's dispel some of the myths surrounding the controversial amendment.

The Equal Rights Amendment

The whole thrust of the ERA is to guarantee "equality of rights under the law." It pertains to government action, public employment, and those small businesses not included in Title VII of the Civil Rights Act of 1964. It will not in any way affect social customs or personal relationships between men and women, nor will it affect those laws that are based purely on differences between the sexes, as in rape laws. It will not cause women to lose support rights. It will eliminate the supposition that the male is automatically responsible for the support of the family, and it will assure that awards upon divorce are made according to each individual's needs and circumstances. It will eliminate the right of husbands, in most community-property states, to have sole control of the marital property. It will invalidate existing laws giving either parent preference in child custody cases (in some states the father is given legal preference for boys and older children); and will assure that judges determine such cases based on what is best for the child.

The ERA will not force sexually integrated public rest rooms, dormitories, school locker rooms, prisons, public hospitals, army barracks, and so on. The 1965 Supreme Court ruling establishing the constitutional right to privacy permits the separation of the sexes in all places that involve sleeping, disrobing, or other private functions. It will put an end to discriminatory Social Security benefits and pensions, and it will assure that a woman, convicted of the same crime as a man, will not receive a more severe sentence, as is often the case. It will put pressure on unions, employers, and insurance companies to treat maternity leave the same as any other temporary disability, and it will end jury exemptions because of sex. It will end discrimination in relation to admission to universities and military academies, and it will end discrimination in regard to military service.

That last point is the stumbling block for all but the most fervent supporters, until the facts are explained. As far as young women are concerned, Congress has had the power to draft them since World War II, and actually contemplated drafting nurses at that time. At present there is no military draft, but several hundred thousand women volunteers are serving in the armed forces. Under the ERA, women would be required to register at their draft boards at age 18, and if the draft were begun again, they would be subject to the same physical and mental tests as would the men, and would receive assignments according to their capabilities. But there are some vital facts to remember. Only one in ten persons in the armed forces ever engages in combat. Women would be entitled to the same draft exemptions as men (marriage and college attendance are usually acceptable for a draft-exempt status). And there probably would be exemptions for any person who has the sole responsibility of taking care of a child. But most importantly, the Equal Rights Amendment would require that any restrictions on promotions and assignments within the services be lifted.

Who are some of the supporters of the Equal Rights Amendment? The United States Congress, President Gerald Ford, the Democratic and Republican Parties, the YWCA, United Methodist Women, American Civil Liberties Union, NOW, AFL-CIO, American Jewish Congress, National Woman's Party, NAACP, League of Women Voters, American Association of University Women, Church Women United, Common Cause, American Bar Association, National Federation of Business and Professional Women, the National Education Association and many other responsible organizations. Among the opponents are the American Communist Party, the John Birch Society, and some specific groups formed especially to fight the passage of the amendment.

The result of passage of the Equal Rights Amendment can mean the end of discrimination of every kind—overt and covert—so that women will be accorded the same rights and privileges enjoyed by men. Will it change America? I fervently hope so. Women have nothing to lose by the passage of the ERA, everything to gain. As Senator Marlow Cook of Kentucky has said during congressional debate, "Passage of this Amendment will neither make a man a gentleman nor will it require him to stop being one." Enough said.

12

COPING WITH YOUR CAR

Was That a Ping or a Pong?

As in any other intimate relationship, love and hate are both involved in your feelings for your car. You will alternately coddle and kick it; love it and loathe it; show it with pride and threaten to scrap it. But indifferent to it you will never be, so when you select your car, prepare yourself for both fun and frustration.

You will be most unusual if you don't need a car. Perhaps you are one of the fortunate ones who lives in a city with public transportation at your doorstep. (Even in that case, you may want a car for weekend trips.) But most of us, particularly those of us in the suburbs, cannot do without a car entirely.

No matter how liberated we become, there are at least two things to which we are still slaves: sex and our cars. We have to come to terms with both, and in some ways, the car is the more difficult.

Our main problem, of course, is our abject fear of and lack of knowledge about cars. Most women know how to get in, turn on the engine, steer, park, back up, and ask for a tankful of gas, and that's about the extent of their familiarity with this vital part of their lives. Cars were always considered to be in the male's province of expertise, and it was thought "unwomanly" if a girl showed any interest in an automobile's innards. Praise be, that's changing. Sixteen-year-old Phyllis McNeal of Houschton, Georgia, was awarded the 1975 $700 scholarship from Firestone Tire and Rubber Company at the 4-H National Congress; she won with a paper dealing with the unscrupulous service tactics of some car mechanics. She knew what she was writing about; she works with machinery on her father's farm, and has worked in a service station during the summer. She started early; most of the rest of us come to car ownership and maintenance later, and then are as timorous as medieval virgins approaching our marriage beds. But fear is usually based on ignorance, so the more you can learn about cars in general and yours in particular, the better for you and it.

What Kind of Car to Buy?

Before you buy your car, whether or not it will be new or used, there are some preliminary things you should decide. You may know nothing about cars, or you may have definite preferences as to make and styling. You should decide if you must have an automatic transmission or if a manual will do. The manual will be cheaper to buy and to operate, but there's no denying that an automatic is easier to drive. You'll have to decide whether you will need a four-door or a two-door car. Your particular driving needs will help you here; how many people will you be carrying? If you'll rarely have more than one or two passengers, the back doors are a luxury you may decide to do without. Should you have a standard-size car or a compact? A station wagon or sedan? Again, your particular needs must be the criteria. The compact will be much less expensive to buy and to operate, and can go anywhere a large car can, but if you travel a great deal you may prefer the increased road stability of the larger model. Will you want optional features such as power steering and power brakes? Remember that every optional you select will increase the cost of the car, so don't choose anything that is not essential to your driving ease and comfort, such as automatically operated door-locks. But do consider carefully the additional cost of things such as power steering and brakes, which can appreciably help in the control and operation of your car. Keep in mind, while you're considering optionals, that every power addition makes more strain on the motor and will decrease your gas mileage and the efficiency of the engine.

Decide what type of engine you will want; some of the four-cylinder foreign cars offer as much luxury as you will find in a larger car, but their initial cost, their upkeep, their insurance, and their taxes will be considerably less. Decide too on the type of gas that you want your car to use. The regular grades are cheaper, yet some American cars require the more expensive premium gasoline. Tests show that the brand doesn't matter. The quality is the same, so buy the cheapest gasoline your car can handle. The important thing for which to look, when you're buying gas, is the octane number posted on the gas pump. This number will tell you how much resistance that particular fuel has against knocking in an engine. The number has nothing to do with "power" of a gasoline, but, as reported in the October 1974 issue of *Consumer's Research Magazine,* many motorists "have been led to assume that the higher price meant more miles per gallon."

The higher the octane number, the more anti-knock resistance the gas has, so check your owner's manual for the recommended number, and use that, or one that goes as much as four points lower. The magazine suggests that you experiment, when your engine is properly tuned, "with successively lower grades and different brands until you find the lowest grade you can use without occurrence of knocking (pinging)."

An auto's body styling is important. As sporty and attractive as convertibles undoubtedly are, they are an unwise choice for a woman. Nothing could be more inviting to a potential rapist than a woman driving around in an open car. Sacrifice looks, in this case, for safety. You're going to be paying extra for federally required safety features in all cars made after 1974, anyway, so the fewer additions you make to the base cost of a car, the better it will be for your budget.

You'll want to consider the size of tires when you're planning your car purchase; compacts use tires that are relatively inexpensive, while tires for standard-sized cars can run quite high. Mileage performance will be a factor to consider; the more miles you can get per gallon, the less your car will cost to operate. The Environmental Protection Agency has a free publication, *Miles per Gallon Rating for 1975 Cars* (write the EPA in Pueblo, Col. 81009). It gives the results of fuel economy tests conducted by the EPA on most domestic and foreign makes and models.

For an idea of the comparative costs of standard, compact, and subcompact cars, here is a rundown prepared by the Federal Highway Administration on the various costs of 1974 cars, showing costs over a ten-year period. These figures don't take into consideration the number of people using the car, or their ages, both of which could determine a difference in the insurance, for instance, so keep in mind that these are not inflexible amounts:

Expense	*Standard*	*Compact*	*Subcompact*
Depreciation	$ 4,201.00	$ 2,860.00	$ 2,360.00
Repairs & maint.	2,939.94	2,365.53	2,119.61
Replacement tires	385.99	330.77	302.72
Accessories added after purchase	57.40	57.40	57.40
Gasoline	3,025.96	2,448.45	1,824.41
Oil	195.00	167.00	138.00
Insurance	1,618.00	1,532.00	1,466.00
Garaging, parking, tolls, etc.	1,960.00	1,960.00	1,960.00
Federal and state taxes and fees	1,509.07	1,158.38	924.96
Ten-year total	$15,892.36	$12,879.53	$11,153.10

After you have decided on the kind and type of car you want, you'll have to decide whether you'll want a new or a used one.

BUYING A NEW CAR

The make of car will probably determine the dealer you select, but before you do business with any dealer, try to talk with other owners who have bought from him. It won't be hard to find the owners; many car dealers attach a metal nameplate onto the rear of each car sold, as a form of advertising. Ask the owner about the quality of the service and the type of sales approach and contract he was given. A dissatisfied owner can tell you more than an ornate showroom, so don't hesitate to inquire.

The service department is a vital part of any dealer's operation, so stroll through it sometime, and ask drivers whose cars are in for service about the kind of treatment they receive (is it prompt, courteous, and is the cost reasonable?). Ask if they would recommend that you buy from the dealer.

The make of car you select can be important in estimating your service costs. Some manufacturers offer a minimum of free care, while some others will service the car and replace parts for little or no charge for as long as two years or 24,000 miles, whichever comes first. Even though you will eventually be able to do some of the routine maintenance yourself, you will want to take advantage of warranty service at the dealer's, so check out his service department with care.

Buying your new car at particular times can save you several hundred dollars. As a general rule, the last four months of the calendar year are best for bargains—any time after the new models come out in September—with the best buys offered in December. When business is bad, as during a period of deflated economy, dealers will offer fantastically good inducements to prospective customers, including rebates up to $500 off the original sales price. If you think you will be any good at trying to talk a dealer down from a stated price, you can bargain better if you know just what his markup is on the model. For instance, on domestic cars, the sticker price of a full-size car shows an increase of 23 percent over the base cost, 18 percent on intermediates, and 14 percent on compacts and sub-compacts. Try talking him down so that he will get about $100 to $150 above base price, and you'll probably make a deal.

Automobile dealers customarily offer other types of deals that can frequently save money. For example, when a dealer offers a "Specially Equipped Car Sale," it is generally of a car loaded with options that the manufacturer has required the dealer to demonstrate in his showroom for a certain period of time, after which the dealer is free to sell it for whatever price he can get. A dealer who still has on his floor a model that has been offered in a "Special Model Sale" for several months will probably let you have it for a greatly reduced price. It will be a car with special paint or engine or other features, and may be one of the few available throughout the country.

Test drive any car in which you are interested; it's the only way you'll know if you are comfortable in the driver's seat, and whether or not the car handles well. Shop around for your car; don't make a hasty decision about what is probably, next to a house, the largest single purchase you will make. Take your time, and make sure you find the ideal car for you.

Selling Your Old Car

If you already have a car, you will want to trade it in on your new one or sell it privately. If you choose to do the latter, ask your bank to make an appraisal and tell you what they would lend a buyer; it will be a good selling point if you can tell a prospect that the financing can be handled by a bank. Advertise in the paper, and tell exactly when you will be able to show the car. Try to have someone with you when the prospective buyer comes, and do *not* allow anyone to take it for a trial run alone—you may never see your car again.

If you decide to trade your car in on the purchase of your new one, there are a few points to remember. Whether you sell the car privately or use it as a trade-in, you can learn what the car should be worth by checking with your bank for the current book value. You should accept no less than this and if the car is in good condition, or if you have just bought new tires, you should be able to get considerably more. If the car is a pre-1967 model, don't expect much more than the book value; cars made prior to that date didn't have such safety devices as dual-cylinder braking systems, energy-absorbing steering columns, padded instrument panels, backup lights, and four-way emergency warning flashers.

The Warranty

The warranty that is given with your car can mean little or nothing, and in some cases you'd be better off with none at all. If no manufacturers' warranties were offered, cars would be included under the Uniform Commercial Code's "implied warranty of merchantibility," allowing you to reject a vehicle that turned out to be less than it was represented to be. You're unable to do that, however, because of the manufacturer's warranty that is actually a means of limiting the maker's liability. Most such warranties agree to correct defects in drive-train parts or workmanship for twelve months or 12,000 miles, whichever occurs first. (The annual mileage driven by the average motorist is estimated at 12,000 miles per year, so they're safe either way; their warranty will last only the first year.)

Many dealers, painfully aware of the shortcomings of the manufacturer's warranty, offer their own "out-of-warranty" repairs and service. Consider the offers made by your dealer and make sure that any out-of-warranty service is written into the contract. Most dealers are reputable people who want to make their customers happy so they will return and will recommend them to other buyers, but there are some who are not so reliable. Check with the Better Business Bureau for a record of any complaints against the dealer, and do not do business with one who is questionable, no matter what deals he offers.

The Sales Contract

Study the sales contract minutely before you sign. Remember that it should have the exact items that any installment contract should have, and which were discussed in Chapter 11. Briefly, it should show the date of the transaction, the names and addresses of the buyer and seller, a description of the car, the trade-in allowance or down payment, the cash price, the credit price, the unpaid balance, the amount charged for credit, an itemized list of any other charges, coverage and amount of insurance, the number and amount of payments, and the consequences if you pay late or fail to pay. Be sure that all these are on your contract, and be sure to read all the fine print at the bottom or on the back of the contract. If you have any questions about it, ask for a copy to show your banker or lawyer. A reputable dealer will give you one without hesitation.

Automobile Financing

It is better and cheaper not to finance through the dealer; you will be able to get a lower interest rate from your bank. Automobile loans are subject to legal ceilings, and must fall at or below the maximum amounts determined by your state's banking authority. You can learn what the rate is in your state by contacting any consumer group or by asking the banking authority itself. There may be one of two kinds of interest, true annual rates or add-on rates. The true annual rate is simple; if it is 7%, for example, the lender cannot charge you more. If it is an add-on rate, however, it can become complicated. To find out what a lender can legally charge you in add-on interest, find out what the legal limit is, multiply it by two, multiply that amount by the number of payments you will make, and divide that total by the number of payments plus one. (Remember, the shorter the term, the less interest you'll be paying.) Say that your state's annual add-on percentage rate is six, and you're going to be paying for the car over an eighteen-month period. Multiply six by two to get twelve, multiply that by eighteen to get two hundred and sixteen, and divide that by nineteen, to get 11.37%, the simple annual interest rate you should be charged. If a lender offers you an eighteen-month loan with monthly payments reflecting an interest rate higher than the 11.37%, therefore, he would be in violation of the law. This is an example, of course; you can use the same simple formula to arrive at the correct amount for your state.

However you decide to finance your car, be sure to add credit life insurance onto the loan as you would onto any other loan, and don't overlook a disability policy that will cover payments if you are unable to make them because of accident or illness. The cost is small, and the benefits are large.

Everything thus far applies to both new and used cars, with the exception of the new-car warranty, but there are a few differences to note if you decide to buy a used car, either privately or from a dealer.

Buying a Used Car

The dealer offers various types of used cars; most of these will carry the dealer's own warranty that is usually for a shorter period of time than is the manufacturer's, generally running for about thirty days or 1000 miles. The warranties are usually free, but some dealers may charge you a few dollars. It will be well worth the cost to have the dealer take care of any trouble that is likely to appear in a used car during those first few months. Whenever you buy any automobile, if you know a good mechanic, ask him to look over the car for you; it will cost a few dollars, but may save hundreds before the year is out. Test drive the car, paying particular attention to the brakes; that's one of the most easily spotted potentials for danger. Beware of a car emitting clouds of white or black smoke; this, too, is a danger signal. (I'll discuss other things you should watch for in the section on repairs and maintenance so that you can buy a used car intelligently.)

To find out what the car should cost, check with your bank; its book value information includes used cars, too. For a simple guide for high-mileage cars, considering the standard 12,000 miles per year as average, deduct a certain amount from the price for every 1000 miles above that amount—for instance, about $15 per 1000 miles for smaller cars, and about $30 to $35 for larger models. Surprisingly, the best buys in older cars are usually the standard-size American makes; some compacts, because of their low maintenance costs and high gas mileage actually increase in value. Avoid station wagons, convertibles, and sports cars; their repair costs are higher than sedans. Don't worry about buying a high-mileage car that is in otherwise good condition. Anything under 120,000 miles is not unreasonable if the car has been serviced and has been driven properly. (You wouldn't want a high-mileage car that has seen only in-town driving; that's the hardest kind for a car to withstand. One that has been driven on Interstates for extended periods will probably be your best buy.) Don't be concerned that the odometer will not register the correct mileage the car has been driven; the Federal Odometer Law requires that the dealer must give you a written statement of the true mileage on the car when you buy it, and you may ask to see the statement given him by the previous owner. When you see it, write down his name and address and contact him if you have any questions about the car.

Don't let the salesman pressure you; if he says that there is another buyer considering the same car, and you'd better snap it up right then or lose it, tell him to let the other buyer (who is probably fictitious) have it. If you are really sold on the car, however, you may want to put a binder on it while you arrange for financing. The binder would be considered as part of the purchase price.

Two kinds of used cars that you might want to investigate are dealers' demonstration cars and rental cars. There is very little to be said against the "demos"; even though they have been driven by many drivers for short periods, and may have been available for use by the salesmen, they have usually been kept in excellent condition. After all, the demonstrators are the cars used by the dealers to sell other cars, so they *have* to be the best. You can get a current-year car for many hundreds of dollars less than the retail price, and generally carrying a new-car warranty.

The other kind of new-model used automobile that you might want to consider is a rental car. Most rental and lease agencies sell their cars when the new models come out or after a certain number of miles, and the cars are a bargain. They are generally kept in good condition and are maintained well, but they have been driven by hundreds of people under a variety of conditions, so have a mechanic check out the one you're interested in and ask for some type of warranty to cover at least the first two months.

LEASING

You may want to investigate the possibilities of leasing instead of buying. Most leasing companies operate identically; you can select the make and model you want, and can usually stipulate the color and options you desire. There will probably be a deposit of about $100 plus the first month's payment; after that you will have a regular monthly payment just as if you were buying a car. The advantages are that you don't have to shop around and make deals, and you won't have to worry about depreciation. (A car depreciates in value the minute you drive it from the dealer's lot.) You won't have to make a hefty down payment that can run as high as 25 percent of the total cost, and when your leasing period is over, you won't have to worry about selling a used car; the lessor will take it off your hands and you can lease another, newer model.

A disadvantage to the arrangement is that you will be responsible for the insurance and maintenance. You may want to have an open-end leasing agreement whereby you could buy the car at its depreciated price at the end of the lease. The advantage is that you'd get a used car driven only by you, and whose mechanical history you would already know. If you are entitled to deduct car expenses on your tax return, the cost of leasing will also be a legitimate expense.

The disadvantage of leasing is that you will have no equity in the car, just as you would have none if you are renting a house or apartment. You must weigh the cost of ownership against the nonrecoverable cost of renting.

CAR INSURANCE

I told you earlier that car insurance is entirely different from any other, and can be one of your costliest expenses, depending on many variables, such as your age and driving record, your driving habits, the make and model of your car, and the number and ages of any other drivers who might use it. Shop around for your car insurance as you would for any other; policy costs vary from company to company and from state to state. You can get the most sophisticated coverage or the minimum required by local law, and the difference can be several hundred dollars a year.

In Georgia, for instance, everyone who has a motor vehicle registered with the state must carry liability insurance, and cannot purchase a license tag without proof of coverage. The insurance is "no fault," which means that the insurance carrier pays directly to the insured regardless of the damage circumstances. The insurance must be in the minimum amounts of $10,000 each person and $20,000 each occurrence on the bodily injury portion of the policy, and a minimum of $5,000 per occurrence on the property damage liability section. Not complying with the law is a misdemeanor, and carries a $1,000 fine or a year's imprisonment, or both.

I cite this 1975 Georgia law as a good illustration of the type now required in many states, following the 1970 examples of Massachusetts and Puerto Rico. It offers the most basic coverage, and you will be wise to increase it as much as you wish, within reasonable limits. Don't let an agent pressure you into "exotic" coverage of amounts in the hundreds of thousands per occurrence; unless you have a great deal of money and could be sued by an accident victim, the basic coverage will be ample.

Most policies offer coverage for medical payments, comprehensive (against loss) and collision payments, towing and labor costs, property damage, and protection against an uninsured motorist.

To give you an illustration of the way age, make, and model of the car and other factors vary insurance premiums, I'll use my policy as an example. There are three cars covered, driven by three people who are listed as principal drivers, and carried on one policy so that I can be given a multiple-car discount.

I am in my forties, drive a 1969 eight-cylinder four-door Pontiac sedan, have never had an accident, and ride public transportation to work. Elaine is twenty, drives a 1969 four-cylinder foreign-made compact, has never had an accident, has had driver's training, receives a good student discount, and rides public transportation to school and work. John is 18, drives a 1972 four-cylinder foreign car, has never had an accident, has a good student discount, and uses his car to drive to school and work because public transportation is unavailable in those locations. My annual premium is $166.60; Elaine's is $177; and John's is $373.80. The reason for the difference in his and Elaine's is accounted for by the fact that she has had driver's training, she parks and rides a bus, and—most importantly—she is a female. John is in the group for whom insurance costs are highest; he is an unmarried male between the ages of 16 and 26—this group has the worst driving record.

Mark's insurance is carried separately and because he has had two accidents his premiums are a whopping $600 a year. Fortunately, both policies are on a budget-payment plan, so that we can pay quarterly. I have excluded towing and labor costs from my policy because I belong to a motor club that pays the charges for the first five miles of towing, but if you don't have such a membership, I recommend that you pay the small additional cost to have it included on your policy. Depending on the age of your car, you may want to carry a deductible amount on your collision and comprehensive coverage. I carry no deductible on the comprehensive and $100 deductible on the collision provision. This means that if my car is stolen or damaged, I would recover the total cost, but if I have a collision I would pay the first $100 for repairs and the insurance would cover the rest, to the amount of the car's actual cash value at the time of the accident.

After the car is a certain age, insurance may cost more than the car is worth. If your annual premiums cost more than the recoverable amount if your car were totally destroyed, it is senseless to insure it for collision or fire or theft, although you may still be required by law to carry the liability insurance.

Review your insurance regularly and report any changes to your agent. Car-pooling, for instance, will entitle you to the same discount you'll receive for commuting by public transportation, and the savings can be as much as 15 to 18 percent of your annual premium. Check to see if in your state you can save (in some cases as much as 10 to 20 percent) on your premiums by purchasing a package policy covering all the items I've mentioned, rather than buying these coverages separately. And ask if any of the new safety equipment entitles you to a premium discount.

If your policy is ever canceled for any reason, appeal immediately to your state's insurance commissioner; carriers must give you notice of an intended cancellation of your policy so you'll have a short period to investigate or to try to get new coverage. Perhaps your agent can get a policy for you with another company. Practice good defensive driving; the fewer accidents you have, the fewer problems you'll have with your insurance. Companies don't like to insure high-risk drivers.

CAR-POOLING

I've mentioned car-pooling, and it's a good idea with automobile operating expenses as high as they are. Before you go into it, though, there are a few things you will want to know. According to the Internal Revenue Service, "the cost of repairs, gas and similar items in connection with operating an automobile used in a car pool to and from work are personal expenses and are not deductible. Amounts received from the passengers are not included in income. These amounts are considered reimbursement for transportation expenses incurred. However, this rule does not apply to the situation where a particular car owner has developed his car pool arrangements to the extent he can be said to have established a trade or business . . . from which a profit is derived."

I don't think that you're considering going into car-pooling as a business venture, so let's discuss it as a means of saving money. Total your monthly car expenses, including maintenance, gas, insurance, and toll and parking fees. Say the cost is $60 a month; with one passenger it would be half that, and so on. The savings can be substantial.

Many companies have a list of employees' living areas so that neighbors can get together to form a pool; if there is no such list, circulate one, and sign up four or five other drivers who live in the same area. Agree with your co-drivers on pickup times, and be sure that all of you adhere to them; if you have a chronically late member, drop him or her. You can do all the driving yourself in your own car, or you can agree to use a different member's car each week. When it's your turn to drive, be sure that your car has a full gas tank before you begin, and keep the car clean and in good condition. Arrange with a garage to allow all the cars in the pool to use the same spot on a monthly rental basis to save parking costs. Be sure that your brakes and steering systems are in good condition; the extra passengers put an additional load on them. You'll probably have to increase your car insurance. Minimum amounts recommended for car-poolers by the Insurance Information Institute are $100,000 per individual claim and $300,000 per accident.

For more information about operating a car pool, write to the Highway Users Federation (Dept. WD, 1776 Massachusetts Avenue, N. W., Washington, D.C. 20036) or to the Public Affairs Department of the Shell Oil Company (1 Shell Plaza, Houston, Texas 77001), and ask for its free booklet, *Secrets of a Successful Car Pool*.

Whether you car-pool, drive a load of children, drive alone, travel, or just use your car occasionally, you'll want it to be in the best possible condition, and that will require time, effort, and money. You can't maintain a car properly without knowing a little about it mechanically, and the more you know about it and the more you can do about repairs yourself, the more money you will be able to save.

THE CAR'S ENGINE

I, who used to boast that I knew nothing about a car more than the correct way to turn on the key and to steer the car where I wanted to go, have learned at least a few of the basics of the operation of the internal combustion engine, and enough about my particular car to be able to do some elementary repairs and replacements.

Using the simplest terms, the World Book Encyclopedia has described the operation of the car in language the most uninformed layperson can understand. Remember that three things make your car run—electricity, gasoline, and air—and the following will be more readily understood.

> When you turn the ignition key and press the starter, the starter motor uses electric power from the battery to give the engines a spin. This starts the crankshaft turning and moves the pistons and rods up and down. After that, the engine will keep going as long as gasoline and air are fed to the cylinders and electricity flows to the spark plugs. Burning of gasoline and air in the cylinders forces the pistons and rods to move up and down and turn the crankshaft. Power from the turning crankshaft runs through the transmission to the rear wheels and makes the car run.

I know—it's like trying to learn to read a foreign language without having learned the basics, but it really isn't all that complicated. Take it step by step, and it will make more sense. The ignition key turns on a flow of electricity to the starter and spark plugs. (The battery has stored electricity just for this purpose.) The fuel pump sucks gasoline from the gas tank through the fuel line to the carburetor. At the same time, the generator fills the electrical system with current when the engine is running, and the distributor sends electricity individually to each spark plug. The spark plug, like a match, sets fire with an electric spark to the mixture of gasoline and air now in the cylinder. (As the fuel pump was injecting gas into the carburetor, air was being drawn in through the air intake; the two mix, and the mixture is sent into the cylinder.) The accelerator controls the amount of the mixture sent to the cylinders, and an explosion in the cylinders drives the pistons and rods up and down (like bicycle pedals) to turn the crankshaft. The clutch connects the crankshaft, so that when the connection is made, the transmission carries power to the drive shaft. Gears in the transmission control the speed with which the drive shaft turns, and can make it turn slower than, or opposite to (as in reversing the car) the crankshaft. All of this is happening for one purpose, to get power to turn the wheels; the power from the pistons and rods, the crankshaft, clutch, transmission, and drive shaft goes to the rear wheels, because they really drive the car. The rear axle (the axle is the bar running from one wheel to the other) carries the power from the drive shaft to the rear wheels, and the differential gears let each wheel turn in a different radius so that you can turn corners.

While all this is happening, water circulating through the radiator has been cooled by air drawn in by the fan, and is preventing an overheated engine. (If your car has an air-cooled engine, the air does the job alone.) Oil enables all of the moving parts to move freely without damage to one another, and is as vital to the successful operation of the engine as are air, electricity, and gasoline.

As I said, this is a simplified version of what's going on inside your car, but will give you a better grasp of some of the problems that can arise, and what should be done about them.

There is no sense in pretending that you will become a master mechanic by learning all about your engine and transmission (although there are some excellent courses being offered in colleges, high schools, and vocational schools), but you can at least do some of the more simple repairs, learn how to see that your car receives proper maintenance, and have a passing acquaintance with the terms used by a mechanic. (And insure that you won't be "taken" every time your car goes for service.)

CAR MAINTENANCE

Car Manuals

The first thing that you must do as soon as you get your car home is read the owner's manual. If it's a new car, read the first few pages before leaving the dealer's; there will be important points to note about driving it for the first few hundred miles. If you have bought a used car, insist that the dealer or former owner supply you with a manual. If it has been lost, ask them to get one for you from the original dealer or the manufacturer, but insist that you must have a manual. Look in the back of the little booklet and see if there is an address to which you may write to order a shop or diagnostic manual. Don't hesitate; order it at once. It costs about $5. If there is not an address, ask the dealer to order a manual for you; write directly to the manufacturer yourself, if necessary, but *get* a manual. It can save you a great deal of trouble and money.

Study your owner's manual, beginning with "How to Start Your Car" (there's a right way and a wrong way) right through to the end. Familiarize yourself with the index and the table of capacities and requirements of such things as oil, anti-freeze, gasoline, and so on. It will tell you the size of your engine—learn this as quickly as you learn the make of your car—and will probably tell you the size of the tires. Learn all about the optional equipment your model may have, and about any special maintenance it may require. The manual will tell you the type of gasoline your car should have, and if new, all about the emission controls. Check out all the equipment again (you did it first before accepting it from the dealer or owner, of course), and if something doesn't work, get it back to the dealer or previous owner—fast.

Oil

The owner's manual will give only the most cursory explanations about the operation and parts of the engine, but while you're waiting for your shop manual to arrive, ask at the library or at the dealer's for a copy that you may borrow. Study it, and take it with you when you look under the hood at the engine. *It* isn't going to hurt *you,* and *you're* not going to hurt *it!* Learn the location of some of the parts, such as the carburetor, battery, and engine block. Find the oil dip stick (it will have a slender curved handle like a fencing foil), and pull it out. It will show you if you need to add oil. Get a rag, wipe off the end, and stick it back down into its sheath. It may not go in easily; twist it gently until it slips right in. Pull it out again and look at the end. There will be little marks and arrows showing you the proper oil level, and if the oil is below that line, you'll need to add some.

When you buy oil, get the best grade; oil is one item on which you cannot scrimp. Buy oil at discount stores, not from service stations, for savings of from twenty to thirty cents a can, and buy a pouring spout at the same time. It will cost under a dollar, and will enable you to add oil whenever necessary. The spout has a sharp v-shaped opener opposite the funnel, and is pretty hard to push into the can. Put the oil can on the ground and push the sharp opener into the can with both hands. Pour the oil directly into the place designated by your manual; it will *not* be the place where the dip stick stays, and is different on different cars, so check to make sure. After you've emptied the quart can, remove the spout, clean it, and store for the next time. You've just performed one of the easiest but most important services you can give your car.

Supplies

When you buy your oil and pouring spout at the discount store, you can buy some other items you should have in your car or trunk at all times. Buy a set of jumper cables; it will be needed if your battery is low and you need to get a power "jump" from another car. Instructions for its use will come with it, so keep it with the cables and check it when needed. Buy an empty gasoline can to keep in your trunk in case you ever run out of gas and need to buy a few gallons from a service station or another motorist. (Be painstaking about keeping your gas level up so that you *won't* run out of gas, but be prepared in case of an emergency. It's a good idea to have your gas tank refilled as soon as the indicator shows that you have half a tank.) Never carry extra gas in the can in your trunk; gasoline is highly explosive and the fumes are dangerous if inhaled.

Buy an air gauge so that you can check the air pressure in your tires; an incorrect amount—either too much or too little—can cause damage to the tire tread and hamper good driving. Your car manual will tell you exactly how much you should have and unless you buy a different type entirely (for instance, steel radials), all tires for your car will require the same amount. Keep a flashlight in your glove compartment and check the batteries regularly. Do *not* keep an extra set of keys in your glove compartment; that's the first place a car thief will look. (I keep one extra set in my wallet and another at home.) Look in your car manual for the location of your fuse box. (Didn't know a car had fuses, did you? It does, and can blow them just as a house can.) Find in the manual the sizes of the fuses needed for various things such as headlights, radio, courtesy lights, and so on. Buy a set of the different sizes you will need, and a few replacement bulbs for the trunk, dash, and overhead lights, as well. The fuses and bulbs all cost under a dollar each.

Buy some all-weather coolant (anti-freeze keeps water from freezing in the winter, but is necessary for cool operation in the summer, too) and keep that in the trunk with the cans of oil and some transmission fluid. Prepare a simple tool kit, with pliers and screwdrivers, and add a roll of duct tape to repair any leaks in your hoses. Keep a cloth for wiping off the dip stick, and a clean one for wiping the windows and headlights after a rain. Keep a scraper on hand for winter weather, and a small bottle of windshield wiper fluid for quick refills. You might want to keep a jar of a vinegar and water mixture, or some carbonated soft drink for cleaning off oily smears from the windshield, and some pre-moistened towels for quick clean-ups. It's a good idea to keep a record in the car of all repairs, purchases (tires, battery, so on), oil changes, and tune-ups. Keep the owner's and shop manuals in the car, with your warranty, registration (in your wallet, if allowed in your state), and the policy or account numbers of your insurance and automobile club, and the telephone numbers of your agent and a towing service.

Gas Mileage

Keep a record, especially for the first month or so after you buy a car, of the gas mileage you're getting. Write down the odometer reading when you get gas, and when you buy more, note the amount needed and the mileage shown at that reading. Subtract the previous reading from the current one, and divide by the amount of gas you just bought to find out how many miles per gallon you're getting. For example, if your current odometer reading shows 10307 miles, and the previous reading was 10102, you've driven 205 miles since you last bought gas. If you've just gotten twelve gallons, you know that you are getting a little more than seventeen miles to a gallon of gas. Do this every time you buy gas for a few weeks or months, and even though the amount may vary a few gallons, depending on the type of driving you've been doing, you will be able to tell pretty accurately the mileage you're getting.

This is important, not as a conversational opener, but because it is the best indication of the efficiency of your engine's operation. An engine badly in need of a tune-up will cut the mileage down a quarter or a third of the amount it should be getting. Another good reason to know your tank's capacity (it's listed in the manual) and your mileage is that this is an excellent way to plan your driving and stops on a trip. If you know that your tank capacity is twenty-five gallons and you're getting seventeen miles to a gallon, you'll know that you can safely drive for about 425 miles on a tank of gas. (I don't recommend it; when I travel, I like to stop every hundred miles or so to stretch and to let the car cool off for a few minutes.) During times when you may have difficulty getting gas, or in locations where service stations are far apart, knowing your driving range can be a great advantage, so keep tabs on your mileage all the time.

Tires

Probably the first major purchase you will have to make for your car will be a new set of tires. Those put on at the factory are usually of inferior quality and will not wear well, and it will be most unlikely that you were able to buy a used car that won't need good tires before long. Cars are like people—they don't want their "feet" to hurt—so the correct size and type tire for your car and your driving needs will be of prime importance to the safety and maneuverability of your car.

If you plan to buy new tires, there are several points to consider. Safety experts frown on mixing types of tires—that is, having some radials and some standard. It's best to have the same kind of tires on all four wheels, but if you *do* mix, the Tire Industry Safety Council urges you to be sure that the radials are in the rear. In this case, when the tires are rotated (and this should be done every 6000 to 8000 miles), don't allow the rear tires to be moved forward; see that they remain on the same axle.

Belted and radial tires will give you good wear and mileage, and you'll probably get the best service from a steel radial, but prepare yourself for a bumpy ride when you first get in the car. The steels settle when they're parked, and don't resume their normal round shape until they've heated up a little; they really do ride like square tires when they're cold. But their safety factor is something to be considered; although they cost much more than standard tires, they withstand more hard driving. Depending on the size of your car, steels can run from $20 to $40 more per wheel than the standards, but are worth it. Whatever tire you buy, be sure that you receive a warranty and that the tires are registered.

The warranty should guarantee replacement of any tire that is defective due to workmanship, and should offer a price reduction on any tire replaced because of wear or road hazards. In other words, if the tire was put on the car in a defective condition, you would be entitled to a new replacement without cost to you (try to have labor included); and if the tire is damaged because of bad alignment or something it picked up on the road, you would get a discount on a new tire that can cut the cost to more than half, depending on the age of the tire. I have such a warranty and have had to have two tires replaced because of cuts received by glass and a nail. The cost was minimal. (I have steel radials, so in both instances, even though the objects penetrated to the tube, the tires merely developed slow leaks and saved me from a blowout. The tires are worth the extra $35 per tire for that, if nothing else.)

Where you buy your tires is as important as the kind you buy. I've never had good service from a tire bought at a service station, although I know people who swear by them. My preference is the tire department of a national catalog store; the tires I buy carry their brand name, but are manufactured by one of the best European makers of racing tires. The warranty is air-tight and the service is generally prompt and courteous. They will balance your wheels (a must for satisfactory wear), and will align the wheels for better mileage. These may be mandatory for the warranty, and the date of the sale and service will be entered on the warranty you'll keep. It will also have the odometer reading, because most warranties will be for a certain number of miles or months. Mine is for four years or 40,000 miles, whichever comes first, and I've never had the slightest problem with replacements. The dealer has a book with the formula giving the amount of discount to which you are entitled, so there's no guesswork as to the price of the new tire.

Besides the warranty, insist on receiving your tire registration. Many dealers won't tell the customer about the registration, but it is required by law, and will protect you against driving on a damaged tire liable to recall for defective workmanship. This is different from the workmanship covered by your warranty. The registration covers tires released with known defects that are later subject to mass recall—after some have blown. The manufacturers, in attempting to comply with new federal regulations, experience difficulty in recovering these tires because sellers have seldom sent the tire number and names and addresses of purchasers to them. But that *is* the law, so when you buy a tire, be certain the dealer records all the necessary information and forwards it to the factory. The law went into effect on May 22, 1971, and all tires produced after that date must be registered and carry a DOT (Department of Transportation) imprint and a series of letters and numbers that are that particular tire's registration. Some dealers may still have some of the older tires in stock, so verify the DOT and serial numbers before you buy. *Insist* on the registration, and if the salesman tells you that it isn't necessary to have one, go somewhere else to buy your tires. Your life could depend on those little numbers.

As with everything else, shop for bargains. All tire dealers regularly have sales in January, July, and on Labor Day, but watch for other chances to save. If tires are advertised as being cosmetically blemished, they are safe buys as long as they have the Department of Transportation initials and numbers. They may have blurred whitewalls, for example, but be perfectly safe. You may want to consider retreads, especially for your spare. In that case, don't buy tires already recapped, but have your own done over. (The terms "recap" and "retread" are used interchangeably; "to retread" means to put new tread on a worn tire casing, and "to recap" means to put the new tread on by vulcanizing it to the original tire.) The savings can be astounding. Mark recently bought new tires at $42.50 each for his Toyota, but decided to have one old tire recapped and kept as a spare; it cost him only $12.50. I don't mean to imply that retreads are safe used only as spares; if the job is done by a reputable company, they are quite satisfactory for ordinary use, although I wouldn't advise that you consider using them for any high-speed driving.

Before you buy your tires, check to see if there are any tire mounting costs, and call a few service stations to compare charges. Take the tires to the least expensive, if it doesn't endanger your warranty. The charge to put the tires on should be no more than $2 or $3 per wheel, but the balancing and front-end alignment will cost more.

Care of your tires will play an important part in their life and wear. Follow the recommended tire rotation suggested by the Tire Industry Safety Council, and have bias and belted (these terms simply refer to the ways in which the layers of rubber are made into the tire) rear tires moved straight forward, and the front tires diagonally transferred to the rear. This is contrary to an old method, so don't let a serviceman tell you you're wrong when you request the newer, better way. If you drive radials, they should never be rotated diagonally, but should be exchanged with the tire on the same side. Proper tire rotation at the recommended times is a necessity; if neglected it can cause a dangerous lack of response to your steering.

The Tire Industry Safety Council publishes an excellent free booklet,

Consumer Tire Guide, that tells you the proper inflation and load-tables for domestic passenger-size tires, and most tire sizes for the more popular foreign cars. The recommended inflation for your tires will be in your manual, but may change if you buy radials, for instance. Follow the suggestions of the manufacturer, in either case. (The address for the booklet is Tire Safety, Box 726, New York, N.Y. 10011.) Enclose a stamped, self-addressed, business-sized envelope, and if you would like the Council's *Tire Safety and Mileage Kit,* for $1.50 you will get the booklet plus an accurate air-pressure gauge, a tread-depth gauge, and four spare valve caps.

Now that you've gotten your feet wet, you're ready to move into other areas of car care and maintenance. There are many jobs you can do to care for your car that will save time and money later. They're not complicated, and if done regularly will add to the life of your car and its parts. It's too bad that we can't buy a car, keep it filled with gas, give it a loving pat occasionally, and let it go at that, but we can't. It would be lovely to have a mechanic on hand at all times. (When my children were small, I daydreamed about having a resident pediatrician; now I'd settle for a part-time mechanic.) But since that's impossible, and the professionals seem to raise their prices from one visit to the next, you'd better learn to do as much as you can yourself, and to be able to identify problems.

By simply being able to analyze the source of a problem you will be better able to deal with a mechanic when one is necessary, and you may be able to spot and fix the trouble alone. I certainly don't make any claims to being a mechanic, but with the help of my service manual and a little common sense, I am gradually overcoming my awe of those high-priced specialists, and have done quite a few money-saving repairs myself.

CAR REPAIRS

For instance, recently both my turn-signal indicators and my air-conditioning failed, and I was horrified at the anticipated costs involved. I finally sat down and analyzed the problem. It seemed too coincidental that two electrically operated systems should fail at once, so I guessed that the trouble might be a blown fuse. I checked the fuse box (usually located in a hard-to-reach place behind the steering column), and sure enough, that was the trouble. I pulled the burned-out fuses, bought two more for twenty cents, replaced them, and was ridiculously elated when I saw my handiwork succeed.

The next time was better; the dashlight indicating that my engine was overheating came on, and I didn't have any problems with my diagnosis or with a prompt remedy. A check of the water level in the radiator showed that it was low, although I knew it should have been full of anti-freeze.

I checked the radiator for leaks and found none, but located one on the underside of the hose connecting it to the engine. A replacement hose cost about $1 plus fifteen minutes of my time. (A warning: Whenever you remove the radiator cap, try to give the engine time to cool. If you can't wait, use a heavy rag to unscrew the cap, loosen it first, and stand as far back as you can; the pressure will be terrific, and the water will be scalding.)

Car Care

The ten most overlooked car-care jobs, according to a survey conducted by the Car Care Council, include several that any untrained woman can do for her own car. The maintenance jobs most ignored by car owners were neglect of the battery cables, the spark plug wires, the radiator cap, and the radiator hose; failure to maintain proper transmission servicing and headlight aiming; and failure to replace faulty shock absorbers, heater hoses, fan belts, and weak batteries. Although they didn't include it on their list, there are two more items that should take top priority: frequent oil changes and replacement of dirty filters. Your oil should be changed according to the manufacturer's recommendation, usually about three to four times a year, and the oil filter should be replaced each time. If you don't feel up to changing the oil yourself (and it isn't that difficult, once you have your service manual), you can save the cost of having the mechanic replace the filter by doing it when you go home. Find out the correct size you need, and buy it at an auto parts store or the automotive section of a discount department store. Follow the steps in your manual exactly as shown, and reverse the order when putting everything back together.

The other filters, gas and air, are equally as important as the oil filter. In fact, the air filter is one of the most vital pieces of equipment on your car. It is located on the top of the carburetor, and cleans the air that mixes with the gas to run the engine. The mixture must be clean for the car to operate efficiently and economically, so the importance of the air filter cannot be overemphasized. Your car needs 12,000 gallons of air for every gallon of gas it uses! No wonder a clean air filter is so necessary. It's simple to replace, and costs only a few dollars, although some stations prey on women by telling them of their dirty filters and selling them a new one for much more. The gas filter costs about the same as the air filter, and should be changed as often—about two or three times a year.

Among the items listed on the survey that should pose no problems for you were care of the battery; replacement of hoses, fan belts, and radiator caps; and maintenance of transmission fluid levels. See that the level of water in your battery is maintained correctly; don't let it be too high or low, and don't use water that has a high mineral content. You can buy bottled water to keep at home for your battery, but it isn't necessary if the water is of a normal quality. Make sure that the battery cables are free from corrosion and are tightly connected to the terminals. (Do this when the motor is turned off, of course.) The posts to which the cables are connected should be brushed clean with steel wool occasionally, and petroleum jelly should be used to encase them. When you buy a new battery, buy a heavy-duty one guaranteed to last several years. Check out the heater and radiator hose for leaks, bulges, or hard or soft spots, and replace them as needed. Normal life is about two years or 24,000 miles, but check them regularly every 2000 miles after the first year. They are easy to replace, and inexpensive to buy. Fan belts should be examined for damage and wear. With the engine off, pull gently at each belt and try to move the fan. If the belt slack is more than one-fourth inch or if you can turn the fan by hand, replace the belts at once. Check them over for any cracked or worn spots, too, and replace as needed. Make sure the radiator cap's rubber seal isn't worn or cracked, and replace it, if necessary, with a make specified by the manufacturer. Check the level of your transmission fluid, and keep a can at home for needed refills.

Unless you take a mechanic's course, you probably will not be able to handle the other jobs listed on the survey, but they are not complicated, and you should know what service to request. Every time the car has a routine tune-up (at least twice a year, but more often if needed), request the mechanic to examine the spark plug wires with his test equipment. The usual life of the wires is about three years, but let him check them anyway. Have him aim the headlights during the tune-up, also, with his special equipment; it will only cost about $6 or $7, and will eliminate a hazardous night driving condition.

The shock absorbers should last about two years, and should be replaced as soon as you notice that your car dips abnormally when you stop or go over bumps in the road. An easy test is to rock your parked car by forcing down on the front or rear bumpers; if the car rocks down and up once and stops, the shocks are all right, but if it keeps rocking, you'd better plan to buy some new ones soon. When you replace shocks, buy the heavy-duty type for better service and wear; they have larger parts and greater fluid capacity.

For an inexpensive way to check out your car's condition take it to one of the diagnostic centers found throughout the country. Occasionally a gasoline company will offer the service free, but generally there will be a fee that can range from a few dollars to $35. In states requiring vehicle safety inspections, the diagnosis will be included in the small fee, but some of the inspections are cursory, so you may want a second opinion. Check with the local automobile clubs and safety councils in your locale; they frequently conduct clinics and charge a minimal fee.

A Mechanic

If you discover that your car needs attention you can't give it, you'll have to select your mechanic with as great care as you would your doctor. The ideal is to stay with the dealer from whom you bought the car, if it's new, or an authorized dealer for the used car you bought, but that may not always be practical. If you can't get to his service department conveniently or promptly, or if you don't like the service you've received, start looking for another person to whom you can entrust your car. Ask your neighbors (especially any teenaged boys) for recommended servicemen; shop around for estimates of the cost for the work to be done; look at the cars belonging to the mechanics—you can tell a great deal about their work by the condition of their own vehicles; see if the mechanic is a member of any organization that might guarantee his work. The mechanics employed by service stations are responsible to the owner; if the station is part of a chain, the oil company is ultimately responsible for quality of service, but if the station is franchised, you'd have to deal directly with the owner if you have a complaint. There are unscrupulous owners and mechanics, and the parent company will remove the franchise after a certain number of legitimate complaints, but that won't help you after you've paid out several hundred dollars for a non-existent repair job. You will generally be safe with a company-operated shop or with one owned by a member of the Automotive Service Council (formerly the Independent Garage Owners of America); they maintain standards of performance, and endeavor to give good, honest service. If you are ever told that you need some high-priced repair job, insist that you be permitted to bring another mechanic for his opinion; a reputable serviceman will never object.

Prepare a list of exactly what you want done (lubrication, tune-up, repairs, whatever), and give a copy to the mechanic. Get an estimate of the cost in writing, and instruct him not to do anything else without your permission. Don't let him call you later with some sort of scare story; tell him to hold off on the work until you can have someone else check it out, or tell him to do only the work authorized, and you'll take care of the other later. But be wary; if you refuse to pay for unauthorized repairs, he can exercise a "mechanic's lien" and keep your car. Protect yourself by having him put all the items listed above (things to be done, estimate of cost, nonauthorization to do any other work) on his worksheet and give you a copy.

Brakes

Although I am a strong advocate of economizing whenever possible, I believe in using the best for my car—the best oil, the best filters, the best battery, the best tires, and the best brakes. A cheap brake job can— literally—be a killer, so be prepared to pay about $50 to $100 for a good, complete brake job by your dealer's service department, an automotive department of a store, or a reputable mechanic who specializes in brake jobs. The wheels should be done in pairs, never one at a time, unless there is a leak in one that must be replaced. Have the brakes checked every 10,000 miles, and expect to have a complete brake job at 25 to 30,000 miles. A complete four-wheel job will include rebuilding or replacing wheel cylinders (it costs twice as much for new ones); replacing wheel-bearing grease seals, return springs, and brake linings; flushing and replacing brake fluid; and checking the brake lines, drums, and master cylinder. It is rare for the master cylinder to have to be replaced, but if your brake pedal sinks slowly to the floor, you may need one. The repair or replacement of disc brakes will cost slightly more than standard brakes, but don't let a serviceman tell you that the difference will be more than $25 or so for the complete job.

When you pick up your car, try to go a little early so you can watch the mechanic put the wheels back on; it isn't complicated, and will help if you ever have to change a tire. You'll need a good jack (some of the ones that come with cars are difficult to operate; try some at an auto parts store for ease of handling), a lug wrench to remove the wheel lugs that hold the wheel on the axle, and a tire iron to remove the hub cap from the wheel. Practice a few times at home, so that when it's necessary for you to change the tire you'll be able to do it with no difficulty.

Weather

Cars are temperamental about weather—they don't like it to be too cold or hot. Be sure your cooling system is working in hot weather, and avoid letting your car overheat; when you've been driving for long distances at high speeds, let the engine idle for a few minutes before you turn it off. Vaporlock in the fuel line on a hot day can prevent an engine from starting by blocking the flow of gas to the carburetor. Raise the hood to let the engine cool. The air in your tires will expand in hot weather or after driving, and can register as much as six pounds more than the actual pressure. Check pressure only after the car has been parked for at least two hours. Keep anti-freeze in your car even during the summer; most types have all-weather protection for the cooling system. If you have air-conditioning, make sure it has enough coolant. If you live close to the ocean or in a snowy climate, have the car's underbody rust-proofed.

Prepare your car for winter by checking the anti-freeze level and adding more if necessary. You can have it checked free at any service station or you can buy a little device that looks like a baster to check for yourself whenever you wish. The tester costs about a dollar, and is easy to use. Be sure that your engine is in tune. (You'll probably need to have the car lubricated twice a year, and may be able to get by with one tune-up annually, but two would be better. It can add gas mileage and months of service to the engine.) Make sure that your car heater is in good condition, and is well-vented; and run your air-conditioner about twice a month for a few minutes even in the winter. Don't waste gas on a warm-up in winter, but start off slowly to let the fluids gradually heat up to operating temperature. If your door locks are frozen, heat your key with a match before inserting it into the lock. If you must drive in snow, start slowly and drive at half the posted speeds. Don't brake on icy roads, and carry a snow shovel in your trunk. Tire chains may be a necessity, but remove them as soon as possible. You might want to carry a sandbag in your trunk for added traction in the snow, but be sure your tires have the correct recommended pressure for the additional weight. Keep your gas tank full to avoid freezing of any condensation of water vapor in the tank.

In General

Never shift a car with an automatic transmission into "park" until the car is completely stopped. If your car is emitting heavy blue smoke from the tail pipe, you probably need new piston rings, but black smoke means a carburetor adjustment is in order. Avoid prolonged idling; it's a waste of gas. If the engine doesn't start immediately, wait a few seconds before trying again, to avoid wearing the battery down. Avoid rapid starts and stops; they're hard on your car and wasteful of gas. Drive slowly through water and puddles to avoid damage to the engine and brake linings. Buy a locking gas cap and have a duplicate key made in case you lose one. Use self-service gas stations for saving on your gas bills, and use only the type of gas recommended by the manufacturer. Save money by washing your car yourself; use a mild detergent solution for the outside, rinse well, dry completely with one towel for the windows and one for the body, and wax twice a year, winter and summer. Clean the windows with a glass-cleaning solution, and the interior with the appropriate cleaner for the upholstery. Watch your dashboard gauges—they're the best indication you can have of potential trouble. If you use gasoline company credit cards, check your statements carefully. It's a good idea to have cards with several companies for convenience when you're traveling. Try to get one with a company that allows you to pay 10 percent of the amount due with no finance charge on the balance.

There are two booklets that I think you might want to have. One is sold by the Ford Motor Company for fifty cents, and is called *Car Owning Made Easier* (Ford Motor Company Listens, The American Road—JP Dearborn, Mich. 48121). The other booklet is free from Gulf, and is called *How Not to Get Stuck When You Get Stuck* (Gulf Consumer Information, P.O. Box 1403-Q, Houston, Tex. 77001).

Although you may decide to trade for a new car every year, there is every reason to expect your present car, with proper love and care, to last you for at least 100,000 miles of good, safe driving. The more you work with it and understand it, the more you will enjoy it and appreciate what a wonderful conveyance it really is, and you will join the rest of us in the great American love affair with our cars.

13

COPING WITH REPAIRS
AND MAINTENANCE

If I *Can Do It,* Anyone *Can!*

There's no question about it—unless you live in a tent (and even then you'd better have a patching kit handy!), you're going to have to learn how to care for your domicile and its appurtenances. There are numerous books and magazines designed for the sole purpose of educating you in the fine art of handiwomanism (if that's not a word, it should be), and you should make a trip to the library or bookstore for some copies. For a starter, though, you should be reasonably familiar with your equipment and should know what you can expect from it.

CUTTING COSTS

The biggest continuing expense will probably be your heating bills, so you can begin saving money right there. Inspect the weather stripping around your windows and doors and replace any that is worn or damaged; this can save you up to 10 percent on your fuel bill. If you live in a climate that necessitates storm windows, make sure they're tight-fitting; if you have air-conditioning, leave them on in the summer—they'll keep 30 percent more cool air inside. Keep your thermostat at 65 to 68 degrees during the day and 60 at night. The difference can mean a 15 to 20 percent saving on your fuel bill. Keep the thermostat at 60 in the winter if you're away, to make sure that the pipes won't freeze. While you're cutting the heat, be sure to maintain a comfortable humidity level, even if it means installing a humidifier. At a temperature of 68, you should keep the humidity at between 45 and 50 percent, but if it drops lower, you'll need more heat. When you're not using your fireplace be sure to close the damper so you won't lose your heat up the flue. Be sure to change your furnace filters as needed, usually once a month.

In the summer, make sure that all your windows are tight in the frames and that you don't have torn screens. You can buy a section of screen and replace it yourself with no difficulty, for only about a dollar or so. You'll need to have the correct size nails, and while you're buying them you can stock up on some tools you should have on hand. Buy an assortment of nails and screws, and get some woman-sized screwdrivers (particularly a Phillips head), a hammer, some pliers, a wrench, a tool to open jars, a plumber's snake, various sizes of washers, some sandpaper, household oil, fuses, and duct tape. Unless it's always been your ambition to own your own electric drill, don't buy anything expensive that can be rented when necessary. If you get into painting, plastering, or extensive plumbing you will need specific tools for each job, but don't buy anything you're not likely to use frequently. While you're in the hardware store, look over its stock of small-appliance replacement parts; instructions come with them, and you can easily put a new element in a percolator, for example.

PAINTING

If a room needs painting, you have three choices: hire a professional, do it yourself, or hang interior walls with material or some of the great new stick-on wallpapers.

If you decide to try a professional, you will have three choices of jobs from which to choose. If a painter offers a "premium" job, he means that the paint will have the most excellent finish possible for maximum dura-ability. (Of course, it will add to the cost, depending on the size of the job, probably by more than $70 to $100; painters, like plumbers, do not work cheaply.) A "standard" job means that it will be well-painted, with usual durability, and a "minimum" job offers exactly that: minimum dura-bility and appearance. Although I can't possibly quote comparative prices because each job will differ with the kind of paint you want, the size and shape of the room, and the going rate for painters in your area, I can tell you that in this case you will get precisely the job for which you pay. Unless you know that you will be happy with the selected paint for a num-ber of years, the premium job isn't necessary; the standard is acceptable and can save you money.

Shop around for painters just as you would for any other person you hire to do any kind of job, and get written quotations from several before you decide. They can only do this by visiting your home to see the area to be painted, and by knowing the colors and types of paint you want; paints vary according to types and some colors have to be specially mixed for the job. When you have selected the painter, follow the suggestions of the National Paint, Varnish and Lacquer Association about the terms of the contract. The organization recommends that it clearly specify a price; list all areas to be painted; list all types and brands of paint to be used; the number of coats to be applied; the anticipated date of job completion; an assurance that drop cloths can be used and that furniture, floors, carpets, and draperies or lawn and plants will be protected; and an assurance that all leftover materials will be removed. The Association doesn't mention this, but I would suggest that you add that you will be entitled to keep any remaining opened cans of paint for future touch-ups.

If you decide to tackle the painting job yourself, your first task will be to understand the types of paint so that you can choose the best for the place to be covered. If you will be painting ceilings anywhere and walls in an adult's bedroom or in a living or dining room, water-base latex paint will be fine. It's easy to use—you can clean up yourself and spills with water—and it dries within an hour or two. It can be washed easily, touched up quickly, and can be put on the walls with a roller to save time and brushes. (They can be washed out with water.) The paint comes in a variety of colors from different manufacturers, and you can have a special color mixed at the paint or hardware store at no extra cost. I recommend any water-base paint for the beginner; mistakes are so easily washed away.

You'll have to be more careful with oil-based alkyd paint. It dries more slowly, smells strong when wet, and requires the use of turpentine, mineral spirits, or benzine for cleaning yourself, spills, and brushes. The semigloss takes much harder wear than the latex paint, and is suited to kitchen, bathrooms, and the bedrooms of smaller children. A gloss alkyd enamel is recommended for woodwork, and a flat paint—either latex or alkyd—should always be used on ceilings to minimize glare.

Most paint manufacturers recommend the kind of primer you'll need, but you can use an inexpensive latex paint as primer on plasterboard, masonry, new plaster, and old, damp plaster. Special alkyd primers and primer-sealers should not be used on plasterboard or new plaster, and primer-sealers known as "stain-killers" should be used on wood to prevent knots from bleeding through the finish. Always use only the primer recommended by the manufacturer; the wrong one could decrease the durability of the finished surface. It's generally wise to use the best paints you can afford, especially in rooms that receive hard wear, such as the kitchen and bath. You may be tempted to save money on brushes, but it's usually a false economy; you may find yourself spending a great deal of time picking loose hairs from your drying paint. Nor should you allow yourself to be sold the top of the line; a good medium price should be about right, and will give good wear. You'll have to have several sizes and kinds of brushes. You shouldn't use the same brush for latex paint that you've used for alkyd, for instance, and you'll need wide brushes for walls and smaller ones for woodwork and tight spots. Get a brush with synthetic bristles for latex, natural for alkyd. Try the weight of the brush before you buy it, and imagine how it will feel when it's soaked with paint. Nothing is more uncomfortable than using a brush that is too heavy or unwieldy, even though its wider surface can save some time in getting the job finished.

You're going to need some other material, too. The store will probably give you a free cardboard bucket for paint mixing, but you may want to buy another for soaking brushes used with alkyd paint. If you use a roller with latex paint, you'll need a tray for the paint. Buy some turpentine or mineral spirits if needed, a plastic drop cloth, a ladder, some masking tape to protect hardware and walls when you're doing woodwork, and a putty knife and spackling compound if you'll have to repair cracked plaster.

The surface to be painted should be cleaned well before you begin. If there are many layers of paint needing removal from a small surface, you can use a chemical remover, but if the area to be stripped is large you may have to hire a professional. The job is difficult and can best be done with an electric paint remover which can start fires easily. On normal surfaces that don't require such extensive preparation, however, a good wash should be sufficient. Use a solution of trisodium phosphate, known as TSP in paint stores and as Soilax and Spic 'n Span in supermarkets, scrub the surface, and rinse thoroughly. Use ready-mixed spackle to repair small cracks or holes in plaster, and fill the crack or hole higher than the surrounding surface, because the compound will shrink as it dries. Sand off any excess when it is dry, add your undercoating, and start to paint. Ventilate the room well if you're using alkyd paint.

Wallpaper

If you want to wallpaper an area instead of painting, the new stick-on types are perfect for you. They come in an assortment of patterns and colors, and are as easy to use as are the other stick-on materials with which you're already familiar. I don't recommend a pattern for a beginner unless it is one that will be very easy to match at the seams, but look at the variety offered and see if you think it will be too hard to manage. Depending on the paint you've used and the type of wallpaper you've selected, the paint will probably be cheaper, but you won't need as many extras with the wallpaper; a ladder, scissors, and smoothing implement should do it. If you hire a professional, though, follow the same procedure as when hiring a painter.

Antiquing

If you have some furniture that would benefit from a change of appearance, buy an antiquing kit, follow instructions to the letter, and the pieces can look as good as old. There are several kits on the market, and they include everything you'll need for the job, including sandpaper, steel wool, and soft cloths. The paint can be used on unfinished furniture, too, and you can choose from a variety of wood tones and colors for any article you wish to antique. The result is very effective and can rejuvenate a piece that has seen better days. If you get tired of the finish you can always remove it with the commercial paint removers available at the paint store, and begin anew.

Besides painting, there are other jobs you can do to keep your home in good repair.

PLUMBING

The bathroom probably has more repair problems than any other room of the house, and there are some that don't require a plumber and his astronomical bill.

You should have sink washers on hand to stop leaky faucets; these inexpensive little rings can save several dollars a year in wasted water. You'll need a screwdriver and fairly heavy wrench to remove the faucet handle, but that's all for this particular job. Before you begin working, shut off the water at the valves that are generally located under a basin or sink, and behind a tub. To be sure you've cut all of the water off, run some while you're turning the valves until the water stops, and remember to shut off the faucet. If the faucet handles have "H" or "C" on the top, they are probably on the top of decorative screws, so put your screwdriver in the letter and turn until it is loose enough to remove. As you remove pieces from the handle, place them somewhere in the exact order in which they came off so you won't have any difficulty replacing them in reverse order when you finish. When you've gotten to the faulty washer, remove it and put the new one on, replace all the parts, turn the valve, and your problem should be solved.

While you're in the bathroom, take the top off the toilet's water storage tank and look inside. You'll see a small water pipe to one side; it brings clean water into the tank, and the water should be up to the marked level for proper pressure to flush the toilet. You'll see a large floating ball; that controls the height of the water in the tank, and its arm can be gently bent to raise or lower the desired level. There will be a standing pipe to control any overflow of water, and a flat bar extending from the handle on the front of the toilet to a rod inside, on the end of which is another ball sitting on an opening on the floor of the tank. With the lid off, flush the toilet to see the functioning of the parts. The handle lifts the bottom ball to allow water to run into the toilet to begin the flushing action. While this is going on, the top ball will float down as the water level drops, but will float up with the water as the tank refills until it reaches its prescribed level, then the ball will stop the water. To see its action, gently lift the rod to which it is connected while the toilet is flushing; it will stop the water immediately.

Now you can understand the problem you may have with a toilet that won't stop running; it's usually due to worn-out rods or trouble with the float at the top or the ball closing the valve at the bottom. If jiggling the handle stops the water, the problem is that the lower ball does not fit tightly onto the outlet valve at the bottom of the tank. Check the rod connecting it to the handle; if it is bent, straighten it, and look to see if the ball is seated closely on the valve. You may need to clean the mouth of the valve with steel wool, or you may need a new ball; you can buy one at the hardware store, and simply screw it back onto the rod. If that doesn't solve the problem, lift the floating ball slightly; if that shuts off the water, the rod may be bent or the ball need replacing. Bend the rod downward a little to see if it stops the water, and if that doesn't do it, buy a new ball at the hardware store and replace it as you did the other. These items cost little and are simple to remove and replace.

REPAIRMEN

There are bound to be repairs that you won't be able to handle alone; you'll find that you'll need a repairman for the washer or television or range. If possible, call only a serviceman authorized to repair your particular appliance; he'll be more familiar with any possible problems and will have more ready access to the necessary replacement parts. If your neighbor has recommended an honest, capable repairman you may want to try him instead, but in either case, get a written estimate for the work to be completed; know exactly what the charges include, and request an itemized bill after the repairs have been completed. Check to find out if the new parts have any warranty and for what length of time the repairman's work is guaranteed. Don't hesitate to call back if you are not completely satisfied or if the problem for which he has been paid persists.

A good television repairman will do his best to complete repairs on a large set in your home, and most of the time will need only to replace a few inexpensive tubes. The costliest item to be replaced, of course, is the picture tube, but it has a long life span (six to eight years or more) and most faulty pictures can be remedied with a couple of other new tubes. Unless your set is very old and you have confidence in the repairman's integrity, don't let him remove the set for a picture tube replacement without having another repairman verify the diagnosis. Have the second one come at another time and don't tell him what the first said; let him make his own determination of the problem. If it *is* the picture tube, select the repairman who offers the lower price and the quicker service; if it is not the picture tube, you've paid for two service calls, but you've saved a needless repair job that can cost over $100.

You'll have to use the same caution with any repairman; most are honest, but some (particularly those specializing in home improvements)

prey on the unwary. Be especially careful with any door-to-door contractors who call for business. Some perfectly honest ones may have to
go that route, but in any case, there are some precautions you should observe. Check to see if the man is licensed or if the Better Business Bureau
has had any complaints about him. Find out how long he has been in the
area and get the names of any customers he has had whom you can contact
for references about his work. Call them and ask if there were any problems
with his work and if so, whether he responded promptly to correct them.
Get estimates from several other contractors before deciding on one, and
when you select one, do as you did with the contract for painting—get a
commitment on the amount, the date the job will be finished, a complete
description of the materials used, and an assurance that all damage to
shrubbery or anything else will be repaired. Make sure that the contract
doesn't have any hidden clauses stating that you will supply materials; they
should be supplied by the contractor and are included in his estimated cost.
Under no circumstances accept an open-end contract; the cost could sky-
rocket. It is reasonable to allow a little leeway, but no more than 10 to 15
percent of the original estimate should be necessary. Have the contract set
up a schedule of payments, and pay nothing in advance; if he doesn't have
money of his own to buy supplies, he shouldn't try to conduct a business.
Don't let him talk you into allowing him to use your hardware store charge
account; insist that he will have to buy the supplies he needs as he goes along
on the job. After he has worked on the job for a few days, have the city
permit office send out an inspector to look it over. If it is satisfactory, have
the contractor continue; if not, have the work stopped immediately until
the changes necessary to comply with the inspector's standards are made.
When the work is completed, have the inspector return—these inspections
are usually free—and if the work is all right, you may sign a completion
statement and make final payment.

For information concerning all types of home improvements and the
things for which you should be especially watchful in your dealings with
contractors, write to the Assistant Director for Rulemaking (Bureau of
Consumer Protection, Federal Trade Commission, 7th and Pennsylvania
Ave., N.W., Washington, D.C. 20580).

Home Improvement Loans

If you find that you will need a loan to finance your home improvements,
there will be several choices open to you. You can take out a loan on your
savings or life insurance, as mentioned earlier, or you may want to go to
one of the lending institutions specializing in such loans. Many banks and
other institutions offer special home improvement loans that are insured
by the Federal Housing Administration. For loans over $2,500, these give

slightly lower interest rates and longer terms than found with a conventional loan, but for smaller amounts, the regular loan will be best. The FHA Title I rates run from 9 to 10½%, depending on the amount and length of the loan; conventional loans generally range from 10½ to 12%. Make sure you understand the annual percentage rate (APR), the total cost of interest plus principal, the monthly payments and length of term of the loan. See if life insurance is included on the conventional loan; it isn't with the Title I loan. You can investigate getting a loan through your credit union, an advance on your bank credit card line of credit, or the contractor may take out the loan with the agreement that you will repay him. Make sure he doesn't add onto the cost; the total should be exactly the same as if you had taken out the loan yourself. You may have to go to a finance company for a loan, but remember it will have high interest rates—up to 22%.

Maintenance and Thrift

Preventive maintenance is the best way to cut down on repairs, whether you do them yourself or pay to have them done. Follow the manufacturers' care suggestions on everything from your furnace to your toaster, and practice thrift whenever possible. Don't overload your washer, for instance, but save by trying to use it only once a day. Do the same with your dishwasher, and use only the recommended detergents or cleansers in both. Save water—and your water heater—by taking a shower instead of a bath; a five-minute shower uses seven gallons of water, but a tub bath takes twelve. (If you vacation during the summer, turn off the hot water heater entirely, to save about $5 a month, but remember to turn it back on when you return. In fact, unplug all the electrical appliances while you're away.) Save on electricity and wear by occasionally cooking your entire meal in the oven and not using the top burners at all, and by cooking two meals at once. Let your percolator have a day's rest and store leftover coffee in a jar in the refrigerator for the next day. Save yourself some plumbing bills by keeping a plunger on hand, and by giving all drains a weekly treatment with a drain-opening solvent. Never put coffee grounds or grease down the sink drain, of course, but if you ever need to open the curved pipe underneath to get at anything in the trap, be sure the water is turned off so the faucets aren't turned on accidentally and water runs all over the floor.

The Freezer

Anyone who owns a freezer is terrified of loss of power; if that happens, there are some steps you should follow to try to save some of that expensive food. If there is a locker plant close to you, get the food there and plan to store it until the freezer is repaired; if you can't do that, get some dry ice, if possible, and put it in the freezer with the food. (Be careful when you handle the dry ice; it can burn your hands severely.) Keep the door closed as much as possible, and estimate how long your food will safely keep. If the stoppage happens during the winter, you can store the food outside in a covered container (a large clean garbage can will do) if the temperature doesn't rise above twenty degrees. In the freezer, the food will stay frozen in a fully loaded cabinet—if the door is left closed—for about thirty-six to forty-eight hours; if there is less than half a load, the food will last less than a day. Baked food in the freezer will not stay cold as long as will meat, and dairy products will last safely for a shorter time than will any other foods. If the power loss was due to a defect in the mechanical system, your food loss, if any, may be covered by your freezer warranty. Most do cover such loss, but you must write to the company immediately with the details, stating the date, and the amount and cost of foods lost. Send the letter by registered mail to ensure its receipt. Call the local dealer to see if he wants to come to inspect the food—some warranties stipulate that you must make this offer—and find out how long you should wait before disposing of the food. Some homeowners' policies cover food lost under certain conditions, so check the policy and notify your agent.

ELECTRICITY

Until you have read a few technical books and manuals about electricity, I don't advise you to try to do much more than change fuses and bulbs, but some of the simpler things such as changing defective wiring on a lamp, or putting in a new switchplate, are easy to learn by following diagrams. Know where the switch is that controls the electricity into the house or apartment, of course, and know how to cut off the power to anything on which you might be working. Don't ever overload your outlets, and check to make sure all exposed wiring is safe and unfrayed. A roll of electrical tape can patch minor tears, but new wiring may be necessary on some of the worse cords. If you have fluorescent lights, take a bulb out of its socket with a gentle twist and look at the little metal thing in the wall bracket; that's a starter, and costs around fifteen cents. If a bulb has been flickering or turning on and off, the starter may be the culprit, and a new one will make the bulb seem like new.

Fuses and Fan Belts

Locate your fuse box and see the kind and size fuses you need. Keep some on hand and practice replacing one before you'll need to do it. Whenever an appliance stops working, think first of a blown fuse. Many dollars have been spent on unnecessary calls by expensive servicemen to replace bad fuses. Make sure the appliance is plugged in—you'd be surprised how many calls *that* causes—and make sure the outlet is receiving electricity by plugging in a lamp or radio. Make sure that all doors and lids are tightly closed, and that the washing machine's load is not unbalanced. If the washer or dryer stops, it may be due to a broken fan belt. Unplug the machine, pull from the wall, unscrew the back panel, and check the belt. If you need a replacement, be sure to take the make and model number of the machine with you; if there is a wholesale warehouse that is authorized to sell parts directly to the customer, you will be able to save a little money. If the warehouse is a long distance away, however, you'll be better off buying from the dealer or hardware store.

EMERGENCY SUPPLIES

It's always a good idea to stock up on supplies and food that you may need during a power failure. Keep a supply of candles, matches, Sterno, kerosene lamps and oil, a can opener, transistor batteries for the radio, clean water, a flashlight, and extra batteries in an accessible place. Keep a stock of nonperishable food on hand, but don't be tempted to cook or heat indoors with charcoal; the fumes are fatal.

PEST CONTROL

If you can afford it, it's a good idea to have a contract with a pest control company for monthly treatment and inspections. Even if you don't feel that you want to commit yourself to a contract for regular care, it would be wise to have a yearly call to inspect for termite damage and to spray everywhere the insects can cause trouble. Deal only with a nationally known or reputable local firm; this is a service that offers unlimited opportunities for the unscrupulous serviceman or company to take advantage of you and insist that you need costly (and unnecessary) treatments.

THE ROOF

Have a good roofing contractor inspect your roof every few years for damage to shingles and for wood rot caused by seeping water onto the roof under the covering. Most roofing materials carry a long-term warranty—usually twenty years, depending on the local weather conditions and the type of roof—but when you know you have a leak, you should have it repaired at once. If you don't know a contractor, ask your friends and neighbors, or call a local building supply store for suggestions. Follow the same procedure as for any other workman; shop around, get estimates in writing, have the same kind of contract.

THE FLOORS

The floors are as important as the roof and should be given good care and maintenance. If you have wall-to-wall carpeting, for instance, the life of the material will be doubled by good cleaning. Vacuum regularly and clean the carpet periodically. There are various types of excellent shampoos and rinses available, some requiring a machine applicator, and some that can be poured or sprayed on, allowed to dry, and brushed off. If you'd prefer the type that must be applied with a machine, the applicators can be rented for a few dollars at most hardware stores and supermarkets. For really thorough cleaning, though, you should consider having a professional service do the job. The cost is figured at about 15 cents a square foot, but the carpet will look and wear as if it were new.

If you have floor tiles that need replacing, different tiles will pose different problems. Rigid tiles such as vinyl-asbestos and asphalt will have to be broken with a hammer, and removed with a chisel. Pliable vinyl tiles can usually be cut down the center with a knife and peeled off the floor. Scrape away any old adhesive until the spot is clean and smooth. Have the proper adhesive for the kind of tile you'll be using, and follow the directions as to the amount needed. You may have to warm the rigid tiles in an oven set on "low" for a few minutes, then press them firmly into place, wipe off any excess adhesive, and put flat heavy objects on top of them while they dry. If you have wooden floors, keep them waxed and clean; grit wears into the grain of the wood. If you find a squeaky floor board, you can put talcum powder or liquid soap into the crack to lubricate the boards that are rubbing together.

As in defensive driving, when you constantly look ahead to avoid serious problems, home maintenance is based on the premise of preventive watchfulness. The small repair jobs prevent larger ones; the small maintenance tasks prevent larger, more costly ones. Do as much yourself as possible, but when you need professional help, get the best. Proper care will add to the life of everything in, on, and around your home.

14

COPING WITH SEX

How to Live with It . . .
and
without It

It's no easier to deny our sexuality than to deny our existence. As sentient human beings, we can ignore our need for sex no more easily than our need for food. Even though it is doubtful that anyone has ever gone so far as to die for lack of sex, it is a basic and vital part of life.

The woman alone is daily—and nightly—confronted with her sexuality and must learn to recognize it and cope with it. She has several choices: She can masturbate; she can try to develop a meaningful and healthy sexual relationship; and she can, when there is no other viable alternative, sublimate. There is a great deal to be said about all of these measures. Masturbation is one way of coping with sexual needs. There is certainly nothing wrong with it morally, psychologically, or physically. It gives an immediately enjoyable relief, and Masters and Johnson even claim that it relieves menstrual cramps! In lieu of a normal sex life, it may be the best thing some women can do for themselves. However, as a sole method of dealing with one's sexuality, it strikes me as unsatisfying as a full-color picture of a seven-course meal would be to a starving man—it merely whets the appetite for the real thing. It should not be thought of as a complete answer.

A sexual relationship with someone is a more fulfilling way of coping with sexuality. But although this may bring sexual gratification, there are hazards involved. There is the danger of being hurt emotionally. There is also the danger of being labeled—and becoming—promiscuous and losing one's self-respect. More on this later.

In his book *Hide-and-Seek*, published in 1967 by Doubleday & Company, Charles H. Knickerbocker, M.D. says of sublimation: "When love relations exist but sex outlets are, for one reason or another unavailable, the stored-up biological tensions need not necessarily induce neurosis. Such energy can be diverted to other creative outlets. Considerable amounts of the best creative work and art are given impetus by such energy. This phenomenon has been called sublimation; it was noticed and studied by Freud."

For most of us, sublimation simply means turning our thoughts away from sex when gratification is unavailable, and channeling our sexual drive into other pursuits. Whether this sublimation is of long or short duration, it in no way affects our femininity or sexuality, which are basic parts of our being, even during a period of abstinence, for whatever reason.

SEXUALITY

There is no "norm" for human sexuality; it differs from person to person. But in the vast majority of people, sex in all its urgency cannot stay submerged for long without serious consequences. The woman alone must learn to pace herself and its demands, so that she can achieve a sexual lifestyle with which she will be comfortable, satisfied, and well adjusted. And recognizing sexual feelings is the first step toward a healthy sex life.

Theodore I. Rubin, M.D., well-known psychoanalyst, says, in the June 1974 *Ladies Home Journal,* "There are a number of people whose sexual feelings are almost totally repressed, deadened and obliterated. These people are deprived of the pleasures sex can bring, and always suffer from serious emotional problems in other areas, too. Having and knowing one's sexual preferences is a valuable sign of being in touch with one's feelings and preferences in other areas of one's life. Many women have never had any sexual satisfaction at all, while still others have not had any sexual experience on any adult level whatsoever. Most of these women suffer from poor self-esteem and confused ideas about femininity and purity. Even today, some women suffer from paralyzing inhibitions and deep-seated emotional conflict and guilt about sexual function and potential satisfaction."

But regardless of the words of such experts, and the fact that modern contraceptive methods have increased the frequency of "safe" sexual encounters (among married and unmarried alike), every woman alone is still faced with that age-old question, "Should I or shouldn't I?" Each of us will have to answer the question for herself.

The question is especially poignant for women who have been married and have enjoyed sex with their husbands. If you have lived your married life as a faithful, virtuous woman, it is going to be difficult to shift mental gears and try to adapt yourself to the new morality. Celibate or Swinger? As harsh as that sounds, you may well be confronted with just that choice. Sex is not something you can put off thinking about until tomorrow, and the pressures you face will be exhausting. Most widows find, to their utter astonishment, that their sexual desire is more intense during the days following their husbands' death than at any time during their marriage. Whatever the reason—it is a fact, and a problem the widow must live with and try to solve.

The problems of the divorcee are just as urgent; not only has she been accustomed to a regular sex life, but now she may feel she must prove to herself that she is still attractive to men. She is too apt to accept the first offers that come, in order to rebuild her self-esteem, but she may find that she has allowed her needs to cloud her judgment.

The unmarried woman, who may not yet have had an affair, may confront the ancient question of the virgin, "Should I wait until marriage, or will it really make any difference?" I don't think that the woman of the late twentieth century will ever be as restricted in her behavior or her thinking as were her earlier counterparts. But my personal opinion is that she will be selective in her sexual partners, if she has any. I don't know that the concept of the virginal bride will ever reappear; maybe that's a good thing, maybe not. The new woman, aware of herself and her potentials, may decide that she wishes to remain a virgin until marriage; but only because it suits her, not to conform to society's ideal. Or she may opt for premarital sex only with men or women with whom she has a deep relationship. In any case, she will decide for herself what is best for *her,* and will not be a puppet adhering to standards not her own. The important consideration is her self-respect; how she will feel about herself in a year or a decade. A woman should never do anything that will make her uncomfortable with herself—she has to live with herself, no matter who else may be around. And *her* opinion of herself is important.

Robert C. Kolodny, of the Reproductive Biology Research Foundation in St. Louis, said that in conducting interviews with hundreds of people, he and his researchers have found that "a strictly mechanical, hedonistic approach to sex, while espoused by some, is relatively rapidly falling by the wayside." Kolodny said that many of those who experimented with the hedonistic approach found it "enslaving, not feeling." The same view is echoed by Professor Amitai Etzioni, a Columbia University sociologist: "It's been discovered in varying degrees that all this sexual spice leads to less satisfaction. There is now more emphasis on things other than sexual acrobatics." And even those erstwhile proponents of the mechanics of sex William H. Masters and Virginia E. Johnson now decry the fact that too much emphasis has been placed on the techniques of sex (what they now call "sex-sex") and not enough on a commitment of love ("love-sex").

In today's world there seem to be indications that women can actually handle the new sexual freedoms better than men. Perhaps it is because in a sense they have had to face human emotional crises relatively alone (bringing up the children, having the babies, dealing with the "domestic" world); while men have typically lived their days within a somewhat compartmentalized, functional workaday environment. Moreover, men have been taught that many methods of tension release (crying, "emoting") are "feminine," and so repress many so-called "natural" responses. If this has some truth to it, it isn't so strange that women find it a bit easier, in many cases, to "go with it"—to accept and internalize freer ways of dealing with their sexuality. A woman, used to a world in which she alone is responsible for changes (from diapering to making the decision about what to do when the roast burns, the cake falls, and Johnny gets chicken pox on the afternoon of a dinner party) can perhaps find it easier to reorganize. A man who is brilliant in the office may fall apart when, having lost his wife, he finds that he has no clean shirts, the coffee is gone, and the electricity has gone off. Someone has wisely observed that today women alone set about changing their lives; men alone look for new wives!

In this section I will be addressing primarily the problems of women who have suddenly found themselves alone after a number of years of marriage, rather than younger women who may not be married. For them the area of dating is not so apt to be so new or mind-boggling.

DATING

I envy the younger women who have grown up in the last few years; their choices and decisions are not as difficult as for those of us who are older or who have been married for most of our adult lives. For us, the shock of re-entry into the world of dating is great. The woman who is just starting an entirely new kind of social life suddenly realizes that a lot of time may have passed since she was an eligible young girl, and the field of the males she can date has dwindled dramatically. If you were married for a decade or two, you'll be astounded to realize that the young men who were your contemporaries may now be middle-aged, paunchy and balding, probably married, and often with an eye for nubile young girls instead of mature women. You will feel that time should have stood still; that while you were living your life nothing on the outside should have changed, and now that a part of your life is over, you should be able to pick up at the earlier spot and go on from there. But time has changed all that, and both the world and you are older. To an attractive woman whose husband always made her feel beautiful and desirable, it is a shock to realize that she has suddenly become something different in the eyes of the world. It didn't matter while she was married; her husband was her contemporary.

The perceptive man who looks beyond the patina of a few added years and sees the warm, vibrant woman beneath is wise and rare indeed, and the woman who finds a loving relationship with one of these men is fortunate. Even so, there is developing a gradual awareness of the older woman's sexual potential. Some experts on sexual behavior think that this problem of peak sexual growth could be resolved neatly by abolishing the social convention that mates women with men who are older. They feel that a woman of 35 and a boy of 18 might be ideal sexual partners, in terms of sexual appetite, capability, and energy. A Russian sexologist, Abram Svyadoshch, says that "men often overestimate a younger woman's needs for sex while they underestimate an older woman's needs."

But this is easier to theorize and agree with than to implement. The fact is that we must deal with *our* situations, *our* possibilities, *our* needs. If we are sure within ourselves that the quality of sexuality is ageless and are comfortable with this knowledge; and if we strive for mature and fulfilling sexual relationships, age—ours and his—will be a secondary consideration.

Although older women will have no more difficulty finding men interested only in a sexual encounter than will their younger sisters, quality, rather than quantity, is what is wanted and that's in short supply. Meeting men is not as much of a problem as is meeting the right *kind* of men.

Men to Avoid

I know you've all heard the old "My wife doesn't understand me" pitch. Then there's the man who tries to shame you into sex, usually by telling you that you're probably frigid or implying that you may have homosexual tendencies. He's in the "natural sex" advocate's league. You know the type—"Nothing is more natural than sex. It isn't healthy to deny your true desires." And how about the, "I've paid for a dinner and an evening on the town; you owe me something" bit? All you owe him is the pleasure of your company and a not-so-fond farewell. Watch out for the flatterer. He's one of the most dangerous ones you'll meet, because at times you may feel particularly lonely and gullible. His kind can spot the vulnerable woman across a crowded room, but you won't have an enchanted evening with *him*. Then there's the "Everybody's doing it" advocate. Fine, let him go join the action somewhere else.

Of course, there are always the wrestlers who apparently got their concept of correct male behavior from their prehistoric forebears, and think that women are turned on by a little rough stuff. But even they are better than the weepers, those poor souls who like to play on your emotions and hope to make you feel sorry enough for them to comfort them in bed. And beware of one who uses the "Tea and Sympathy" come-on; *he* says he isn't sure that any woman can ever arouse him again, but what woman wouldn't want to accept the challenge? Watch out for the employer—married, naturally—who wants to take you to dinner to discuss some business problems. You will know his interests aren't on the latest Dow-Jones if he tells you he's taken a room at a local motel. Married men are always to be avoided; they can lead to nothing but trouble, and the sooner you say "Goodbye" the better. Unfortunately, the number of unmarried women is far greater than of unmarried men—more than 23 million of us, over 16 million of them. Thus some women consciously seek a relationship with a married man because he is there and available, and because she really isn't happy in the dating game; she wants some sort of romantic and sexual stability. She knows that there's no future for their affair, but elects to settle for the temporary security of a one-to-one involvement. As long as she is aware of the probable end of the affair and is willing to be the "other woman," she may be able to achieve some kind of happiness, but it will be tenuous at best.

Another insidious approach of men to avoid is the "It doesn't matter to me one way or the other; if you don't want sex with me, there are plenty of other women who do." Good! You can show him out and not have to worry about him one minute, since he's so successful. Avoid the borrower; he will begin with a few dollars and may wind up with your car and your life savings. If he's having financial problems, offer to introduce him to your banker. Don't let him give you that old business about putting everything into a joint account before marriage (this one usually proposes, and can convince you that he honestly intends to marry you).

Two of the worst offenders in the dating losers' sweepstakes are the indifferent lover and the jealous one, and either should not be given an extra minute of your time. The indifferent ones will make dates and not show, or tell you they'll call and then forget, and constantly treat you with a casualness bordering on cruelty. They are determined not to let a woman "run" their lives or think she has any control over them, and can cause many a sleepless night and tear-soaked pillow. They're not worth one tear, so unless you are a latent masochist, get rid of them fast. The jealous type is a special exhibit in this gallery of failures; after one date he will think that he owns you, and that your every waking minute should be devoted to thoughts of him. Woe to any woman who has a career and thinks her time is her own. He will dismiss her career as a female foible, and will make it clear that *he* should be her prime concern. You will never be able to have an adult relationship with this type.

Because these types of men abound, as they always have, many women are becoming cynical, and reach a point when it is tempting to say, "It just isn't worth the fight. There are worse things than sitting at home alone."

What an adult, mature woman needs is an adult, mature man (the two are *not* synonymous). Then any decision about going to bed together will be made because of affection, respect, and common interests and not just because of desire.

Finding Men

Where to go to meet eligible men? Through your work—not necessarily a co-worker, but someone who works in the same building, or someone who travels in the same commuter train. In organizations and classes and group therapy sessions. At church. Through friends. Through your hobby. At stores you frequent. Blind dates (but only if your friend who arranges it knows your interests and the type of man you like).

When you date, try to avoid embarrassing situations. If you don't know him too well, leave yourself an out by saying you'll have to leave at a certain time; if he turns out to be all right you can always change your mind. Perhaps you'd feel more comfortable on a first date meeting him somewhere, especially if you drive; that way you can leave whenever you like, and it eliminates any possibility of your having to fend him off at your front door. Don't go to his apartment until you really know him well. Keep in mind that you never have to justify refusing sex with any man; say "no" and let it go at that. If he never calls again you'll know he probably was after only one thing. There are intelligent ways of refusing a man that don't threaten, insult, or belittle him. In fact, if you are clever as well as honest, you may intrigue him!

Sexual freedom means different things to men and women. To us it means a freedom from guilt and inhibitions—and an awareness of ourselves, our femininity, and our sexuality. It means that whether or not we choose to be intimate is beside the point; the point is that whatever we do, we do because *we* want to do it, not because it is the custom or because it is expected of us. In sex, as in every other area of our lives, we should aim to be our own women, to live as we see fit according to our own standards, needs, and religious or moral beliefs. Many people too often think that sexual freedom means freedom from the necessity of any preliminaries to a possible sexual encounter. They think it means freedom to live out their sexual fantasies at the expense of another, using that person as an object. No matter how important sex is, people have more than that to offer one another—unless we are wantonly promiscuous, we want kindness almost as much as we want sex.

How wonderful it is to meet men who offer kindness, understanding, companionship; who are witty and bright; who are mature enough to let a relationship grow until sex will be a natural result. Rare is the man who understands that a woman may be lonely, but not desperate. But then, rare and valuable is *any* person we want to have in our lives as a close friend.

Computer Dating

There are so many businesses that are profiting from the human fear of being alone that you will have to be careful you don't fall prey to one that is unscrupulous. There are computer dating services that will match you with men with similar interests, but the fees are pretty steep (they can run up to $200 for the first three names, with additional fees for more names), and you will have no money-back guarantee of satisfaction. Even more risky are the organizations that advertise in the paper with a question such as "Widowed? Single? Divorced?" and give you a number to call. You are likely to be refused any information unless you sign a contract for their services, which may turn out to be another computer dating business.

AFFAIRS

Suppose you do find the man with whom you want to have an affair—not a passing encounter, but a real love affair? Remember that you don't necessarily sacrifice your independence and your "liberation" by making the man in your life feel attractive, desirable, special. That's the way you'd like him to make *you* feel, isn't it? And that's what equality is all about. Treat a man with the same deference and consideration you would give to any friend. Keep in mind that he's not just a man; he's a person, too. Take it from there.

To make for easier reading, throughout this Chapter I refer to a lover or mate as "he." It would be ridiculous to ignore the fact than uncounted thousands of women are lesbians, and find satisfaction in homosexual affairs. Added to the risks and rewards involved in any close relationship, they have additional problems that arise from the way in which society and the law regard the fact of their difference, but the joys and heartbreaks in any romantic relationship are very much the same, no matter what the sex of the partners.

Before you enter into an affair, there are several things that must be taken into consideration. If you live alone, there will be no problem about where you'll meet, but what if you have roommates or have children at home? You probably will be restricted to meeting at his place, and if *he* has roommates or children, there is a problem. Meeting at motels is sordid—and expensive—so you'll have to work something else out. There are several options—and they all involve patience and understanding. If you're lucky and well-to-do, perhaps you can find a small apartment. Or, if you have understanding friends, you may be able to arrange to borrow their places while they are away. (Try to make it a matter of a leisurely afternoon, day, or weekend—"quickies" are apt to be unsatisfactory and tense.) Your children's schedules, ages, and maturity will have a bearing on whether or not you can use your home (or his) for those special personal times of togetherness, but this is something every couple has to work out individually and with consideration for the feelings of other involved people.

You may as well prepare yourself from the beginning to recognize that an affair may end someday, so unless you can face the emotional upheaval that will then inevitably follow, think hard before you become too involved. Contrary to some modern misconceptions, fostered by the *Playboy*-type philosophy, most people cannot jump in and out of beds with no emotional attachment to others involved. There is still the knowledge that our bodies are very special, and that when we give them we give part of our beings.

As with most other areas of your life, there will be many times when you'll need to talk over your problems with someone who can offer advice about coping with your sexuality. It is difficult to feel free enough with a member of the clergy to discuss your needs and problems with him, unless you know one another fairly well, but there are numerous counseling services available to you. Look in the yellow pages of your telephone directory under marriage and family counseling. There are free services and those requiring fees. The costs will be similar to those specializing in counseling with children, and there are, in some cities, services dealing specifically with divorcees and widows.

SUBLIMATION

You may be advised to sublimate your sexuality, at least for a time. You won't want to be as drastic as St. Francis when he jumped into the snow to cool his unwanted ardor, but a cold shower sometimes helps, believe it or not. The object, of course, is to take your mind off sex and to keep it off for as long as necessary. This is not at all easy in our sex-oriented world. Sex is presented as the ultimate solution to everything from bad breath to postnasal drip! And there *is* a lot of truth to the idea that relief of sexual tension makes us feel better. But the fact remains that it isn't always possible, and at those times deliberate sublimation may be the wisest course.

In such a time, try to guard yourself from any unnecessary stimulation. Avoid the erotic. *Don't* go to sexy movies or read any books that will keep your libido in an uproar. There are many things that can be absorbing and will help.

If you have a job, throw yourself into it and learn all you can about it. Take courses that will help you do your work better or more efficiently. (You may receive the additional reward of job advancement, which won't hurt, either.) If you are a housewife, don't stay home and brood. Even with a houseful of children, there are many times when you will be alone. Study a foreign language; brush up on your college major; take guitar lessons. Go swimming at the YWCA; bicycle, play tennis, exercise. Garden, knit, sew, read, clean house, scrub the floors, work on your car. Take a course in something practical such as plumbing or banking or preparing income tax returns. Do volunteer work, write letters, take up something new and absorbing.

You *can* do it, for an afternoon, a week, or however long it is necessary. It *is* possible to deal intelligently with your very real sexual needs, even though it may not be easy. It's a constant, conscious struggle, but other woman are doing it, and so can you. Remember that maturity is the ability to cope with reality (even if you don't like it).

Marriage

What about marriage? Or remarriage? Or a permanent or long-term commitment to someone in which you both decide to live together without the traditional marriage arrangement?

More and more people of all ages are entering into non-marital living arrangements that may or may not result in marriage. From college dormitories to retirement villages men and women are choosing to live together without marriage, and without fear of condemnation or censure. Many young couples, put off by the rising divorce rate, have decided on a no-strings-attached arrangement that is often as stable as a marriage but can be terminated without the cost or messiness of a divorce. Many older people choose to live together without benefit of marriage in order to retain their full Social Security benefits, which would be decreased if they married.

The financial arrangements in any of these cases are flexible, but are usually divided evenly between the partners, and at the dissolution of the relationship, there are rarely problems about distributing the household goods, as there would be following a divorce. Generally, and of course there are exceptions to every case, furnishings are not bought jointly, so ownership is not in question. The entire situation can be viable, fulfilling, and completely satisfactory for both partners.

But what if you meet a man you love who returns that love, and you decide to make the momentous commitment of marriage? You'll have to be sure of the reasons you're marrying. Is it love? Or sex? Or companionship? Hopefully, it will be all three, but for some women, security will be the deciding factor. I think that a marriage based primarily on the hope for a secure future will have the roughest going of all; what would hold it together if the husband could no longer provide? Another divorce and two more unhappy people.

A First Marriage

If you are contemplating your first marriage (with or without traditional legal and/or religious sanctions), you will have fewer decisions to make than the widow or divorcee, but all women face the same basic decisions before they take this momentous step. The most dangerous thing is mistaking loneliness for love, and if you have been married before, you are particularly vulnerable. How can you tell if it's love? Would you rather be with *him* than with anyone else in the world? Are you miserable when you're apart? Is his happiness important to you? Is it agony to imagine life totally without him? If the answer to all these questions is "yes," you are probably in love.

If you've never married, you'll enter your first marriage with some preconceived ideas about the way it will be; try to be realistic. Marriage is not a cure-all for any problems you may have. Don't enter marriage as an escape, but only as the vehicle for a new way of life that will involve you and another person—a partnership of equality for sharing your lives, including the good and the bad. If there are certain things about the man you don't like (and there will be), don't delude yourself that marriage will change him. There is not a woman living who has not nurtured the secret belief that her love could reform the worst drunkard, the most notorious womanizer, the most shiftless man alive. If you really believe that, try to name *one* case in which that has happened. It isn't worth the heartache to find out if you're a rare exception to that rule.

Two rules from which you should never deviate: Never criticize your husband to *anyone* except a marriage counselor; and neither live with parents (his or yours) nor invite them to live with you. It just doesn't work.

Remarriage

It isn't quite so simple if you are remarrying. You'll have to use the same criteria for deciding if this is the right man for you, and if you have children, you will have to remember that you will be involving their lives as well. If the *man* has been married previously, and has children, that's another complication.

You will have to think practically; you're not a young girl going un-encumbered into marriage. You are a woman of property and responsibil-ities, and they are not easily ignored. There are many questions to be asked before the marriage; don't wait and hope that they will work them-selves out with time. As in every other area of your life, planning ahead eliminates future problems.

For instance, where will you live? If you have a house, will he move in with you? Will you keep the title in your name or add his to the deed? If you decide to sell or rent your house and move in with him, what will become of the money from the sale or rent? If you live in a community property state you won't have to worry about all these things, but what if you live in one of the others?

If you both rent apartments, before you decide to move into his, make sure his lease permits children, if you have any. Will you be able to get out of your lease or can you sublet? You must consider all this or you may find yourself paying rent or upkeep for two residences. (I would suggest, if you have children, to try to stay in your own place; they don't need another change unless you are sure it will be for their special good.)

If you die before he does, who will inherit anything you have, your children or your new husband? What will you do about your savings and your hard-won credit rating? Are you going to get credit cards as "Mrs. Second Husband"? Do you plan to put all your money into a joint check-ing or savings account?

If your children are small, do you want them to be adopted by your new husband? If you both have children, do they seem compatible? Do you and his children like each other? What about your children and your suitor? These are serious questions which have to be settled before the wedding, to prevent a great deal of misery for all concerned if you act without forethought.

My advice, as far as your house and money are concerned, is to keep them in your name, and through your will, guarantee that your children will inherit whatever you have. They are the children of your first hus-band, after all, and are entitled to benefit from any fruits of his labors. If you have children by the second marriage, you probably will want to maintain this condition, and have the later children provided for by their father. This is something that you must decide before you remarry, letting your relationship with your second husband be a determining factor.

If you are considering his adopting your children, and are a widow, keep in mind that they will lose their Social Security benefits; it might be best to avoid legal adoption unless you are sure that your new husband will be able to raise and educate your children without the money. If you are a divorcee, the children may lose their support benefits from their father unless you remembered to have a stipulation in the decree that remarriage and/or adoption would not affect their payments. In any case, think long and hard about legal adoption; it is not always the best course to follow.

There is one other consideration if you are a widow: Can you cope with the possibility of becoming one again? Statistically, the chances are good that you will outlive another husband, so you will have to give a great deal of thought to that eventuality. However, to turn your back on happiness because of the fear of pain is to shut out a portion of life that is vital to your being a whole person. You cannot live in fear of loss, but must go forward to meet whatever life brings, the good *and* the bad.

If you have weighed all the pros and cons and your decision is for remarriage, don't bring the ghost of your former husband to the new marriage. Don't compare your old love and your new love, and don't expect the two to be alike. It would not be fair to the living or the dead.

That doesn't mean that you won't mention your first husband; it would be unrealistic to act as if an important part of your life had not existed. Just don't dwell on it—live your life *now* to the fullest, and appreciate your new husband for his own attributes. If you are a divorcee, your greatest hazard is in selecting a man who is either the same as your first husband or exactly the opposite. Consider the man on his own merits, and give him a chance to show his own qualities.

Whatever the circumstances, keep openness and honesty between the two of you; talk over any problems, and respect each other for the individuals you are. No woman has ever lost anything—her independence, her personality, her individuality—in a good love relationship. Work at it, and make yours one of the good ones.

15

COPING WITH TRAVEL, HEALTH,
INCOME TAX

The World, the Flesh, and Uncle Sam

What is more fun, or a better way to get away from it all, than to travel? More and more women are traveling alone; we are becoming one of the most widely traveled groups in America. There have always been the tour groups of widows; the busload of well-coiffed, nicely dressed, sixtyish ladies being shepherded around by a weary guide is a common sight. I always used to pity them but I've come to admire them more and more; at least they are out with other people, seeing new places and doing new things, and aren't sitting at home looking at blank walls.

Today, women alone can travel much more easily than in the past. And we don't have to go in pods—we can, and do travel anywhere in the world alone. Although we may still encounter some problems with desk clerks who expect to see a male when we register, there are few places to which we may not travel alone, from a camel ride in Afghanistan to a camera safari in Africa, from a trip to the remotest reaches of the South Pacific to a wilderness trek in upper Canada. We are limited only by our time, money, and energy. There are trips that are perfect for a weekend or a season; that cost very little or a great deal; that can be relaxing or exhausting. The ideal, of course, is to plan a trip that you can afford, that will last long enough for you to see and do everything you wish, and that will leave you exhilarated but refreshed. You may not find that ideal, but today there are so many alternatives that there is no excuse not to travel at least once in a while. It's good for you!

TRAVEL

TRAVEL ABROAD

Want to go to Europe?

American Express offers a fifteen-day, fully escorted tour of seven countries featuring stops in London, Paris, Amsterdam, and Rome, for a very reasonable price, including air fare from New York. The cost includes two meals a day in many cities, and all land travel by motor-coach. Swissair will give you a week in Europe with a car and accommodations during the winter, at a low cost that doesn't include meals or air fare. These are just two examples of travel opportunities offered to people who can save the money and take time to travel abroad. And there are many more, ranging from very short and economical theater trips to London to long and luxurious jaunts to the continent.

However you get to Europe, a Eurailpass is a good investment. Purchase it before leaving home in order to avoid paying a surcharge if you travel first class, and be prepared for excellence in service and equipment if you ride on one of the luxurious Trans-European Express (TEE) trains. For $60, for instance, you can travel from East Berlin to Moscow, if you're so inclined, in two and a half days, in a two-passenger compartment furnished with Oriental rugs, bronze lamps, blue wallpaper, blue draperies and a table (not blue). You guessed it, you'd be on the famed Blue Express, traveling at the height of luxury offered by Europe's expansive rail system, so you can imagine for what little cost you would be able to travel first- or second-class all over the continent. And for even greater savings, if you qualify, there is the Student-Railpass, like the Eurailpass good in thirteen countries, but offering second-class accommodations (usually eight persons per compartment, or six in a "couchette" compartment, in which the beds pull out of the train walls). When you reach your destination, avoid the higher-priced hotels and use the charming guest houses and pensions that are available. Some offer food of excellent quality, and as a bonus, you will be able to meet other travelers.

If you're not in a hurry, consider going to Europe by ship. Your choice of vessel is limited—your best bet is the Queen Elizabeth II, but only at certain times of the year. (She's busy in the Caribbean during the winter.) Beginning at the end of March each year, you can travel on the giant liner for a leisurely six-day trip in a medium-price outside room for four, including all meals and shipboard facilities and entertainment. The price is for a round-trip ticket, and compared with the usual round-trip air fare, it is a bargain. The main difference to be considered is the length of the voyage—six days as against six hours by air.

Of course, you're not limited to Europe. You can go to Africa for a tent safari; or take a twenty-eight-day caravan trip through India; or go on a cruise through the Pacific islands that make up Micronesia; or make an odyssey to the Orient; or circle South America. Travel to Australia; or make a journey to the Middle East; or go on a round-the-world voyage on a standard liner or a freighter. Prices vary according to carrier and destination, but the difference between the cost of an airliner and a cargo-passenger ship is substantial. Freighter travel means only up to ten or twelve fellow passengers, which may appeal to some and not to others. The accommodations are similar to a room in a good hotel, and there is superior food, plus the benefits of duty-free bargains on shipboard of cigarettes and alcohol. Bookings must be made well in advance of departure date for freighter travel, owing to the limited accommodations. There is no doctor on board because maritime law requires one only if the passenger list exceeds twelve, so take that into consideration before you book on a noncommercial liner.

For information about any trip, ask a travel agent or the carriers who go to the spot in which you're interested. There are a variety of offerings as to tours or individual trips, and there is no fee charged by the agent who helps you plan your trip. (If your department store has a travel department, you can charge the trip to your account.) You may even want to join one of the many travel clubs that offer interesting trips, group rates, and yet allow you to be as alone as you wish.

Tipping

When you travel overseas, you should have a convenient guide to the currency so that you will know how much to tip and what your correct change should be. Americans tend to overtip when they're abroad, probably through a lack of familiarity with the foreign money, so here's a simple guide to help you. On any non–first-class ocean voyage, a rule of thumb is to tip about $1 to $1.50 per day for the cabin attendant, and $1.50 to $2 a day for the dining attendant. If you travel first class, double these figures. Don't tip the maitre d' unless he's been especially helpful, and then count on giving him about $5 for the week. You should expect to tip the wine steward, if you use him, and the deck stewards about $3 per week. Tip at the bar as you buy, about the same as in the States, 15 percent. If you're on a cruise or trip that takes ten days or less, tip at the end of the trip; otherwise, at the midway point and the end. If you are averse to tipping, book passage on a ship operated by the Holland-America line, where none is allowed. On land, tip exactly as you would in this country for your food and services. (Ten to fifteen percent for meals, a quarter to fifty cents per bag for luggage, a dollar a day to a maid, and the same to any other hotel attendant would be ample. Some countries add the tip into the price charged, so be sure you don't tip twice for the same service.)

TRAVEL IN THE WESTERN HEMISPHERE

What about our own hemisphere? You can fly to South America from Miami for a fifteen-day trip during our spring and summer months (their winter months). Caribbean cruises, by both ship and plane, are offered by almost every travel agency in the country. Or if a cruise ship is not for you, how about a ten-day voyage before the mast of a windjammer for very reasonable prices? (You can write for further information to Windjammer Cruises, P.O. Box 120, Dept. 10S, Miami Beach, Florida 33139.)

How about Mexico? Again, you can travel there by ship from Miami or you can fly. Interested in a ski vacation in Canada? Eastern Airlines offers programs that include air transportation, a rental car, chalet condominium, and ski-lift tickets. If you're interested in fishing, swimming, boating, hiking, camping, riding, or relaxing, you can do all of these on a Manitoba Farm Vacation. Begun in 1972, the Manitoba Farm Vacation Association has fifty farms in the program, and costs include accommodations and food. If you're a train buff and enjoy the leisure of a relaxing trip by rail, you can travel, one-way, from coast to coast, for a very low fare which includes meals and a sleeping berth. The trip takes three days if you make no stops, but you can get off anywhere you like and re-board at any time within a period specified on your ticket. Canadian trains cross the country, and are well-run and maintained. They make connection with Amtrak trains at Vancouver, Montreal, Detroit, and Buffalo. The Canadian lines offer economy travel on Monday, Tuesday, and Wednesday during the summer, and meals may be purchased on board for reasonable rates. (Information about specific routes and fares may be obtained by writing to the government-owned Canadian National Railways, 935 Lagauchetiere Street W., P.O. Box 8100, Montreal, Quebec H3c3N4, or to the corporate-owned Canadian Pacific Rail, P.O. Box 6042, Montreal, Quebec HcD3E4.)

TRAVEL IN THE UNITED STATES

The traveler who wants to journey by train in the United States will find the current picture much brighter than a few years ago, thanks to Amtrak. There is still much to be desired as far as connections and schedules are concerned in some areas, but the trains in service are adequate, and personnel is usually courteous and efficient.

Train

In June 1974, two of my children and I traveled from Atlanta to Williamsburg, Virginia via Southern Railways and Amtrak. We were enchanted with the trip; it was smooth and uneventful, although some road beds in this country are not maintained as well as they should be. We left on time and we arrived early. The cost was reasonable, we saw a lot of the countryside without the bother involved in driving a car, and we loved the relaxation and elegance of the train. I can heartily recommend at least one train trip to anyone who is interested in seeing our own country.

There are other travel adventures that evoke the past, the most nostalgic being a journey up or down the Mississippi on a genuine paddlewheel steamboat, the Delta Queen. You can board at New Orleans, St. Louis, Cincinnati, Pittsburgh, or St. Paul, and there are weekend cruises available as well as longer ones. (For a brochure and cruise schedules see a travel agent or write to Delta Queen, Dept. RJ 02-09, 322 E. Fourth Street, Cincinnati, Ohio 45202.)

Bus

Unless you drive, one of the best ways to get to out-of-the-way places is by bus, and it's a good bargain anytime. If you think of buses as second-class travel, you haven't see some of the large luxury cruisers traveling the highways today. Greyhound's Americruisers and Continental Trailways' Silver Eagles are similar to giant jets. The seats are comparable, the interior noise level is about the same, and the ride is almost bump-free. These buses all have air-conditioning and bathrooms, of course, and both companies offer, on their special runs, fewer seats for greater leg room, lounge areas, galleys, stewardess service, taped music, and free snacks. The special runs don't operate on all routes and it's necessary to make reservations. The special service is only a few dollars more than the regular.

Don't go by bus if you're in a hurry, but if you have the time to see the scenery and make a couple of stops along the way, you can buy a special go-anywhere thirty-day pass on either line (the other will honor it). This is the best bet if you're going to be traveling more than 6000 miles, and it allows you to vary your itinerary as you wish, with no reservations. There is a small additional charge if you go by special bus, and on any line, you will be able to bring along up to 150 pounds of luggage. There is usually at least one stop every three hours, with comfort stops (for buses without restrooms) lasting about fifteen minutes, and meal stops about forty-five.

All major lines offer guided and individual tours of every part of the country, and their costs are generally lower than standard tours. The escorted tours are more expensive, but are on special buses that don't have to make non-tour stops. (For information about tours, contact any bus line or write to Greyhound World Tours, Inc., Greyhound Tower, Phoenix, Ariz. 85077, or Continental Trailways Tours, Inc., 315 Continental Avenue, Dallas, Tex. 75207.)

Plane

If you travel by plane, check to see if the airline is offering any kind of special rate for that particular time of the year, and try to avoid traveling during a holiday or vacation season. Use the airline's early-morning and late-night flights for appreciable savings, and save even more by flying tourist class (generally about $30 difference).

Car

If you travel by car in a foreign country, be sure that you know all the traffic laws and safety regulations, and abide by them faithfully. If you travel in this country by car, do get a travel guide from your automobile club or one of the major oil companies. You can also ask for their free tour-planning services and excellent maps showing roads under construction, toll roads, and location of gasoline and comfort stations. Of course you will have your car in top condition for the road, with good tires, a good spare, all your usual car-care equipment plus a fire extinguisher, and a thermos for good hot coffee. Stop at motels to use the public restrooms rather than using those at service stations, which generally leave much to be desired in the way of cleanliness. As you enter a new state, stop at the Welcome Center. This is a good place to stretch your legs, get some folders about the state's attractions, pick up maps, travel information. Those that don't offer free soft drinks have water fountains, and all of the centers are well-kept and clean.

If you *do* have car trouble on the road, be careful from whom you accept help. If you'd like to wait for a while, most Interstates are well-patrolled, and a state patrol officer should be along shortly. Be reticent about accepting help from men who are traveling alone or with other men. If any stop, and you are suspicious, tell them (through a window rolled down no more than an inch or two) that the patrol has already stopped and is sending help; they won't linger if they think a patrol car will be back. You are generally safe if a long-distance trucker stops. Most of these drivers know the road and the distance to the next service station, and many drive radio-equipped trucks and can call ahead for help. There are, periodically, reports of women drivers being robbed or raped by male motorists who have cars equipped with flashing red lights. If you're not sure whether or not it's really an official car (if you know it isn't, keep going), don't roll down your window lower than just mentioned, and ask for identification; only when you're satisfied the man is an officer should you give him your license. All your doors are locked already, so don't unlock any of them, and don't get out of the car. It is always a good rule to travel by daylight so you can get help when needed.

A self-contained camper is a good answer to cutting travel costs, but it requires a good deal of care and you should be cautious about stopping in isolated places for overnight parking. Campers are ideal for stays in national parks and for intercity travel, however, so if you can afford the cost, investigate buying one at reduced prices from Labor Day to Christmas, either new or used. Depending on the type you buy and the condition it's in, the price can vary by several thousands, so before you invest, be sure the savings you will realize in food and motel costs will be substantial.

Before you travel, write to the Chamber of Commerce of the United States (1615 H Street, N.W., Washington, D.C. 20006) for the names and addresses of chambers of commerce in any area of the country; they can give you complete information about things to see and do in each locale. Stay in motels that are just outside town for lower rates, use the coffee shop instead of the dining room for savings, and stop at the lower-priced motels without pools and color television for as much as $5 or $6 a day difference in most locations. Use your tour-guide information to plan your sightseeing so that you will save time and gas, and visit local libraries, museums, and colleges for any special free programs being offered during your visit. Some colleges even rent rooms during the summer.

If your funds are practically nonexistent but you love to travel, you can get a job for the summer as a tour guide either here or abroad, or with one of the national parks or tourist spots. You can even work as a maid or cabin attendant on a ship (you'll probably have to join a union for that one, but it's worth investigating).

Don't overlook the three-day and weekend specials offered by most airlines to Florida, New York, or Las Vegas. A short trip in the doldrums of winter should hold you until your real vacation.

Other Places to Go

You will be in the majority, of course, if you travel by car, and there is no limit to the things you can see. You can visit one of the summer festivals that are held in every section of the country, from the Gathering of the (Indian) Tribes, held in Hayward, Wisconsin in the first week of July, to the Stratford Shakespeare Festival in Stratford, Connecticut. If you're interested in music, you have offerings as diverse as the Newport Jazz Festival in late June and the Aspen Music Festival, through July. A rodeo? You can't beat Wyoming's Cheyenne Frontier Days in late July, and if flowers are your thing, Richmond, Virginia will hold its Rose Festival in June, and Atlanta its Dogwood Festival in April. Your travel agent can give you more information about all these.

Interested in a camp just for women? You'll have a chance to explore new interests or old hobbies at camps such as The Offshore Sailing School (5 E. 40th Street, New York, N.Y. 10016), which offers a week-long session at Martha's Vineyard, Massachusetts. How about combining fun and credit toward a college degree? You can enroll in a one- or two-week session at the Arrowmont School of Arts and Crafts, (Box 567, Gatlinburg, Tenn. 37738) while getting credit at the University of Tennessee. If you'd like a week of learning new dishes from an expert, write about the course conducted by Libby Hillman (17 Lawrence Street, New Hyde Park, N.Y. 11040), or if you want to brush up on your golf game, you can take a four-day course in September or February conducted by Peggy Kirk Bell (Pine Needles Lodge and Country Club, Southern Pine, N.C. 28387). You can get further information about cost, meals, and lodging by writing directly to the camp that interests you, and you can contact universities in your area about any special courses offered during summer months.

Wilderness Trips.   The opportunities for exploring the American wilderness under the guidance of an expert are almost limitless. You can select the area of the country and of your own interest (botany, archaeology, geology, or whatever), and spend as much time or money as you like. Write to the American River Touring Association (1016 Jackson Street, Oakland, Cal. 94607) for information about riding such rivers as the Colorado and Rogue. Or find out about individual instruction in rock- and ice-climbing from the Eastern Mountain Sports Climbing School (Box 514B, Main Street, North Conway, N.H. 03860). The Sierra Club (1050 Mills Tower, San Francisco, Calif. 94104) offers "Wilderness Threshold" trips that include hiking, camping, and learning about the outdoors. The Wilderness Society (4260 E. Evans, Denver, Colo. 80222) will take you on journeys all over the West, and even into Alaska. None of these wilderness exploration organizations is exclusively for women, so they offer a good opportunity for you to meet others with similar interests.

Whether you travel by car or camper, our national parks are a source of pure delight at small cost. The national park system is one of our greatest natural resources, and offers a variety limited only by the scope of the grandeur of this country's scenic pleasures—there is no limit to their wonders. There are coastal wildlife sanctuaries, there are undersea parks that must be visited by snorkel and swimfin, there are caverns and lava beds, volcanoes and glaciers, there are swamps and deserts, historic landmarks and battlefields, forests and mountains. In other words, anything that you might want. And more parks are added each year. You will have to make reservations for cabins early (write to the Department of the Interior, Washington, D.C. 20240 for particulars), but there are parks in every part of the country, and all are well-kept and patrolled by polite, capable park rangers and other personnel.

Of course, it's more fun to travel with someone with whom you can share the adventures of the trip, but don't hesitate to travel by yourself, if necessary, if that's the only way you'll be able to go. Just exercise the ordinary safety precautions that you would observe at home, and don't be too trusting simply because you are in strange territory. You can have something stolen as easily in downtown Chicago or Denver or Detroit as in Rome. Maintain watchfulness and you should have no trouble.

In General

If you wear eyeglasses, be sure to take an additional pair on any trip with you, and take along any prescriptions you might need. You won't need immunization shots if you go to England, but you will elsewhere; check with your doctor and the travel agency, and if you do need them, get them well in advance of the trip in case of any adverse reaction. Carry the minimum amount of clothes you'll need, with lots of mix-and-match pieces in your wardrobe, and be sure that as much as possible is washable. The best time to buy luggage is in January and May. Be sure to get the best, most durable kind for your particular type of travel. If you're going to fly, make sure the luggage is sturdy, but car travel requires minimum handling, so you can economize. For air travel, buy a "carry-on" bag that will fit under your seat, and pack in it a complete change of wardrobe and all your essentials, in case you're separated from your other luggage. If you rent a car at your destination, shop among the services available; they vary a great deal. Wherever you go, check all your bills before you pay them. If you're going to be away from home for more than two weeks, ask your telephone company about suspending service (and charges) for that time, be sure to stop your paper delivery, and ask the post office to hold your mail. If you need help in any sizeable city, appeal to Traveler's Aid in this country, an embassy or a consulate overseas. Carry your makeup and other personal items in a separate bag, put as many items as possible in plastic containers, and add a supply of premoistened towelettes. Make all your preparations far enough in advance so that you won't be a nervous wreck before the departure date; then relax, enjoy the scenery, the change, and the people, and most importantly, have fun and return refreshed in body and spirit.

HEALTH

Traveling or staying at home, you'll want to do everything possible to stay at your peak physically, so a program of good health care is vital. Of course you'll be going regularly to your doctor and dentist, but there are some things that you should be concerned with between checkups. Such as your weight. You know that maintaining the correct weight for your age, height, and bone structure makes you look and feel better, but it is a necessary preventive health measure, too. You may be among the 60 percent of overweight Americans, and obesity can lead to many problems, not the least among them heart trouble and diabetes, so keep an eye on the scales and establish sensible eating habits. Don't starve yourself, but eat all the things required for adequate nutrition. There are numerous organizations that will help you with your regimen (I recommend Weight Watchers), and the inspiration you may need to diet is as close as one of their meetings. If your problem is underweight, consult your doctor; he may recommend one of the food supplements in the supermarkets. Either way, to gain or lose, do nothing without the approval of your physician.

I don't have to repeat the damage that stress can do to you; it can make you prey to all kinds of ailments, and can make you suffer as much distress from psychosomatic pains as from any that are organically caused. Try to get at the source of your problem. Seek counseling, if necessary, and if at all possible, try to change the cause of your trouble, whether it is work, living conditions, or the people with whom you associate. Getting away from all three may be the answer. Don't keep suffering in a situation you can change; stress can kill, too. Nothing is as harmful as frustration and resentment.

The Pill

Unfortunately, there is no help in sight for the middle-income wage-earner who has doctor's bills not covered by insurance, but you can avail yourself of free examinations and limited treatment at your county health centers, and can go for tests to such organizations as the American Cancer Society no matter what your income. Check with your local health department about free Pap smear tests, and see if free vision and hearing clinics are offered. You can get most of your immunization there, as well as the Pill. As you probably know, there is still controversy about the use of oral contraceptives, and the misinformation and misconceptions are as widespread now as when the Pill was first introduced in 1960. So far, there is no proof that the Pill can cause cancer, although research shows that when it is used for at least two years, it appears to protect *against* the formation of benign breast tumors, ovarian cysts, and uterine fibroids. The formation of blood clots (thromboembolism) is recognized as a definite risk; for this reason, users of oral contraceptives should have regular checkups. In some cases, users develop an increased degree of high blood pressure (hypertension), but this can be treated with medication, and the pressure returns to normal when the Pill is discontinued. It is possible that your blood sugar level will rise, but again, it will return to normal if use is discontinued. (You can see why it is vital that you see a doctor before using these contraceptives, and why a specific type and dosage must be prescribed for you.)

Because there may be a correlation between birth defects and the use of the Pill during early pregnancy, Dr. Dwight T. Janerich, director of genetic oncology (study of tumors) at the Cancer Control Bureau of the New York State Department of Health, urges doctors and users to be sure the patient is not pregnant when use begins. Two important findings relating to vitamin deficiency among users of the Pill show that women using the contraceptive have markedly lower levels of folic acid and vitamin B-6 than do nonusers. Also, depression is thought to be caused by this lowering of the necessary B-6 level. Correct nutritional balance should counteract this deficiency, but your doctor may want to prescribe additional vitamins and an anti-depressant. Conversely, the Pill seems to increase the iron and copper levels, so users should not be troubled with anemia. There has been found to be an increase in vaginal and urinary tract infections, but so far it hasn't been determined whether this is due to the use of the Pill or increased sexual activity. In either case, prompt treatment is mandatory. Great Britain's Royal College of General Practitioners has published a report stating that there is an increase in cases of viral infections (particularly chicken pox) among users, indicating, perhaps, a weakening of immunity to such viruses. The Pill has also been connected to an increase in the incidence of a rare tumor of the liver; the tumor is benign, but should be treated, of course, immediately; but the chances of your having one are slim. You should also have your doctor check you for any gall bladder disease which may occur among some users. The Pill is certainly the most effective method of contraception, but you must be aware of all possibilities of danger before using it, and should contact your doctor at once if you suspect trouble. (You can learn more about the Pill from the free government booklet 143B, *The Pill,* and can write for it to the Pueblo, Colorado address.)

Other methods available, and offering varying degrees of effectiveness, are vaginal foam, IUDs, and diaphragms. Of the mechanical means used by women, I think the diaphragm is the safest and most trouble-free. Foam is the least effective, and there have been too many problems with IUDs to guarantee effective and safe contraception. Some women expel them spontaneously, some experience bleeding (some experience pregnancy!); think twice before using an intrauterine device unless your doctor is convinced it is the best method for you. Normally you will ovulate on or about the twelfth to the fourteenth day after the first day of the previous menstrual period, and are most apt to become pregnant during this time. Intercourse from at least two to three days before and four to five days after ovulation (if you can actually pinpoint it that accurately) is apt to cause pregnancy unless you have taken the best preventive measure available to you. Keep in mind that mistakes can happen to your body's calendar or your arithmetic, so use the contraception that is most efficient for you. If you don't want to go to your own doctor for information, ask Planned Parenthood for help. When you contact them, you might want to inquire about abortion. In addition to books and pamphlets available at each office, you can call their toll-free number, 800-523-5302, for further abortion information.

Venereal Disease

Be especially watchful for venereal disease; take prompt action if you see any signs of it. According to the U.S. Center for Disease Control, gonorrhea is the nation's number one communicable disease. It is easily contracted, but just as easily cured. Be wary of any vaginal discharge, and seek medical attention immediately. The symptoms of syphilis may include vaginal sores, a body rash, and a sore throat. All symptoms may disappear for a while, so that the victim is deceived into believing that she is all right; the time for medication is when those first signs are noticed. Venereal disease can be a serious—even a deadly—problem, so *get medical attention as soon as you suspect infection.* Your private physician can treat you, as can the public health department clinics.

Hormones

If you are approaching menopause (it can happen in the thirties), talk with your doctor about hormone replacement therapy. Again, the rumors and speculations abound, as with the Pill, but most medical experts agree that for most women hormone therapy is advisable.

Robert Greenblatt, M.D., Professor Emeritus of Endocrinology at the Medical College of Georgia, divides doctors into four groups in their opinions about the use of hormone therapy. He says there are those doctors who refuse to interfere with nature; those who prescribe small doses for short periods to relieve the most severe menopausal problems; those who believe hormonal therapy should begin before the onset of menopause and continue throughout life; and others who believe that most, but not all, women need and should be given the replacement hormones. Why replacement? As a woman reaches middle age, her body's output of the vital hormone estrogen decreases, and its lack adversely affects her blood, heart, skin, muscles, hair, eyes, and general feeling of well-being. The generation of women now in their forties and fifties are the first who have been offered widespread use of hormone replacement, so studies are continuing as to their safety, but research indicates, according to the American Medical Association, that fear of cancer caused by the drugs "does not seem justified on the basis of available evidence."

Although some doctors don't want to interfere with nature's plan, many physicians see no reason to subject their patients to years of the discomfort of hot flashes, palpitations, sweating, and indefinable pains. Nor do they think their patients should suffer the anxiety, insomnia, depression, and frequent loss of sexual appetite that occurs in some women during menopause. They generally give their patients controlled, cyclic dosages of as small amounts as possible, and watch them carefully for any adverse signs such as irregular bleeding. Tests show that women whose levels of estrogen are maintained during the middle and later years are less prone to heart disease and broken bones, and they are spared the menopausal symptoms above. It must be a decision reached by each of you with your own doctor, but I feel that if it is deemed safe for you, then neither you nor any other woman should have to suffer discomfort when a comparatively harmless medication is available.

I feel the same about anti-depressants; I don't think any woman of any age should have to struggle unaided through bouts of depression—whatever their cause. I think she should ask for and receive the most effective medicine and/or therapy she can obtain.

Operations

Before you agree to an operation as radical as a hysterectomy (removal of the womb), if it is suggested, get other professional opinions. There were 716,000 such operations performed in 1973; this is second only to the number of appendectomies. Only about 20 percent of these were done because of cancer. Some were performed because of fibroid tumors, some because of recurrent bleeding, some for simple chronic backache. It's generally a good idea to get a second opinion about any operation, but it is certainly mandatory for anything as traumatic as a hysterectomy or breast removal. Mastectomies are probably the most publicized operations of the past few years, and millions of women are more aware of the dangers of neglect as a result of the publicity allowed by courageous women like Betty Ford and Happy Rockefeller. The importance of both professional and self-examination is now known by most women. If you have any questions, contact the American Cancer Society; most branches conduct free examinations, and will teach you how to examine your breasts for any unusual lumps or other danger signals. Don't delay if you find a lump; only one in fifteen is malignant, but why take a chance? Go to your doctor immediately, and ask for a mammogram, if available in your area, or a biopsy if there is any question in your mind about the diagnosis.

If you must go into the hospital for any operation, try to avoid going on a Friday; the hospital will not be fully staffed until Monday, and you will have paid an additional two days' room rent for nothing.

Many county medical societies maintain a free telephone tape library so that you can call, ask for a numbered tape (a list is available through the society), and hear a short discussion on everything from heart disease to correct dental care. These tapes last about two to three minutes, and are quite informative.

Your Teeth

When you need dental care, be sure you discuss fees with your dentist before the work begins. Check his charges with the local dental society, and if you feel that his charge is high, go to another dentist. The dental society will give you a referral list, or you may want to check with friends or a local dental school. (See about free dental work offered by most of these schools; it will be done by a student, but under the supervision of a teacher.) Dental care is expensive, so if you want an idea of the prices that should be charged for different types of work, write to the Pennsylvania Insurance Department (108 Finance Building, Harrisburg, Pa. 17120) and ask for *Shopper's Guide to Dentistry*. (Residents of the state can get a copy by sending a self-addressed pre-stamped nine-by-twelve envelope; non-residents will have to add a dollar, and write to Consumer Insurance, 813 National Press Building, Washington, D.C. 20004.)

A recent advance in dentistry is the perfection of tooth implants that put a permanent tooth, complete with the man-made equivalent of a root, into a gaping socket. The work costs about the same as tooth capping or fixed bridgework. (A list of dentists who are members of the American Academy of Implant Dentistry can be requested from 469 Washington Street, Abington, Mass. 02351.)

In General

Ask your doctor about the best vitamins for you to take, but don't overdose; taking too many vitamins (particularly Vitamin A) can be as dangerous as taking too few. Whenever you are given a prescription, be sure to ask your physician to give you the generic name of the medication; it will be several dollars cheaper than if you buy it by trade name.

If you're troubled by insomnia, drink milk before going to bed; it's thought to work on the body's amino acids and assure you a good night's sleep. (I don't know the cause, but I know that it works for me better than anything else I can take.) Try not to take your worries to bed with you;

they'll make you lose more sleep than anything will. When you have a problem, sit down and think out all the ramifications, explore the possibilities of solution, then reach a decision about your course of action. Indecisiveness will cause as much trouble as will the problem itself. In every case—and I cannot emphasize this too much—try to control or eliminate anything that causes tension and stress. These will cause you to become prey to every kind of illness, real or imagined, and will make you vulnerable to every kind of ailment, from hypertension to colds to heart attacks. Relax, and give your body a chance!

INCOME TAX

One cause of distress to millions of Americans annually is their income tax return; but, as in everything else, planning and preparation will eliminate most problems. If during the year you have kept accurate records of income and expenses, if you have prepaid taxes, and if you are careful about filing your return correctly, there should be no difficulty. Don't let it all wait until April 14th; keep a running record during the year, and keep all necessary information accessible in one place. Buy an alphabetized accordion file for your records and canceled checks, and hang on to most of the records for at least five years. (A good idea, anyway, in case you ever want to average your income, and would have to use the previous years as a base.) Cut down on the things you keep; your canceled checks will be sufficient to substantiate a claim, in most cases, and you can throw out the bills themselves. A good rule of thumb to determine if a document is worth keeping is whether it shows evidence of a legal transaction such as a loan or bill of sale for a car or appliance; whether it proves your ownership of anything; whether it defines your legal rights or obligation (your lease would fall into this category); or whether it will enable you to check on possible errors made by someone else (your bank statement, for example). Keep all records of stock transactions and sale or purchase of property, and a note of the value of any property you have received by gift or inheritance, so you will have the amount to use for computation if you ever sell the property.

I suggest that you retain permanently all copies of your income tax returns, not only for income averaging, but for later verification of your Social Security benefits. If you need a copy of one of your returns, send one dollar for the first sheet, plus a dime for each additional copy or sheet, to the IRS Service Center in the area in which you filed the return.

Whoever said that line about nothing being certain except death and taxes was not overstating the case; there is no way to avoid paying taxes of some kind, no matter how little you make, own, or spend. Almost everything we use, earn, eat, live in, travel on, wear, drink, or touch is taxed in one form or another. The taxes are here to stay, so you may as well resign yourself to a lifetime of record-keeping and tax-paying. However, you can make the task a little easier on yourself by having a clear understanding of your rights and responsibilities in relation to your tax liability. I've explained certain taxes and the way in which they affect you as we've come to them, so I'll touch them again only briefly. The best way to examine the tax picture as it relates to you is to take a return, item by item, and go right down the form to its final line.

Who Must File

You must first determine whether or not you must file at all. Following are the rules set by the Internal Revenue Service. (In all cases I am relating only those things that concern a woman alone.)

You must file a U.S. Income Tax Return if you are

1. Single or a widow under 65 and your gross income (all income that is not exempt from tax by law) is at least $2,050
2. Single or a widow 65 or older, and your gross income is at least $2,800
3. Single; you could be claimed as a dependent on your parents' return; but you must show dividend income, interest income, or other *unearned* income on your own return of at least $750
4. A person with income from sources within U.S. possessions
5. Self-employed and your *net* earnings from self-employment are at least $400

If income tax was withheld but you are not required to file a return, you should file one to get your refund.

Filing Status

Let's define some terms. You were considered married for the entire year if on December 31 (for most taxpayers) you were married and living as husband and wife; living together in a common-law marriage recognized by the state in which it began; married and living apart, but not legally separated; or separated under an interlocutory decree of divorce. If your spouse died during the year, you are considered married during the entire year, and if you did not remarry before the end of the tax year, you may file a joint return for yourself and your deceased spouse.

You may file as a single person if you meet all the following tests: You file a separate return; you paid more than half the cost to keep up your home for the tax year; your spouse did not live in your home at any time during the tax year; and for over six months of the year, your home was the principal residence of your child whom you claim as a dependent. If you are divorced by a final decree on or before the last day of your tax year, you are considered single for the entire year.

When it is time to file your income tax return, your next decision must be which form to use. You may use the short Form 1040A no matter what your filing (marital) status or whatever number of dependents you claim, if you do not itemize your deductions and if you did not have interest income of more than $400. You may use the short form no matter what your income, but if you have more than $10,000 of Adjusted Gross Income (AGI), you will undoubtedly want to itemize although you may itemize no matter how low your income.

On either form, you must next determine your filing status. If you are single with no dependents, there is obviously no problem; you check the block on Line 1 marked "Single." This will establish your tax rate when you look it up in the tax tables or the tax rate schedule. You may as well accept the fact that you will pay more tax because you are single; the cards are stacked in favor of the married female taxpayer who has children and who files jointly with her spouse. For example, if both you and she claim two exemptions, do not itemize, and have AGIs of $3,700, her tax would be $130, but yours would be $134. By the time the two of you have an AGI of $6,800, her tax will be $625, while yours will be $695. And so on up the scale. However, there are tax breaks for the widow with a dependent child, and for anyone qualifying as head of household.

If your husband died within the two years preceding the one for which you're filing, if you were entitled to file jointly with your husband the year of his death, you have not remarried, you have a child who qualifies as your dependent and for whom you furnished more than half the cost of maintaining your home, you will be able to claim a special tax benefit. You will be able, the year of the death, to file a joint return, and during the next two years to file in the same tax category as someone who is married and filing a joint return. Later, if you qualify as head of household, your tax rate will be lower, too. For example, consider a woman with one dependent (entitling her to claim two exemptions), who does not itemize, and with an adjusted gross income of $4,530. If she files as single, her tax will be $263; if she files as head of household, her tax will be $256; and if she files as a widow under the above circumstances, or as married filing jointly, her tax will be $249.

There are obvious advantages to being able to file as head of household, but the qualifications are strict. Generally (all this tax information is taken from the IRS Publication 17, *Your Federal Income Tax,* 1975 edition), you can file as head of household if you meet *all* the following requirements:

1. You must be unmarried on the last day of your tax year
2. You must (a) maintain a household and (b) contribute over half the cost of maintaining it
3. Your household must be the principal residence for at least one relative for the entire year. A dependent related to you in any of the following degrees need not live with you for you to claim him as a dependent; your child, grandchild, stepchild, brother, sister, half brother, half sister, stepbrother, stepsister, your parents, grandparents or other direct ancestor (but not a foster parent), your stepfather or stepmother, a brother or s:ster of your parents, a son or daughter of your brother or sister, your father-in-law, mother-in-law, son-in-law, daughter-in-law, brother-in-law, or sister-in-law.

That's pretty inclusive, but remember those crucial words about "paying more than half" the cost of maintaining a household? You will have to be very meticulous in your computation of these costs, which include such things as rent, mortgage interest, taxes, insurance on the dwelling and premises, upkeep and repairs, utilities, domestic help, and food consumed in the home. Do *not* include the cost of clothing, education, medical treatment, vacations, life insurance, or transportation. Do *not* include the rental value of a home you own, and remember that these items are not necessarily the same as those used in determining whether or not you have provided over half the support of a dependent. The above are to be used solely to decide if you will be able to file as head of household.

Exemptions

The next order of business is deciding your exemptions. Your personal exemptions are determined by your age and eyesight. If you are under 65 and your eyesight is better than 20/200 with corrective lenses, you may claim only one exemption; if you are over 65 you are entitled to an additional exemption, and if your eyesight falls below the above standard, you are entitled to another, no matter what your age.

The tests to determine whether or not you are entitled to claim any *dependency* exemptions are five: gross income (the dependent's); relationship or member of the household; citizenship; joint return (the dependent's); and support.

To make it easier, let's take it one step at a time. If you answer "Yes" to all the following questions, you will be able to claim another person as a dependent.

1. The gross income test is the easiest. If your dependent earned more than $750, you may not claim him unless he is your child *and* (the italics are the IRS') he is either less than 19 years of age *or* a full-time student during some part of each of five calendar months of the year. The five months need not be consecutive. In other words, you may claim an exemp-

tion for a child who is under 19, no matter how much gross income he had (provided the other four tests are met, of course). You may also claim him regardless of age or gross income if he was a full-time student for at least five months of the year.

2. The relationship or member of the household test is easy, too. You may claim a qualifying relative (all of those listed in the head of household test, with the exception of a half-brother or half-sister, and with the addition of a cousin who lives with you or who is institutionalized). An adopted child or a foster child who has lived with you the entire year is considered your child.

3. The citizenship test is simple. The dependent must have been a U.S. citizen or a resident of Canada, Mexico, the Panama Canal Zone, or the Republic of Panama for any part of the tax year.

4. The joint return test is easy, too. If your dependent filed a joint return with his spouse because they were liable for taxes (not if they filed only to claim a refund, and had no liability), you may not claim him.

5. Now we come to the hard one, the support test. It's so easy to confuse the requirements for this and for head of household that you should go over them each time a question arises. To claim the dependent, you must have furnished over half of his total support during the year. To know what "over half" is, you will have to determine the total cost of support provided by you, by the dependent, and by others. Total support is the sum of the amounts spent for food, clothing, shelter, medical and dental care, education, recreation, operating expenses, transportation, and other similar necessities. A pro rata portion of the total costs of food, utilities, and other household expenses will be accepted by the IRS in lieu of actual records, but you should keep as accurate an accounting as possible.

Tax-exempt income, savings, and money borrowed by you or your dependent for support expenses should be included in total support. Some of the tax-exempt income to be included are Social Security benefits, state benefit payments, Veterans Administration payments, and Armed Forces dependency allotments. As you can see, certain types of income that are not included in gross income are included in total support, so be careful not to confuse the two. Other items may be considered as support depending on the facts in each case. For example, payments to others for child care, or for disabled dependent care, may be included in support, even though you may be entitled to deduct them as an itemized expense on Schedule A.

The fair rental value of your home, whether you own or rent, is the amount to be used when you pro-rate the portion used by your dependent, and is the amount you could reasonably expect to receive from a stranger for the same type of lodging. It includes in the dependent's pro rata share a reasonable allowance for the use of furnishings, for heat, and for other utilities. Fair rental value may be used instead of rent, taxes, interest, depreciation, insurance, and the cost of furniture and appliances. But do be careful when you determine this amount; don't let wishful thinking cloud your judgment as to the amount a stranger would pay. If you want to be absolutely certain that you are figuring correctly, you can get a real estate agent to tell you the amount he thinks you could expect to charge, but he may charge you a fee, and it really isn't necessary if the amount you use is sensible and realistic.

Using the standard formula to determine if you have contributed more than half toward your dependent's support, put everything *you* contributed in the numerator and divide it by the total support in the denominator for the answer. Say that you have a dependent for whom you furnish support totaling $3,000, and the dependent received Social Security benefits of $1,200. The figure in the numerator would be $3,000, the denominator would be $4,200, the answer would be 71.4%, so you would be able to claim the individual as a dependent.

Some items not included in total support are scholarships, life insurance premiums, purchase of an automobile, or other capital expenditures such as furniture and appliances, taxes paid by the dependent from his own income, Social Security taxes, and funeral expenses. If you are not the only person contributing to a dependent's support, you both or all will have to file a multiple support agreement, whereby only one of you who contributes more than 10 percent of the support may claim the person as a dependent. This declaration, Form 2120, may be obtained at any IRS office, and must be filed with the return of the person claiming the exemption.

The 1040

A concerted effort has been made over the past few years to make the 1040 as simple as possible, and if you follow the directions accompanying it, take it line by line, you should have no trouble with the remainder. For instance, the part pertaining to your income is self-explanatory, but be sure to include everything you have earned. On the first line of the section you will put your total wages, tips, and other compensation paid to you by an employer. (If you are self-employed, your business profit or loss, after you have deducted expenses, will go on the back of the form on the first line of the part for other income. You will show the amount of your self-employment tax in the section for other taxes, and will attach to your 1040 both Schedules C and SE.) You must be sure to attach your W-2 forms with your return, whether you use the short or long form; only your employer can issue a W-2, and no substitute is acceptable. The employer is required by law to furnish you with a completed form by January 31, but if you have any trouble getting one from him, contact an Internal Revenue Service office with the details.

The instructions that come with the two forms, both long and short, explain about the dividends that qualify for a $100 exclusion; if the corporation distributing the dividends cannot tell you if it qualifies, contact the IRS for the correct information. All your interest income must be shown on the designated line, but be sure to remember that even though they may be called "dividends" by savings and loan associations and credit unions, they *are* interest and must be included in this total. If you have had gain (or loss) from capital assets, whether stocks or a residence, for instance, the amount will be shown on the back of the form on the correct line, with a Schedule D attached. (If you do show a loss, enclose the figure in parentheses on the return.) If you have received funds from a pension, a trust, an estate, an annuity, rent, or royalty, the amount must be shown in the same section on the 1040, with an explanatory Schedule E&R, and your itemized deductions for such things as medical expenses, taxes paid, contributions, interest expense, and so on will be entered on a Schedule A&B, and it, too, will be attached.

It isn't as formidable as it sounds, but I repeat: You *will* have to keep accurate records, read the instructions, and complete the forms precisely. Don't hesitate to call on the IRS for assistance, and watch out for the most common trouble-causing errors. Be sure that you attach all schedules and your W-2 forms; be sure to give your complete address and correct Social Security number; check the appropriate blocks; itemize all your deductions; be sure to list all your income on the proper lines; if you have more than $400 in interest income, itemize its source on the reverse of a Schedule A&B; and sign your return. (You'd be surprised at the number of taxpayers who fail to follow these directions, thus delaying their refunds. And equally careless are those who move after filing but forget to notify the post office specifically about having IRS mail forwarded to them.) Beware of fly-by-night tax preparers, and *never* sign a paper allowing them to cash your refund check; you may never see it—or them—again!

No matter who helps you with the completion of your return, *you* are responsible for its contents, another reason for care with the amounts shown. Claim everything to which you are entitled, whether it is educational expenses or charitable contributions. Some of us think we ought to get an extra deduction just for making it through another year—the IRS won't go *that* far, but it will help you to realize as much savings as is legally possible.

EPILOGUE

Don't Just Sit There—
Do Something!

The saddest thing in the world is to see a woman reach her final years alone and friendless—not because all her family has died or moved away, but because she has become the kind of person no one likes or wants to be with. The fact that is too often overlooked, however, when we see such a lonely old woman, is that she didn't become 70 or 80 overnight; she has spent her entire life becoming the woman she is today.

If she was a tyrant or a shrew at 25, she is likely to be one at 75; if she was kind and loving and joyous at 30, she will probably be the same at 60—and she will never want for company and companionship. She will still be interested in people and the world around her, and will be as active as her physical strength permits.

Why do I speak of growing old? Because we age from the day we are born, and like it or not, old age will happen to us all. But although everyone ages, not everyone matures, and therein lies the secret of laying the right foundation *now* for all the years ahead. What is maturity? It has been defined by many, but I think that it simply means accepting whatever cannot be changed, challenging those things that we want to and can change (including ourselves), learning from past experiences, looking forward to a better future—and doing everything possible to *make* it better. Maturity means patience, perseverance, and dependability. And it means having a vital sense of one's own worth and ability and freedom.

I have never had any patience with any woman who sat back and expected life to come to her. I have even less sympathy for an old person who sits back with folded hands, expecting the world to pay homage because she happened to outlive her contemporaries. She will complain that no one cares about her anymore, yet she will make herself so unpleasant that she is avoided by one and all. Instead of complaining, she should seek to do something for others not quite as well off as she. She should try to care for others, and in so doing, will find that others will come to care for and value her.

I admire the old gentleman from Tacoma—Walter C. Jones, aged 102—who bought a mobile home in which he planned, during 1975, to make a one-year tour of the United States. I admire my great-aunt Hannah, who personified the spirit of *carpe diem*—seize the day. At 98 she was still lively, witty, alert, and interested in the world around her. She was sought out for her sprightly company by both young and old. Not for *her* the lifeboat theory—the philosophy that one must spend life preparing for the future with no thought for the pleasures of the day, making the entire life journey in a lifeboat instead of being on deck and enjoying all the drama of the voyage. Don't misunderstand; you know by now that I strongly urge preparedness for every eventuality. But you can stock your lifeboat and still participate in life itself.

The woman who eagerly embraces life and is intimately involved in living knows that in order to be loved she must be lovable, whether she is 18, 28, or 80. She enjoys the world and everything in it, meets it head-on, and gives of herself to everyone with whom she comes in contact. She knows that the only way to be fulfilled is to open herself up to life, to experience it. She remembers that other people accept a person according to that person's own evaluation of herself, so she keeps an upbeat attitude about everything she does. There will be bad times—sometimes they may seem to outnumber the good—but each day should bring a new experience from which to learn and profit.

A wise man once said that the three ingredients for a happy life are to have someone or something to love, to have something to do, and to have something to look forward to.

The first ingredient, having someone or something to love, simply means giving of yourself. The love can be of any type—sexual, maternal, filial, platonic. It can be the love you feel for a friend, for a group, for an ideal. It means giving not things, but yourself, to the forgotten, the unloved, as well as to those people who are easy to care about. It means doing things for others—because you want to. It means total involvement with the world.

As for the second ingredient, having something to do, there is no reason—and no excuse—for anyone in this world to be bored. And yet thousands of people succumb to ennui, boredom, a lackluster existence, when the world is so full of wonderful and useful things to do! With people to love, how can there *ever* be nothing to do?

There are so many things that can enrich your own life and those of others. Even if your money is limited, being busy doesn't necessarily cost anything. There are so many free offerings in even the smallest communities that your days can be filled with learning, with delight, with useful activity.

You can be a member of a volunteer program to help the less fortunate; you can take courses; you can use your library to borrow books, records, reproductions of great paintings; you can involve yourself in any number of groups which meet for the prime purpose of understanding human existence better.

But no matter how much you have to do, no matter how busy you become you will have to exercise a little judicious selfishness and save some time for yourself alone. You will benefit from your contacts with other people, but you also want to be a person in your own right, independent of anyone else's needs or support. And this involves the third ingredient—having something to look forward to.

Your work and family will be the most absorbing parts of your life, of course, but you will have to set some kind of goal—for you alone—toward which you will be working. It need not be anything earthshaking or momentous; it can be long- or short-term; and can be as modest or as ambitious as you like. But it will give you something to look forward to.

Your goal or project can be simple or complex. You can plan to paint a room; or lose five pounds; or learn a new language; or read all of your favorite author's books. Whatever you do, don't let your life become routine. If you have always changed the beds or washed your hair or bought the groceries on a certain day of the week, do those things on different days occasionally, and you'll be surprised at the way your outlook changes. It helps you take joy in the anticipation of simple pleasures. It makes you clear your mind of cobwebs and think of *new* goals and plans. It helps you to be happy.

In the last few years I have found that I receive pleasure from such simple things as looking forward to a particularly entertaining program on television; or from finding an out-of-print book for which I've been searching; or from the success of a new recipe I want to try out for friends. I find special pleasure in meeting someone new and knowing that this may ripen into a lasting friendship. I even enjoy letting some things go while I finish a new project, and realizing, without a qualm of remorse, that they will be right there waiting for me when I get around to them tomorrow or the day after. In essence, I can set a goal, work to attain it, enjoy myself, and keep my spirits raised by success. I can also resist being shattered if I can't quite achieve all I'd like to do.

Socrates said, "The man [woman] who most truly can be accounted brave is he who most knows the meaning of what is sweet in life and what is terrible, and then goes out undeterred to meet what is to come."

That's the lesson I've learned during these years alone. Yes, there are days when I wonder if I can cope with everything life presents me, and there are times when I am almost crushed by the pressures of living, but I've learned that these too shall pass, that things won't seem so terrible tomorrow, and that I will be able to resolve problems in some satisfactory way. I think that's a measure of maturity, too—knowing that you are never defeated. I also think that I've finally become an adult. I no longer have George to depend on, and I know that it's all up to me from here on out. I know *me*—at last; I know where I am and what I want to do. I recognize and honor my limitations and my capabilities, and I know how to pace myself. I know enough not to fragment myself by doing too many things at once; I must do one thing at a time and do it well, and yet my periphery of interests is constantly expanding.

I hope someday to be a good mother-in-law and grandmother; I know that there are yet many new roles for me to play, and that I will enjoy every new facet of my life. I also hope that I will continue to grow. I will never again live in another person's shadow, or live vicariously through another person's life. I'll never be able to do that again, either as a wife or a mother, because I've learned something about coping with life—alone.

By no stretch of the imagination could I be mistaken today for the woman I was in July 1970. A new woman has emerged, one who is no longer sheltered in a cocoon of comfort and protection. A little harder, infinitely more self-reliant and independent, I have gradually come into focus, like a picture in a developing tray. I even think the new woman is better; I don't think that I would ever return to the old.

I know now that whether I have thirty years left to me or three, I'm going to live life to the hilt, to the very maximum limits of my productivity and enjoyment. I am eager to try new things—to travel, to meet new people, to constantly learn and share and give and love.

Why do I tell you all this? Because I know that if I have been able to survive and cope and triumph, ill-equipped and unprepared as I was, I know that you can, too. But don't fold your hands, sigh, and wait for something to happen—go out and *make* it happen. Confront life, *cope*—but on your own terms. Make of life what you will. Don't just sit there—*do* something!

Index